Date Due

BOLLINGEN SERIES XLV

The Collected Works of Paul Valéry

Edited by Jackson Mathews

VOLUME 15

PAUL VALÉRY

MOI

Translated by
Marthiel and Jackson Mathews

BOLLINGEN SERIES XLV · 15

PRINCETON UNIVERSITY PRESS

THIS IS VOLUME FIFTEEN OF THE
COLLECTED WORKS OF PAUL VALÉRY
CONSTITUTING NUMBER XLV IN BOLLINGEN SERIES
SPONSORED BY BOLLINGEN FOUNDATION.
IT IS THE FINAL VOLUME OF THE
COLLECTED WORKS TO APPEAR

ISBN: 0–691–09936–7
Library of Congress Cataloging in Publication Data
will be found on the last printed page of this book

Type composed at the University Printing House, Cambridge, England
Printed in the United States of America
by Princeton University Press, Princeton, New Jersey
DESIGNED BY ANDOR BRAUN

CONTENTS

ACKNOWLEDGMENT   vii

Autobiography   3

Moi   12

Three Wakings   15

Mediterranean Inspirations   19

Impressions and Recollections   36

My Early Days in England   41

A Timely Recollection   55

Valéry–Fourment Correspondence, *a selection*   60

Valéry–Gide Correspondence, *a selection*   108

In Marcel Prévost's Time   265

Graduation Ceremonies at the Collège de Sète   274

Remarks About Myself   287

My Work and I   335

The Avenues of the Mind   343

Reply   349

Memories of Paul Valéry, *by Pierre Féline*   354

NOTES   391

INDEX   409

ACKNOWLEDGMENT

IN THIS FINAL volume of *The Collected Works of Paul Valéry*, the editor thanks all of the writers who collaborated on this long and difficult translation into English of the works of a difficult writer. He wishes to acknowledge most of all the support of John D. Barrett, president of the Bollingen Foundation, whose knowledge of, and interest in, Valéry were at the inception of this project. And he records his gratitude to Mme Catherine David, whose sensitive knowledge of both French and English was of unfailing help.

J. M.

MOI

Autobiography

I WAS BORN at Cette [Sète] on October 30, 1871.

My father, a native of Bastia, was a customs official there. I have few or no memories of my earliest childhood. But the pageant of a seaport, things belonging to the sea, the boats below our windows were food for my eyes in my early years, after which we *see* nothing except by effort.

As a I child I lived in *imagination*. Horror of violent games. I began to read fairly early.

I was very impressionable. My sensitivity caused me to suffer cruelly. Childhood terrors.

In 1878 I was enrolled in the town grammar school (after attending various small schools).

The location of this school was remarkable. Halfway up St. Clair "Mountain" (180 meters in altitude) on which the town is built, overlooking the port. The playgrounds were terraces, one above the other, from which the sea and the comings and goings of ships were in view.

I suffered in leaving all this, in 1884 when we went to live in Montpellier. There, the playgrounds were like wells.

The classes at Cette were so small that I necessarily stood high. I was first out of four without much effort. When I was twelve, I was seized with a passionate desire to be a sailor. The visits of the fleet drove me out of my mind. I suffered from this intense love as one suffers from love. But my father did not look favorably on my imagined vocation, and, besides, I did not understand the first thing about mathematics.

Montpellier, in 1884.

The lycée had the dreariest possible effect on me. I felt lost in the corridors of the third form. No personal relations with my teachers. The few efforts I put forth produced very meagre results. Boredom overwhelmed me. I was a very mediocre student and remained so to the end of my studies. To me, the teaching seemed completely uninspired and repugnant, and in short nothing more than coercion. The simple and foolish idea of the baccalaureate dominated everything. The baccalaureate: a bogey and an expedient.

Little by little I made an "inner life" for myself.

I read a great deal of Hugo and Gautier. We begin with the picturesque and the romantic.

In the second form, this predilection became more specific. I fell in love with Architecture, to the point of setting out to read Viollet-le-Duc. I took the notion of making a résumé of the great dictionary—which I began, even copying the illustrations, but gave up before finishing the letter *A*.

The following year, 1887, my father died and was buried at Cette in the cemetery which I called "Le Cimetière marin" [The Cemetery by the Sea].

I passed the baccalaureate examinations despite my professor's predictions. Passed philosophy also and entered law school in 1888.

I began the study of law as many others have done, without having the vaguest notion of what I wanted to do.

I wrote a few poems.

Our student life was very easy. We passed our time in conversation, walks, a few classes, after which we held forth in the beautiful gardens of Montpellier or at a café. All sorts of odd things began to interest me—even anthropology. I measured skulls!

But it was only in the following year that literature took deeper hold of me.

In September of '89 I read Huysmans' *A Rebours*, which made a tremendous impression on me. It was a manual of art and the most "advanced" literature of the time. The names of Verlaine, Mallarmé, and Villiers appeared there with quotations from their work.

The literary fever made astonishing progress in me in those few weeks.

Then in November, when I was barely eighteen, I volunteered for military service to profit by the law of 1872 which had just been replaced by the law of 1889. I was refused the deferment I had hoped for, and joined the 122nd infantry regiment to begin my year of military service.

A very hard year for a very young and very frail volunteer. I was of a nervous temperament. No muscles.

I do not know how I stood it. We were subject to a mechanical regime in the intensive use of weapons. Boredom and constant pressure. Nothing to feed the mind. Corporals were being created, not officers. The initial good will of the sixty-nine volunteers changed to loathing for the profession.

On Sundays I shut myself up at home, and as a reaction against the stupidity of the week I wrote poetry.

That period of my life has affected me deeply. I recall that, in order to protect myself against that lethal boredom, I trained myself during the long marches or during hours of guard duty *to imagine* with all my powers other scenes and landscapes, completely different conditions—imagined so *precisely* that I was able to create for myself another life to mask the deadly reality.

In the month of May 1890, the celebration of the sixth centenary of the University (1290–1890), four days of leave. On the fourth day, by pure chance, I made the acquaintance of Pierre Louÿs. *A capital event.* An encounter at a café. A correspondence began between us, an intense exchange of likings and desires.

Pierre was already deeply involved in the movement. From him I learned what was going on. He founded a little review, *La Conque*, and induced me to send him some poems.

My first poem, "Narcisse parle," had a success that astonished me. Unexpectedly, Chantavoine praised it in the *Journal des Débats*.

I was then in my second year of law.

My law studies suffered as a result of my preoccupation with poetry. I met André Gide, who sent me Mallarmé's poems, then impossible to find in the provinces.

And I discovered Rimbaud. These two poets had a most powerful influence on me. Moreover, they made me despair —one for his perfection the other for his intensity. I thought I had seen the limits of the art of expression.

On the other hand, I read a great deal of Poe, in whom I found a scientific bent, a taste for precision, rigor, and reasoning that joined forces with my old love of Architecture.

I felt developing in me a sort of will toward an *intellectual* art, premeditated works requiring the presence of all the faculties of the mind. I posed to myself many questions about aesthetics, and gave great importance to reflections on *Ornament*.

At the same time I became acquainted with *Music*, that is I saw operating in me the liaison between music—an art I knew nothing about beyond simple works and popular operas—and my own preoccupations.

Beethoven's *Pastoral* Symphony and the prelude to *Lohengrin* sent me into transports. Wagner's great influence on me dates from that period.

Those few months of 1891 were for me very full ones. I changed visibly.

I went to Paris in the month of October. Pierre Louÿs took me to see Mallarmé.

I returned home for my third year of law.

All the preceding *themes* were aggravated.

I could write poetry only with great difficulty. A love affair finished me.

Finally, having taken my law degree—and just barely— I went to spend a month in Italy, where I suffered an acute mental martyrdom. Despair in every direction. Extra-lucid nights.

And I passed through my inner 18 Brumaire which led to the advent of "Mr. Teste".*

This meant that I resolved to think with rigor—to *not believe*—to consider as null and void everything that could not be brought to total precision, etc. ...

I began to construct for myself a "philosophy"—which was, moreover, the exact contrary of philosophy—and I set about looking into the exact sciences.

I went to Paris in November 1892.

I lived in the rue Gay-Lussac, in a student hotel. Mixed company—professors, foreigners from all countries, prostitutes, etc. ...

* Valery's English.

I went to Mallarmé's, to Heredia's. I saw Huysmans fairly often.

I attended the Lamoureux concerts.

And I did nothing. Nothing visible. My friends began not to understand. Even I did not know where I was headed. No profession, no regular studies, nothing produced, not even any projects.

But enormous mental activity. I studied mathematics, but in a very odd spirit, as a *model* of acts of the mind. I met Schwob, who showed me what erudition could be—until then I had despised it.

Furthermore I owe an infinite amount to my friends and acquaintances. I have always learned from conversation. Ten words are worth ten volumes.

It was at about that time that, greatly bothered by my totally hidden future and by living without any justification in the eyes of my family, I agreed to write an article on Leonardo which Mme Juliette Adam had asked of me at the suggestion of Léon Daudet! Knowing very little about Leonardo, and in short being surprised by her request, I accepted for the reasons stated above and I imagined a Leonardo of my own! In 1894 I went to London, which attracted me. There I saw Meredith and various other English writers. I greatly enjoyed that city, which is so foreign to us.

In 1896, an English friend indirectly found a job for me in London. The story of this incident is very curious. Without knowing what I was going to do there, I fell into the hands of a certain Lionel Dècle (from St. Quentin), an adventurer, explorer, journalist, etc. ...

A berth was found for me in the press service of the Chartered Company, where I observed the journalistic tricks of a great enterprise.

I soon returned to France, brought home by a severe case of flu.

I had written the article on the German methodical conquest to be printed in England.

At that moment in my life I had not found the politician or the businessman who could have made a career for me.

I was very much interested in all questions of organization and general policy.

It was no doubt an illusion, but I *saw* the modern world and the coming changes with intensity and keen interest.... I saw policy on a no doubt too grandiose scale of time and space.

In 1897, no longer able to endure being without employment and anxious about the future, I was so stupid as to take the competitive examination for the post of draftsman in the War Ministry, and I had the misfortune of being accepted.

Three years of "hard labour"* in the branch of artillery equipment. It was hard work. The period of the 75-millimeter cannon, Fashoda, and the Dreyfus affair—eight ministers in succession. ...

Finally, in 1900, I married.

Mme Mallarmé and her daughter had introduced me to the Mlles Gobillard, nieces of Berthe Morisot.

I married the younger in May 1900.

A month later, my friend Lebey invited me to become secretary to his uncle, Edouard Lebey, director of the Agence Havas.

* Valery's English.

I remained with him for twenty-two years. He was an incurable invalid, afflicted with a progressive paralysis that, to the end, left his mind unimpaired. I took charge of his business affairs and the business of the governing board of the Agency.

My employer was a consummate businessman. He was always affectionate and exceptionally considerate of me. But in order to keep me by him ... he never said the word that in 19– would have made me the director of the Agency, which everyone expected, except me.

From 1900 until 1913 I pursued certain very abstract studies to which I would like to return. I think that I went rather deep into various questions that have been little explored.

I owe to these studies, which were not at all meant for publication, a certain way of thinking that perhaps has its value.

Studies of attention, dreams and waking, time, number, language, etc.

From 1909 to 1914 my life depended on the health of my wife, who happily recovered.

In 1912, Gide and Gallimard kept after me to publish my early poetry. I refused categorically. They got together a manuscript of early poems taken from reviews and submitted it to me. I read through those outmoded verses with a less-than-indulgent eye.

But finally, since I was weary of my abstractions, I decided to write some verses as an exercise.

These few lines grew into *La Jeune Parque*, after four years of work.

They were beginning to interest me when the war broke out. I expected to be called up with the last contingent. But nothing happened, and I did not even stand guard over the most insignificant railroad culvert.

In 1917 *La Jeune Parque* was published in a limited edition of 600 copies, which sold out in three months.

Immediately after, I wrote "Aurore" and "Palme" with great facility.

Soon the poems of *Charmes* began to take form.

To my great astonishment, I found myself taking on the figure and rank of a *poet*.

I tried to put together my ideas about poetry, my general ideas, and my instinctual feelings about music. It was then that I was urged to write, and so became a slave to prefaces, essays, etc. The rest is known. I go into society and pass for one who likes it. The unexpected has always guided me. I have never asked anything—pursued anything outside myself. And I have rarely said no.

I have a rather pronounced inclination for things of the mind. None for the things of life. I do not like facility. And I greatly dread the difficult. I owe everything to my friends. My entry into literature to Pierre Louÿs, into the Academy to Hanotaux and a few others, my work to circumstances and even to publishers.

Etcetera. . . .

P.V.

Moi

PAUL-AMBROISE VALÉRY was born on October 30, 1871 of a Corsican father and an Italian mother. On his father's side, he knew nothing or almost nothing about his ancestry. On his mother's side, he learned from certain bundles of legal documents, certified at the tribunal of Rota (?), that he was descended from a family of northern Italy that numbered such illustrious members as a certain Cardinal de Grassi and the famous Galeazzo Visconti, Duke of Milan and conqueror of Bayard. Although he came of Mediterranean stock, his ancestors bequeathed him his clear blue eyes and his hair. His complexion, moreover, was white before it was burnt by a military sun.

A rather poor student at the university, he came out of it with the usual asinine diploma, bringing from his lessons only disgust for prescribed things and a love for his own fantasy.

At the age of twelve—perhaps before!—he was already possessed with *Notre-Dame de Paris* and certain obscurities known as *Han d'Islande* and *Bug-Jargal*. Then came poetry. He never even read Lamartine, nor Musset, but rather the *Feuilles d'automne*, the *Voix intérieures*, etc.

...Meanwhile the young man drew, painted, and questioned certain objects, searching for multiple light.

He studied the learned arts of the Middle Ages, of Byzantium, and a little of Greece.

Finally Baudelaire conquered him. Then the *Others*. And he could one day claim the merit, himself a provincial among provincials, of having discovered and cherished a few of the secret poems which manifest the solitary Glory of Mallarmé.

The task of explaining his exact mind and of reflecting the various currents of his thought in the too clear mirror of writing is illusory. You might as well try to explain the vagrant Whirlwind!...

Yet here are certain traits that may be real.

He detests what is called sentiment and Rolla is loathsome to him. Not that he does not have his tears and his anguish, but to him it seems ugly to make of them a rule of life or a theory of art. He understands all the kinds of affection, but for him they must be beautiful. He abhors easy weeping and melting over detestable love, with no splendor and no *recklessness*.

He adores the religion that makes beauty one of its dogmas, and Art the most magnificent of its apostles. He adores above all his own kind of Catholicism, a bit Spanish, very Wagnerian and Gothic.

As for pure belief, this is what he thinks (meaning above all to be frank, and above all, with himself):

"The crudest of hypotheses is to believe that God exists objectively.... Yes! He exists and the Devil too, but within us!

"The worship that we owe Him—this is the respect that we owe to ourselves and it should be understood as the search for the Better by way of our strength in the direction of our aptitudes.

"In two words: God is our *particular ideal*. Satan is that which tends to turn us away from it."

Women are for him graceful little animals who have the perverse ability to draw the attention of too many minds. They are placed on the summit of the altars of art, and our elegant psychologists know better, alas, how to note their bitchy sulking and their catlike clawing than to analyze the difficult brain of an Ampère, a Delacroix, or an Edgar Poe.

Finally, to terminate this autopsy, let us say that he has *loved* very little, and always by way of a dream.

He is made up of many different persons and a principal witness who watches all these puppets bobbing.

. . . .

To him the future seems mostly glum. The obligation to work frightens him, for he has always chafed under rules. *However one must live!...*

He regrets writing verse, which can *break* a *career* and make him lose a *good place*; moreover, he writes poorly and makes it too much his own to *please* others.

He has few illusions about things. But many inner illusions. He often thinks that there is nothing outside himself and ends by believing it.

His particular sign: he reduces all theory to schemata and strives to fit it into his practical life.

P. VALÉRY

This is between us.

14

Three Wakings

NIGHT IN THE BARRACKS

TEN O'CLOCK. In my loathing, I wander about the dark stony courtyard, consoled a little by the vast splendor of the night, a night like the somber velvet cushion on which a jeweler pours rivulets of diamonds. A cool soothing calm scarcely troubled by intruder lamps flickering beneath the archways, by the flash of a bayonet, the distant rumble of wheels, or the whistling of an invisible man. A trickle of water purls in the water trough.

The far-off sound of carriages plunges me again into the anguish of my imprisonment amidst the stupidity, the brutality, and the square heads under their kepis.

In the barracks. On a cot without sheets, between my overcoat and a blanket. Voices in the background, whispering. Yawns, flickering of the single dim light hanging from the ceiling. Someone snuffs it out. Now it is only a blue dot in the darkness; it swings rhythmically. A pale light trembles in the narrow windows. Bodies turn over in the covers. Someone swears. Now and then, a patch of light criss-crossed by the black bars of the window grating is projected onto the ceiling, and the whole image revolves across the room as the lantern outside passes by.

I cannot sleep. Sonnets of Heredia, verses of Mallarmé

come back to me. I say them over to myself without savoring them, without enjoying them.

Someone is snoring. One loudly, another softly. Both follow a mysterious rhythm. An oppressive odor bothers me. I cannot identify it because it envelopes me, but I imagine it rotten. I go down to the courtyard.

The cold is pleasant. Morning is coming. It is still dark. The sky is faintly dappled. Suddenly a flicker of light toward the east, between two roofs. A cry of light, still dim and distant. As if in reply, the blare of a bugle tears the silence. A sharp bizarre phrase rising out of two or three notes.

Reveille.

And arms stretch in the cots, while a breath of light comes into the dark room, pits the iron pitcher with white, lights up the metal of the guns. . . .

Uproar in the stairways. Water splashes in the water basins, and a wholesome morning wind bellies the new army overcoats appearing from all sides.

November 17, 1889
Morning

*　*　*

Sometimes I do not know whether I am more awake than asleep or more asleep than awake?

There is a conflict at times between the *one who thinks* and the one who wishes not to think but to sleep, and *that which is thought* and which wants to develop, to see its future.

Thus there are two possible outcomes to this moment.

Some mornings (today perhaps?) when I wake and sit down with this Notebook, I don't quite recognize myself.

I see myself as more stern, more stony than I am by nature, and old. I see myself as an old man, without pity for anything mental that tries to masquerade as total, and insignificant.

For, bear in mind, the *mark of the real* is *absolute insignificance*.

I get up. I go to make my first ritual cup of coffee without knowing whether it acts as substance on my chemistry, or a taste and stimulant through sensation, more than by molecular change in my composition, or a nervous effect of chronometric repetition. For it is possible to make these three hypotheses.

Thus I move about, and on the one hand I feel Ideas (very diverse) invading me, contesting life, etc., etc., but on the other hand I am aware of myself moving about and acting out of total automatism and somnambulism.

I am aware of my own phantom, my regular ghost. Everything I do has already been done. All my steps and gestures can do without me, as the imperceptible and essential acts of vegetable life *can do without us*.

My "lucidity" illuminates for me my mechanical nature. And—the last straw—it belongs to that nature. I am given to discovery and the unexpected at that early hour.

January 1944

* * *

Waking up. There is no phenomenon more exciting to me than waking.

Nothing *tends* to give a more extraordinary idea of... *everything*, than this autogenesis. This beginning of what was

17

—which also has its beginning. *What is*—and this is nothing but shock, stupor, contrast.

Here, a state of equidifference takes place as if . . . there were a moment (among the most unstable) during which no one is yet the *person one is*, and *could again become another*! A different memory could develop. Whence the fantastic. The external individual remaining, and the whole psyche substituted.

May 1944

Mediterranean Inspirations

TODAY I am going to confide in you; I am going to talk about myself. Do not imagine that I would venture to tell you the kind of secrets that everyone knows from his own experience. What I want to talk about has to do only with the relations between my mind and my sensibility in their formative period and the Mediterranean sea, which since my childhood has been ever present to my eyes and to my mind. These will be only a few specific impressions, and a few perhaps general ideas.

I begin with my beginning. I was born in a middling-sized seaport situated at the end of a bay and at the foot of a hill, whose mass of rock juts out from the line of the shore. This rock would be an island if two sandbanks—sand constantly washed up from the mouth of the Rhone and deposited by sea currents carrying the pulverized stone of the Alps toward the west—did not attach or join it to the coast of Languedoc. The hill, then, rises between the sea and a vast saltwater pond where the canal du Midi begins—or ends. The harbor it overlooks is made up of canals and docks connecting this pond with the sea.

Such is the place of my origin, about which I will make the ingenuous remark that I was born in one of those places where I should have liked to be born. I am happy to have been born in a place where my first impressions were those that came from facing the sea and from being in the midst of human activity. For me there is no spectacle to compare with what can be seen from a terrace or a balcony pleasantly situated above a harbor. I spent my days looking at what Joseph Vernet, a painter of beautiful seascapes, called "the various activities of a seaport." From that vantage the eye takes in the intoxicating expanse and the uniform simplicity of the sea, while, closer by, human life and industry traffics, builds, maneuvers. At any moment when the eye turns to nature—a nature eternally primitive, untouched, unchangeable by man and constantly and visibly subject to universal forces—it sees exactly what the first man saw. But closer to land it first notices the erratic work of time continually reshaping the shore, and then the reciprocal work of man— the accumulation of constructions with their geometric forms, straight lines, planes, and arcs—contrasting with the disorder and accidents of natural forms, just as the spires, towers, and lighthouses built by men contrast the falling and crumbling shapes of geological nature with an opposed will to construct—the stubborn and as it were rebellious work of our human race.

Thus, at the same time, the eye encompasses the human and the nonhuman. It is this that the great Claude Lorrain felt and magnificently expressed and, in the noblest of styles, exalted—the order and ideal splendor of our great Mediterranean ports: Genoa, Marseille, and Naples, all transfigured, by the architecture of the port, the contours of the shore, the perspective of the water, making a sort of stage set, where only one actor moves, sings, and sometimes dies: LIGHT!

Halfway up the hill I spoke of was my school. There I learned *rosa, the rose,* without being too much bored, and I was sorry to leave after my second year. The very small number of pupils allowed each of us to satisfy his pride. There were four in my grade, and, by the simple law of probability, I was first one time out of four without trying at all. Those in the final form were even more fortunate since they were only two. Inevitably, one got the first prize and the other the second. How could it have been otherwise? But fairness demanded that the one receiving the second prize should win the first prize in composition, and the other (naturally) the second. And so on. . . . To the strains of a military band, both would march down from the platform on prize-day, crowned with laurels and carrying gilt-edged books. . . .

> Corneille claims that there is no glory without risk:
> *To win without risk is to triumph without glory!*
>
> (*Cid:* ɪɪ, 2.)

But Corneille was mistaken, and the mistake is naïve. Fame and glory depend not on effort, which is generally undetected, but on proper staging.

This school had rare charms. The courtyards overlooked the town and the sea. There were three terraces, one above the other: the *little ones,* the *bigger ones,* and the *biggest* were blessed with horizons of increasing vastness, which is not altogether true in later life! So, there was always something to look at during our recreation time, since there is always something happening at the frontier between land and sea.

One day, from the height of our happily situated school-yard, we saw a prodigious cloud of smoke rising into the sky, much thicker and more voluminous than the usual smoke from the steamers and freighters putting in at our port.

The noon bell had hardly rung when the day-pupils rushed out the doors in a yelling mob to the mole, where a crowd had been watching a good-sized ship burn for several hours. It had already been towed from the docks and left to its fate beside a fairly isolated jetty. All at once flames shot up to the crow's nest, and the masts, undermined by the fire burning furiously in the holds, suddenly came down with all their rigging, as if mowed off, stripped, abolished, while a great jet of sparks leapt up and a sinister muffled roar reached us on the wind. You can imagine that many a student missed class that afternoon. By evening, the beautiful three-master had been reduced to a dark hull, apparently intact but filled like a crucible with an incandescent mass whose fiery brilliance intensified as night came on. The hellish derelict was eventually towed out to sea, and finally sunk.

At other times we would be on the lookout from our school for the arrival of the fleet, which came every year and anchored a mile off shore. How strange the battleships of that time were, the *Richelieu*, the *Colbert*, the *Trident*, with their rams shaped like ploughshares, their sheet iron armor plates at the stern, and, beneath the flag, the admiral's bridge, which filled us with such envy. These ships were ugly and imposing; they still carried a considerable structure of masts and spars, and their bulwarks were lined with the crews' sea-bags in the old-fashioned way. The fleet sent ashore its boats, beautifully kept, decorated, and equipped. These long boats skimmed over the water; six or eight pairs of oars, perfectly synchronized, were shining wings flinging out, every five seconds, a flash and a swarm of sparkling drops. In the foam from their sterns trailed the colors of their flag and the edge of the scarlet-bordered blue rug on which the officers sat, dressed in black and gold.

These splendors engendered many a naval vocation; but between the cup and the lip, between the schoolboy and the midshipman's glorious life, there were very grave obstacles: the incorruptible forms of geometry, the systematic snares and enigmas of algebra, the grim logarithms, the sines and their fraternal cosines discouraged many a boy who despairingly saw, between the sea and himself, between his dream-navy and the real navy, the implacable surface of a blackboard falling like an iron curtain. So he had to be content with melancholy gazing at the open sea, and enjoy only through his eyes and his imagination, and direct his thwarted passion toward literature and painting, for at first it seems that desire is enough to open up those careers which look so attractively easy. Only those who are predestined suspect and exact of themselves at an early age all the imponderable difficulties. For such there is neither a course of study nor an examination.

These dreamers, whether budding poets or painters, contented themselves with the impressions lavished on them by the ever-eventful sea, creator of extraordinary forms and projects, mother of Aphrodite and soul-giver to many an adventure. It could still be said in the days of my youth that History lived on these waters. Our fishing boats, many of them carrying on their prows the same emblems used by the Phoenicians, were in no way different from those used by the navigators of antiquity and the Middle Ages. Sometimes at twilight I would watch these sturdy boats returning to port, heavy with their catch of tunny, and a strange feeling would possess me. The sky, extremely clear, but suffused with fiery rose at its base and its blue fading to pale green toward the zenith; the sea, already dark, with breakers and spume of a dazzling white; and, toward the east, just above the horizon, a mirage of towers and walls which was the phantom Aigues-Mortes. At first nothing could be seen of the fishing fleet but the sharply pointed triangles of their lateen sails. As they came closer in, one could make out the heaps of enormous tunnies they had caught. These powerful fish, some as large as a man, blood-spattered and glistening, would remind me of men at arms whose bodies were being brought ashore. It was a picture of epic grandeur which I was fond of calling "Return from the Crusades."

But this imposing sight led to another, of horrifying beauty, which you will forgive me for describing to you.

One morning, the day after a large catch of huge tunnies, I went down to the sea to swim. First I walked out on a little jetty to enjoy the beautiful light. Looking down all at once, I saw only a few feet away in the marvelously still and transparent water, a hideous and resplendent chaos that made me shudder. *Things* of a nauseating red, masses of a delicate pink or of a deep and sinister purple lay there.... I recognized with horror the dreadful heap of viscera and entrails of Neptune's flock, which the fishermen had thrown into the sea. I could neither flee nor endure what I saw, for the disgust caused by that charnelhouse struggled in me against my sense of the real and exceptional beauty of that confusion of organic colors, of those ignoble trophies of glands from which bloody wisps still trailed, and of pale and quivering pouches held by invisible threads beneath the polished surface of the perfectly clear water, while the infinitely slow movement in the limpid depths sent an almost imperceptible golden shimmer over all this shambles.

The eye admired what the soul abhorred. Torn between repugnance and interest, between flight and analysis, I forced myself to muse on what an artist of the Orient, a man with the talents and curiosity of a Hokusaï, for example, might have drawn from this sight.

What a print, what variations on the theme of coral he might have conceived! Then my thought turned toward the brutal and the bloody in the poetry of antiquity. The Greeks were not averse to describing the most appalling scenes. . . . Their heroes worked like butchers. Their mythology, epic poetry, and tragedies are full of blood. But art is comparable to that limpid and crystalline depth through which I saw those hideous things. Art gives us eyes that can take in everything.

There is no end to my early impressions of the sea! I cannot take time to tell you about everything that diverted me, held me spellbound on the harbor docks; to describe, for instance, some of the boats that now scarcely exist, types centuries old driven out by steam and gasoline; the strange xebecs, for example, of an oriental elegance of form with their slender and curiously designed prows, their tall lateen rigs rising as sharp as a pen stroke, and surely identical with the ships of the Saracens and the Berbers in the days when those fearsome visitors came plundering our shores and carrying off ladies and damsels. My xebecs were used only for the transport of excellent products. Their hulls were painted yellow and brilliant green (a triumph of pure color) and on their decks lemons from Portugal and oranges from Valencia were piled in vivid pyramids. On the calm, green water around them floated some of this yellow or red fruit, either fallen overboard or thrown away.

I will not try here to evoke the heady mixture of odors which make a dock's atmosphere an olfactory encyclopedia or a symphony: coal, tar, spirits, fish soup, straw, copra—

teeming, vying with one another to dominate and sway our associations of ideas. . . .

But in these modest confidences, let me proceed from the concrete to the abstract, from impressions to thoughts, and now evoke simpler sensations, deeper and more complete, those sensations of the whole being which are to colors and odors what the form and composition of a speech are to its ornaments, images, and epithets.

What are these general sensations?

I plead guilty before you of having been truly possessed by light, truly possessed by water.

My recreation, my only recreation, was the purest of all: swimming. I made a kind of poem about it, a poem that I call *involuntary* since I did not go so far as to give it form and write it down. When I made it, it was not my intention to sing of the state of swimming but to describe it—which is quite a different thing—and it verged upon poetic form only because the subject, swimming, moves and has its being in the heart of poetry.

SWIMMING

I seem to rediscover and know myself again when I return to this universal water. I know nothing of harvests and vintages.

The *Georgics* mean nothing to me.

But to plunge into the mass and the movement, to be active from head to toe, to roll in that pure and deep element, breathe in and breathe out the divine saltness—this for me is nearest to love, the activity in which my body becomes all signs and all powers, as a hand opens and closes, speaks and acts. Here all the body spreads itself, draws itself in, understands itself, spends itself trying to exhaust all its possibilities. It touches *her*, wishes to seize *her*, embrace *her*; it goes mad with life and its own freedom of movement; it loves *her*, possesses *her*; with *her* it engenders a thousand strange ideas. Through *her*, I am the man I wish to be. My body becomes the immediate instrument of my mind, and yet the author of all its ideas.

All is clarified for me. I understand to the full what love might be. Excess of the real! Caresses are knowledge. The lover's acts would be models of works.

So, swim! Plunge your head into that wave rolling toward you, breaking over you and rolling you.

For several moments I thought I would never be able to come out of the sea. It cast me up, sucked me back into its irresistible folds. The withdrawal of the huge wave that had heaved me onto the sand rolled the sand with me. In vain I dug my hands into the sand; it drained, gave way, sank down under my whole body.

While I was still struggling feebly, an even larger wave came in and threw me like flotsam to the edge of this perilous place. At last I walked along the wide beach, shivering, and drinking the wind. It was a southwester, which caught the waves broadside, curled and ruffled them, covered them with scales, and burdened them with a net of smaller waves which they carried from the horizon to the breakwater and the surf.

A happy man with bare feet, I walked, drunk with walking on the mirror continually repolished by the infinitely thin wave.

And now I shall raise somewhat the tone of these confidences.

The port, the boats, the fish and their odors, swimming— they were only a kind of prelude. Now I would like to try to tell you about a profounder action of the sea on my mind. It is difficult to be precise in these matters. I am not fond of the word *influence*, which indicates ignorance or a hypothesis, and plays a great and convenient role in criticism. But I will tell you what is evident to me.

Certainly nothing so formed me, permeated me, instructed—or constructed—me as those hours stolen from study, hours seemingly idle but really given over to the unconscious worship of three or four undeniable gods: the Sea, the Sky, the Sun. Without knowing it, I recaptured something of the wonder and exaltation of primitive man. I do not know what book could match or what writer incite in us such states of productive wonder, of contemplation and communion, as I experienced in my early years. Better than any reading, better than the poets or the philosophers, a certain close observation without any definite or definable thought, a certain lingering over the pure elements of the moment, over the vastest and simplest objects, the most powerfully simple and perceptible in our sphere of existence —the habit this imposes on us of unconsciously relating every event, every person, every expression and every detail to the greatest and most stable of visible things, moulds us, accustoms and induces us to measure without effort and without reflection the true proportions of our nature, to find within ourselves without difficulty the way to our highest level, which is also the most "human." In some way, within ourselves, we possess a measure of all things and of ourselves. Protagoras' statement that *man is the measure of all things* is characteristic and essentially Mediterranean.

What did he mean? What does it mean to measure?

Is it not to substitute for the object we are measuring the symbol of a human act whose repetition obliterates this object? To say that man is the measure of all things is thus to set up against the diversity of the world the ensemble or group of human potentialities; and it is also to set up against the diversity of our moments and the mobility of our impressions, and even the particularity of our individuality, our own unique and, as it were, specialized person confined in our local and fragmentary life, a ME who sums it up, dominates and contains it, as a law contains the particular case, as the sense of our own powers contains all the acts possible to us.

We are conscious of this universal Self, who is not our accidental self, determined by the coincidence of an infinite number of conditions and chances, for (between you and me) how many things in us seem to have been drawn by lot! . . . But I say we can feel, *when we deserve to feel*, this universal Self who has neither name nor history, and for whom our observable life, the life received and lived or undergone by us, is only one of the innumerable lives that this same Self might have adopted. . . .

You must excuse me. I have allowed myself to be carried away.'. . . But do not imagine that this is "philosophy." I do not have the honor of being a philosopher. . . .

If I allowed myself to be carried away, it was because to look at the sea is to look at the possible. . . . But to look at the possible is, if not quite philosophy, at least a germ of philosophy, philosophy in a nascent state.

Ask yourself how a philosophic thought could originate. As for me, I never attempt to reply when I ask myself this question, for my mind carries me at once to the shore of a marvelously luminous sea. There, the perceptible elements (or aliments) of the state of mind from which the most

general thought, the most comprehensive question ger-
minates, are brought together: light and space, leisure and
rhythm, transparency and depth. . . . Do you not see that our
mind experiences at such a time, discovers in that prospect
and that harmony of conditions, all the qualities and all the
attributes of knowledge: clarity, depth, expanse, measure. . . .
What it sees represents for it what is in its essence to possess
or to desire. The mind's contemplation of the sea engenders
a vaster desire than any that can be satisfied by the possession
of a particular thing.

It is as if the mind were beguiled, initiated into universal
thought. Do not imagine that I am now leading you into
subtleties. It is known that all our abstractions originate in
such personal and individual experiences; the words that
compose our most abstract thoughts are taken from the
simplest common language, words we have corrupted by
using them to philosophize. Do you know that the Latin
word from which we have taken the word *monde* ["world"]
means simply "adornment"? And you certainly know that
the words *hypothèse* ["hypothesis"], *substance* ["substance"],
âme ["soul"], *esprit* ["mind" or "spirit"], *idée* ["idea"] or
words like *penser* ["think"], *comprendre* ["understand"],
are the names of elementary acts such as *placing*, *putting*,
seizing, *breathing*, or *seeing*, which little by little took on
extraordinary meanings or overtones, or on the other hand
were progressively stripped until they lost whatever would
prevent combining them with almost unlimited freedom.
The notion of *peser* ["weighing"] has almost disappeared
from the notion of *penser* ["thinking"], and *respiration*
["breathing"] is no longer suggested by the words for *esprit*
and *âme*. The creation of abstractions, which the history of
language teaches us are repeated in our personal experience,

and it is by the same process that the sky, the sea, and the sun (which a while ago I called pure elements of the moment) suggested or imposed on contemplative minds the notions of infinity, depth, knowledge, universe—ever the subjects of metaphysics or physical speculation and whose very simple origin I see in the presence of exuberant light, space, movement, in the constant impression of majesty and omnipotence and sometimes of superior caprice, sublime wrath, or chaos among the elements always ending in triumph and the resurrection of light and peace.

I have just spoken of the sun. But have you ever looked at the sun? I do not recommend it. I tried it once, in my heroic days, and thought I would lose my sight. But I repeat, have you ever thought of the immediate importance of the sun? I do not mean the sun of astrophysics, the sun of astronomers, or the sun as the essential agent of life on this planet, but simply the *sun as sensation, sovereign phenomenon*, and its effect on the formation of our ideas. We never think of the influence of this conspicuous body.... Imagine the impression that such a star must have made on primitive minds. All that we see is *composed* by it, and by composition I mean an order of visible things and the slow transformation of that order which constitutes the entire spectacle of a day: the sun, master of shadows, at once part and moment, a dazzling part, and every dominant moment of the celestial sphere must have imposed on the first reflections of humanity the model of a transcendent power, a single master. Moreover, this peerless object, which hides in its own blinding light, played an equal role, visible and convincing, in the fundamental ideas of science. The observation of the shadows it casts must have served as the basis for a complete geometry, the kind called *projective*. This no doubt would not have been thought of under an eternally clouded sky; nor could the measure of time have been instituted, another primitive conquest first accomplished by observation of the displacement of the shadow of the *stylos*, and there is no physical instrument more ancient or venerable than a pyramid or an obelisk—gigantic gnomons, monuments whose character was at the same time religious, scientific, and social.

So the sun introduced the idea of supereminent omnipotence, and the idea of the order and universal unity of nature.

You see how it is that a clear sky, a distinct horizon, and an admirable shoreline can not only be the conditions for attracting life and the development of civilization, but they can stimulate the particular intellectual sensitivity that is scarcely distinct from thought.

And now I come to the dominant idea which will sum up what I have said and which for me is the conclusion of what I will call "my Mediterranean experience." I will do no more than specify a notion that is widely known, after all— that the Mediterranean, by reason of its physical features, has played a role or function in the formation of the European mind, of historical Europe, insofar as the European spirit has modified the entire human world.

The physical nature of the Mediterranean, with its resources and relations determined by it or imposed upon it, is at the source of the astonishing psychological and technical transformation, which in only a few centuries has sharply distinguished Europeans from other men, and modern times from earlier centuries. It was the Mediterraneans who were the first to take sure steps along the way toward precision in methods, in search of the necessity of controlling phenomena by the deliberate use of the powers of the mind, and who started the human race on the extraordinary adventure we are still living, whose developments no one can predict and whose most remarkable trait—and perhaps the most disturbing—is our increasingly marked estrangement from the initial or natural conditions of life.

The vast role played by the Mediterranean in this transformation which spread to all mankind can be explained (in so far as anything can be explained) by a few simple observations.

Our sea is a limited basin; any point on its shore can be reached from any other in a few days of coastal sailing or overland travel.

Three "parts of the world," that is to say, three very dissimilar worlds, enclose this vast salty lake, with many islands in its eastern part. There is no noticeable tide, or if noticeable it is almost negligible. The sky is rarely clouded for long—a happy circumstance for the navigator.

Finally, this enclosed sea, on the scale of primitive man and his means, is situated entirely in the temperate zone, the most fortunate situation on the globe.

The populations living along its shores are extremely diverse, differing in temperaments, sensibilities, and intellectual capacities, and living in close contact. Thanks to the ease of movement I spoke of, these people kept up relations of all sorts: war, commerce, trade (whether voluntary or not), of things, knowledge, and methods; they mingled their blood, their speech, their legends and traditions. The number of ethnic elements thrown together or in contrast throughout the ages, their customs, languages, beliefs, laws, and constitutions have engendered an incomparable vitality in the Mediterranean world. Here competition (one of the most striking characteristics of the modern era) reached a singular intensity very early: competition in markets, influences, religions. In no other region of the globe has there been such a variety of conditions and elements brought so close together, creating a richness again and again renewed.

All the essential factors of European civilization are products of these circumstances—that is, local circumstances have had effects (and recognizable effects) of universal interest and value. In particular the formation of the human personality, an ideal of the most complete and perfect development of man, was sketched out and realized on our shores. Man as the measure of all things; man as the political element and member of the city; man as a juridical entity defined by law; man as equal to any other man before God, and considered *sub specie aeternitatis*—these are almost entirely Mediterranean creations whose far-reaching effects need not be recounted.

Whether in the realm of natural or of civil laws, the type itself was defined by Mediterranean minds. Nowhere else was the power of language, conscientiously disciplined and directed, so fully and usefully employed; language ordered by logic, employed in the discovery of abstract truths, constructing the universe of geometry or the relations which allow for justice; or, again, mistress of the forum, the essential political means and a regular instrument for the acquisition or the conservation of power.

Nothing is more admirable than to see, within only a few centuries, the most valuable and among them the purest of intellectual inventions deriving from these coastal people. It was here that science broke away from empiricism and practical use, here that art cast off its symbolic origins, that literature was clearly differentiated and divided into distinct genres, and that philosophy tried almost all the possible ways to consider the universe and to consider itself.

Never and nowhere else, in an area so restricted and in so brief an interval of time has such a fermentation of minds, such a production of riches been observed.

Impressions and Recollections

AT THE TIME I am speaking of, I had reached the age when the child changes imperceptibly into a man.

Between the simplicity of childhood and the clarity of mature years there is a period of uncertainty and activity, a mingling of enthusiasms and boredom, eagerness and listlessness, as if we were encumbered with several souls contending for the future. The child lives in the moment; his toy conceals from him the sequel. A grown man lives in a future weighed down by his past. But the adolescent lives in the possible; the probable is not his business.

At least it was not mine. I lived abstractedly. My body attended law school; my mind grasped at many things, skimming them and then abandoning them at the least difficulty. I clung to a few books that I had come to think of as essential.

Friendship played a great part in my life. We were two or three comrades closely bound together by our differences, as if some instinct to form a complete being had brought us together. I owe so much to these friends, and to various others, that one day I will try to give them my thanks.

Sometimes I wrote poems which I showed to them, but the idea of publishing, and even more, the aim of choosing this diversion as a career was infinitely remote from my thought. It did not enter my head that anyone could deliberately become a poet, or even that purely intellectual things and all the exceptional fruits of our rarest moments might serve us as objects of a profession. This feeling has only grown stronger in me.

I did not know where I was going; I was waiting, for what, I did not know. It seemed impossible to me that something would not happen to make of me what I could be, even if I did not know what it was. Faced with the mechanics and the practical side of life, I felt like a primitive man confronting nature. To him, everything seems subject to whim. But had anyone told me that my whole fate was to hang on an event that had taken place in the thirteenth century, I would nevertheless have been amazed.

I had interrupted my study of law (if one can speak of interrupting a semblance) to go and learn something about the use of force. The State graciously lodged me, with quite a few others, in a building whose proportions I greatly admire and which must date from the time of Louis XV. We must not tear down this barracks, the Caserne des Minimes, for it was built at a time when the military engineer sometimes yielded to the artist.

There were about fifty of us "temporary volunteers," forming a small, specially trained squad in the regiment. All winter we practiced the infinite refinements of the *goose step*, for this was well before the days of the Flood. At that time in Montpellier there was a Marshal of France and of England in the guise of an artillery captain assigned to the general staff of the division.

Just before entering the service I had been passionately reading and re-reading several volumes of Verlaine and Huysmans' *A Rebours*, which had such a great influence on young literary men of the time. I was suffering from being so cruelly separated from my reveries and my reading. Perhaps the military education of the time was at fault in not providing the cultivated part of the contingent with the attractions and stimulation of whatever is intellectual in the military profession. In times of peace, the enemy is boredom.

I would wait impatiently for Sunday, my intellectual holiday. As soon as I woke I would rush off between yawns of the guard, my overcoat flapping against my buoyant legs. Quickly I would climb to the plateau of the Prefecture. A dim inner light would be fading from the face of the clock as the morning light wakened the gold of its hours and its hands. I would run down the hill toward an ancient house in the rue Urbain-V. There I recaptured my idols and myself. At the back of a small, partly dried-up, partly mouldy old garden was my refuge and my soul. I would spend the whole day writing and rewriting poetry.

In May of that year, 1890, came the event from the thirteenth century that was of such great consequence for me.

The University was about to be six hundred years old. Physical bodies are inconsolable for growing old, but it is not the same with corporate bodies. The University let it be known throughout the world that she was to be congratulated for being so aged. All her sisters sent delegations loaded down with speeches.

The entire town was hung with banners, and the strangest robes moved about everywhere. Never have so many doctors of all colors been so gaily intermingled. It might have been called a carnival of human knowledge, with ignorance looking on.

I remember the illustrious Helmholtz in the magnificent robes of a Berlin professor. His enormous crenellated velvet hat covered a powerful cranium. The face was rugged, the hair red. The discerning analyst of whirlwinds was not apparent in that rough old warrior.

The military authorities graciously granted leave to the students doing military service to take part in the celebrations. We marched in berets among our comrades in uniform. . . . But finally the last day came. It all ended with a banquet at Palavas.

I can see myself on the shore, just before the final banquet, among a group of students from Lausanne. They were charming comrades. I had written my name in the tops of their caps, and from them had received the green and red ribbons of the *Bellettriens*. Another group of young Swiss came along and took us off to a café terrace.

Someone, who was neither blond nor Swiss, sat down beside me. Fate had taken on the features of this delightful table companion. We exchanged a few words. He was from Paris. An album I had placed on the table plunged us into the arts. Sacred or yet unknown names were murmured between us. We were in raptures. . . .

My newfound friend stood up. Joining arms, walking as if in a lyrical world, we strode along in instantaneous intimacy. In low voices we compared our gods, our heroes, and our dreams.

Minds need only five or six minutes to communicate fully. And the time had almost run out. Our Swiss friends were calling us. We lost each other among the twelve hundred banquet guests. I returned to Montpellier before dawn to put on my tunic with its yellow collar. Emptying my pockets, I found a visiting card bearing the name:

PIERRE LOUIS

He had not yet adopted the *Y* and its diëresis.

I would not know how to estimate the number of independent circumstances necessary to our meeting. How many times, in endless conversations with the admirable author of *Aphrodite* and *Bilitis*, have we marveled at this triumph of the improbable!

My Early Days in England

My FIRST VISIT to England? Good heavens, I can hardly remember it; I was seven years old. . . . To cross the Channel then people had to use an extraordinary kind of boat consisting of two hulls joined together, and with this arrangement the rolling could have been hardly noticeable, but all the same I felt seasick. I believe I was justified and that I had a perfect right to feel seasick, for experience has condemned this contrivance and it has now vanished from the seas. This occurred in 1878. All the recollection I have of this first contact with England is merely an impression of a mad fright which I experienced in Mme Tussaud's Museum, which I understand has now ceased to exist. I can still see those horrid masks of famous criminals which were being collected for the Museum. I have also another faint recollection of an operetta called *Fatinitza*, music by Suppé. I retained an exquisite and fairylike impression of it, with slim and charming women, whom even now I can see in my mind, dancing. A shower of snowflakes was falling all over them.

Sixteen years elapsed before I again came to London. On a certain day I felt a sudden desire to go and see that city to which Mallarmé often referred as "very captivating." In those days, French artists used to form a peculiarly gentle and sweet idea of London. They looked upon it as a kind of Babel made up of an infinity of voluptuous and comfortable homes with which they associated, in their flights of fancy, Turner's gigantic painting and the familiar visions they had met with when reading Dickens.

Some among them, however, had a more precise opinion and a more erudite knowledge of England. Their reading had gone beyond Dickens and they possessed notions about English literature often very much deeper than might have been expected of Frenchmen. In making this statement, I am thinking in particular of Marcel Schwob. In some respects I might say that Schwob knew English too well. He was acquainted with the least known and oldest writers, but this is an achievement almost within the reach of all. Schwob, impelled by his natural taste for brigands' stories (toward which his studies on Villon, regarded as a rogue, had inclined him), had made himself familiar with professional slang and especially with the slang of thieves in various languages and at different periods. He had learned the slang of the English populace and more particularly the slang of criminals. All the same, he followed the English literary movement of that age with the same passion. He was one of the first to make known in France such men as Meredith, Stevenson and many others. He corresponded with several of these writers, and when I left for London in 1894 he gave me a precious letter of introduction to George Meredith, whom he had never yet seen himself. During my stay, I lived a long way off the center, in the Highbury district. Below my windows I had a large lawn gently brightened by the golden morning sun in June; it was called the Crescent, where sometimes football matches were being played, while often strollers were lying, lazily enjoying a "far niente," which I should never have thought possible elsewhere than in our southern latitudes. In fact, I discovered on that day that there are lazzaroni in the North. I started roaming about London from morning till evening, very much alone, but in the company of thoughts within, and I found delight in wandering aimlessly and without any purpose in the streets of the capital, either too full of life or else too lonely. For me there is such a thing as a London intellectual intoxication. I can say that my mind was amused at everything, and since then a general impression of nervous and indefinite merriness has remained in my mind associated with the idea of a town and a country that are not generally regarded as calculated to impart such cheerful excitement. I see London —black, red, and white with flashes of crystal and immense green expanses.

I did not miss the opportunity of getting into touch with a few young men of letters. At that time a review was founded, which is now extinct, called *The Yellow Book*. This review, I believe, played a rather important part in the literary movement which corresponded in England to the symbolist movement in France. Numerous writers occasionally met at the house of Mrs. Pennell, the wife of the well-known engraver, who used to live in Buckingham Street close to the Savoy. I remember having had there a long conversation on Toulouse-Lautrec with Aubrey Beardsley, whose art was so different from that of Toulouse. Beardsley highly appreciated the work of the French painter, of whom he spoke with great interest and wonderful intelligence. I very clearly remember Beardsley's extremely delicate, sad, and distinguished features.

I believe I can also recollect having had a long chat with Mr. Gosse about Mallarmé's poetical art and poetry. I have a recollection of a monologue of an hour and a half.

The windows of Mrs. Pennell's apartments overlooked the Thames. Between their conversations the guests enjoyed an admirable view of the river and of the blue expanse on a June night. One evening, about 11 o'clock, a pink glare lighted the sky. Nothing could be more beautiful than the fantastic sight that met our gaze. A great conflagration had broken out in the direction of Finsbury; no flames were visible, but the reverberation of the fire from the sky imparted a rosy hue to the atmosphere. A London as seen in dreams was being produced before us: we saw masses of azure and gigantic turquoise and sapphire forms. The dome of St. Paul's was silhouetted against the luminous sky, and one felt the sensation of seeing a unique masterpiece that would have satisfied all Turner's and Whistler's ambitions combined.

The great event of my journey to London was my visit to George Meredith. Having sent him Marcel Schwob's letter of introduction, I received from him the following reply in French:

Boxhill, Dorking,
le 20 juin 94.

Cher Monsieur,

L'ami de Marcel Schwob se trouve bien dans son droit en me demandant l'entrée de ma maison. Vous serez le bienvenu, et j'espère que vous me ferez l'honneur de dîner avec moi, 7 heures. Cuisine anglaise, malheureusement: mais pour le vin, il est bien français. Je suis chez moi chaque jour de cette semaine à votre disposition après 4 heures soir. Vendredi, samedi, dimanche. Il y a un train de retour 8.25.

Agréez, Monsieur, l'assurance de ma considération distinguée.

GEORGE MEREDITH

On the following Sunday I took the train to Boxhill. After I had reached my destination the train went on, leaving me alone, absolutely alone, at the Boxhill Halt. No one near me, no dwellings, no sign-post. Where and how could I find my way to the house? After a few minutes I began to lose hope. I did not want to leave the railway, as each step I took might be a step farther away from my goal. I already felt doomed to stay at the Boxhill Halt for ever. At last a man appeared. He was an honest-looking fellow, wearing a check cap, with a pipe in his mouth. He approached me with a steady step and leisurely. Having raised his cap, he asked me whether I was the Frenchman expected by Mr. Meredith, and forthwith I declared myself enthusiastically and un-mistakably the very Frenchman expected by Mr. Meredith. Then he said to me "I am the faithful Coles," from which my great sagacity led me to infer that he must be the great writer's servant. We started on our journey, plunging into the verdure of English fields where there are neither walls, boundaries nor hedges; green everywhere.

On the way, good-natured Coles attempted a conver-sation with me. I speak and understand very little English, especially when spoken by the common folk. Nevertheless, I was able to extract some substance from this transitory conversation. Coles informed me that he was very fond of the French. When I then asked him if he knew them, and how and where he had learned to like them, he told me that in 1889 his master, on the occasion of the Exhibition, had paid him his fare to Paris. He had availed himself of an excursion. I then said to him, "You liked Paris very much." "Oh, yes, sir," he replied, and then explained that, having only just alighted at the Gare du Nord, he made the acquain-tance in some way or another of an individual who, he thought, was a constable on leave (perhaps he had taken a postman or bank messenger for a policeman). Howbeit, he spent the three days and three nights, which had been originally allocated to a visit to the Exhibition, in drinking, sleeping, and again drinking with his extempore friend. He had seen Paris under a table. The recollection filled him with joy.

I was beginning to wonder where Meredith's abode might well be. All at once Coles said to me, "Here we are; all you need do is walk straight ahead," and he went off, after again raising his cap with a happy smile. Still I could see nothing before me but green pastures without walls, hedges, or houses. I walked on in the direction indicated. Gradually the ground rose, and I soon observed against the sky, at the top of the hill, a mass of something sweetly reflecting the golden rays of the setting sun and consisting of a few trees clustered together round a hut—the hut in front. I began to distinguish a few persons sitting who, little by little, proved to be ladies and gentlemen having tea. I felt very bashful in thus approaching, in full daylight, Meredith and his guests. I imagined the impression necessarily produced upon them by this little foreign personage, a black marionnette on a green background, advancing awkwardly towards them. Then a somewhat strange looking old man rose with difficulty and came towards me. He wore a blue suit and a red handkerchief round his neck. He walked with difficulty, resting on a stick. When within three paces from me, raising and shaking his cap as a sign of welcome, he missed his footing and fell full length in front of me. I have the strange recollection of having picked up with wonderful ease the very thin body of this rather tall man. I felt confused by the incident, which increased my awkwardness, but Meredith at once manifested so much kindness and such marked sympathy that this painful impression almost at once gave way to the pleasure his gracious reception gave me. He spoke roughly and with difficulty, with a strong guttural and rather indistinct voice. There was great nobility in his face and in his manner. He introduced me at once to his guests, who included Sir Frederick and Lady Pollock and a young girl dressed in yellow. I can very clearly see the color of that dress, even now.

After tea, while talking with Meredith, I began looking at the cottage in front of which we were sitting. I was asking myself whether this represented his whole habitation. He suggested that we should go in. The dwelling consisted of two very small rooms. The walls were covered with books, the larger number of which were in French, and the larger number of these French books were Memoirs on "Le Consulat et l'Empire," which at that time were published in quantities. They included all possible Marbots, Sergent Bourgognes, and Captain Coignets. Meredith was in love with Napoleon. He spoke of him with the greatest fervor, sometimes curiously expressed. For instance, he said, "Napoleon was a man so great, so great, that the Gods could only get rid of him by turning him against himself." Such an opinion is somewhat noteworthy from the lips of an Englishman. He also had a kind of worship for Joan of Arc.

This might perhaps lead to some reflections on the taste, if not on the devotion, which so many eminent men have felt for the Emperor. It is the zenith of glory to be able to attach to one's person or to the idol of one's person, at the same time, the soul and hazy devotion, so to speak, of the people, and the minds of the most deep-thinking men, men so different as Goethe, Byron, Stendhal, Balzac, Hugo, Lamartine, Nietzsche, Tolstoi, Taine and others; and nearly all the great statesmen of the second half of the nineteenth century took a passionate interest in the action and conduct and the probable psychology of Napoleon.

As I was curiously watching the desk on which Meredith was writing, I asked him why he had placed his desk in front of a little window, almost entirely obscured by dark and thin shrubs growing in front of it. Meredith replied, "The brain requires darkness," and, as we started talking about this awful brain, the eternal and invisible collaborator of the man of thought, both a very capricious friend and foe, Meredith said to me, "The brain never gets tired, it is the stomach. ...." Then we went down to dinner, toward the cottage, which until then I had not observed, and which was situated below in a depression of the ground.

I returned to London in the company of Sir Frederick and Lady Pollock. They did not forget to invite me to dinner at their house at an early date. What an exquisite house! I had the honor of being presented to two very old ladies, one the mother and the other the mother-in-law of Sir Frederick, who both spoke the purest and most elegant French. One of them had known Victor Hugo very well, and she had a long conversation with me about him.

I stayed a few days longer in London. I sometimes used to go to lunch at a restaurant which was called "Solferino," and which may no longer exist. There I met a few editors of the *Pall Mall Gazette*. My dear friend Charles Whibley had introduced me to them, and I particularly remember one of them, who bid fair to cut out for himself a brilliant career in literature and particularly in journalism—his name was Steevens. The *Pall Mall* was then very Imperialistic. It was fate's decree, however, that Steevens should die in the Transvaal during the siege of Ladysmith, where he was war correspondent, after having, for some time before, followed

Kitchener's operations against the Dervishes. He described the latter in his remarkable book *With Kitchener to Omdurman*.

I returned from England absolutely enchanted with my stay. I had seen London under the most favorable conditions. The month of June, the facilities I had had to come into contact with so many minds differing so much and, for me, both so distant and so attractive. Briefly, everything left upon me one of those impressions which necessarily create an increasing desire to experience them again and lead us to that strange conclusion that different causes must produce the same effects, and that it is possible to return to the same place as if it were a rendezvous with one's own self.

I therefore seized with alacrity the first opportunity that presented itself to return to London in 1896. Meanwhile, I had been prompted to take this second journey by a charming letter from George Meredith. Nothing could be more flattering to me than the spontaneous wish to see me again expressed by the great author.

Juillet 11ème 1895.

Cher Monsieur Valéry,

Voici que nous sommes en pleine saison de voyages, et peut-être avez-vous l'intention de rendre visite en Angleterre, pour vos études. Il se peut même que vous avez des amis qui peuvent vous attirer et aider à trouver quelques agrémens dans ce pays assez triste pour un étranger. Si cela est, je vous prie de me compter un peu d'entre eux et de venir me visiter. Vous me ferez un vrai plaisir. Sir Frederick et lady Pollock, que vous avez rencontré à ma chaumière, se souviennent de cette occasion avec beaucoup d'amitié. Pour moi, je parcours les Gazettes littéraires pour chercher votre nom et vos oeuvres: je sais que vous travaillez et que vous possédez avec l'habileté cette chaleur qui pousse à de grands resultats.

M. George Hugo m'a parlé d'une étude sur Da Vinci,—mais par grace, ne m'appelez pas, maître, je ne suis que votre frère ainé.

Agréez l'assurance de mes sentiments les plus amicals.

GEORGE MEREDITH

Meredith, with the utmost kindness, had touched the sensitive spot of my conscience at that time.

I was then leading a strange life, empty and yet full, idle and yet occupied, and sterile in regard to its results (for I was only writing a few notes for myself), but possibly fruitful all the same owing to the diversity or, let us say, fickleness of the interest I took in mental affairs—a life which I had devoted to the utmost to all the whims of my curiosity, although I was still following within myself a certain clue which I felt to be continuous, but the end of which I could not see. This singular mode of existence, charming in itself—I say charming, but understand that it was made up of worries—was attended with serious drawbacks from a practical standpoint. I felt too much that I was nothing, and in the end I believed that I was absolutely barred from ever achieving anything. Sometimes the anxiety of the future weighed heavily upon my soul. The worry about my material position penetrated my intellectual powers and introduced into my ordinary problems an anxiety of a more positive character. I lived waiting for I do not know what incident to turn up and change my life. My trunk was always at the foot of my bed as a symbol of the departure I was ready to take upon the slightest token by Fate. I held myself in readiness to obey any call or external intervention giving me the signal to transform this stagnant life. I was therefore ready to go when, about the beginning of '96, I received a letter from London. A post about which no particulars were given was offered me there in a letter signed with an unknown name. I had to decide at once, wire my reply the same day, and leave in the evening.

The next morning I arrived at Victoria and a cab conveyed me to the writer of the letter. I found myself in a house where everything was Negro and all bristling with more or less poisonous assegais and arrows and adorned with obviously equatorial photos. I was then introduced into this home by an individual of magnificent black who, as I afterwards learned, was no less than the son of a king of Bechuanaland or something of the kind. I waited a considerable time among these African weapons and spoils, very anxious to know what I had come here for.

However, this state of suspense and surprise is familiar to me. It is seldom that my mind, when in the presence of new scenes or new experiences in life, is not surprised and as puzzled and taken back as if it were introduced to the moon.

A tall gentleman appeared in white silk pyjamas. He first of all gave me a full account of his life, which did not concern me, but at the same time interested me very deeply, as it was most graphic and varied, and his story was especially the story of the career of a professional explorer in the central parts of Africa.

He related stories which made me shiver, stories of Negroes given up alive to giant ants, stories of Negro kings like the famous Lobengula. He seemed to have known this man, fond of wit, who, it appears, formed words by having the tongue, hands, feet, etc., cut of people who had not shown him enough respect or whom he disliked.

At the most pathetic moment, it occurred to X——— that I must be dying of hunger. I availed myself of this little oasis, in the form of bacon and eggs and tea, to ask him what I was expected to do and why he had asked me to come. This was the time when the Chartered Company, under the able and energetic leadership of Cecil Rhodes, was organising Rhodesia and was trying to annex the Transvaal and the

Orange Republic. In other words, it was the very time of the Jameson Raid. The Chartered Company had rather extensive press departments, and my duty was to watch over the relations of these departments with the French press. In fact, on the next day I went to this press bureau and began to try and form some idea of my new functions.

Nothing could be more curious than the going in and out of strange personages observed in these offices. The Chartered Company had recruited their staff and agents for Africa in a most liberal and eclectic manner which would be very incomprehensible to a continental European. There could be seen there an unparalleled collection of the most diverse types of humanity, that is to say, a humanity of adventurers. Strange wrecks could occasionally be seen, men to whom no other perspective was left than suicide or life in its most dreary form. There were among the officers and "magistrates" of Rhodesia even members of the French aristocracy who had adopted a mode of living sometimes resembling more that of their ancestors of 800 years ago than that which they would have followed in modern France.

I spent a few weeks in these offices, but now the London climate was the weather of February, the season when the fogs did not fail to severely try my southern constitution. Before long I had to give up the Chartered Company in England. Had it not been for influenza, I might have stayed. I had got accustomed to English life, and as I had no literary ambition, I could well have settled there, where I found my substance and livelihood.

During this stay I met fewer men of letters than during my visit in 1894. I have kept a very affectionate recollection of that kindly W. E. Henley. He was then managing *The New Review*, a wonderful review, which has supplied very important articles (including contributions from Marcel Schwob, Williams, Joseph Conrad, etc.), and the extinction of which, possibly due to Henley's death, is to be deplored. It is in that review that Williams published between '95 and '96 the famous series of articles he had written on the development of German competition and the dangers it involved for British economics. These articles appeared under the description "Made in Germany," and the impression they produced was sufficiently strong to procure the passing of the Bill which bears that name. W. E. Henley had the singular idea of asking me to write a kind of philosophical commentary on that same question. At first I felt very much embarrassed by this request, but I finally gave him a general outline of views on the method, which he published in French at the beginning of the year '97.

I returned to England much later in 1922. My friend G. Jean-Aubry had the excellent idea of organising a few lectures which I delivered in London. He seized the occasion of my visit, which coincided with the fixing of a commemorative medallion on the house where Verlaine stayed in 1872, Howland Street, Tottenham Court Road. It was a little ceremony noteworthy, on account of the cold weather then prevailing, by the heterogeneous assembly which attended it, among which were observed a somewhat puzzled policeman, a few passers-by and sundry witnesses, more or less interested in the question. M. de St. Aulaire, then Ambassador in London, made it a point of honor to participate in our secret rites and to speak himself almost officially in honor of the "accursed poet," but this is history which is almost contemporary.

Whether old or new, my recollections of England are among the most pleasant recollections of my life. I have only retained one bitter thought, and that is the hateful sensation of a kind of impotency, which I have never been able to overcome, in expressing myself in English or understanding it as it is spoken.

A Timely Recollection

I WAS in London in 1896, and very lonely, even though I was obliged by my business to see many people every day—people of the most picturesque sort. I liked London, which was still rather strange to me, and rather a "Biblical City," as Verlaine called it. No one has better described it in a few lines of verse.

I was pervaded by the wonderfully strong sensation of being dissolved in the mass of people, of being no more than a perfectly commonplace element in the fluid multiplicity of living creatures flowing endlessly along the innumerable streets—the Strand, Oxford Street, over bridges vanishing in the fog—creatures whose muffled steps on the pavement stupefied me, leaving me with the sole impression of the fatal flood of our destinies. I obeyed; I gave myself over, aimlessly and to the point of exhaustion, to this river of people where faces, postures, individual lives and their certainty of being unique and incomparable, all merged. Among the crowds of passing people I had the overpowering sense that it was our business to pass by, that none of these creatures, including myself, would ever pass there again. I took a bitter and outlandish pleasure in the simplicity of our statistical condition. The mere numbers of people absorbed all my individuality, and I became vague and indistinguishable to myself. This thought is the truest we can have about ourselves.

One day, tired of the crowd and solitude, I decided to visit the poet Henley. Mallarmé, who was very fond of him, had talked to me about him. He had described Henley in this way: "You will see the head of a lion."

William Henley received me more than courteously in his cottage at Barnes, on the bank of the Thames.

I was impressed, as Mallarmé had been, by the somewhat formidable expression of the old poet's face. But with his first words, this wild creature with a strong and truly leonine head, a heavy mane, and a red beard streaked with white put me at ease; and, after a while, a bit too much at ease. Jovial, and speaking French in a warm deep voice with a marked accent, he treated me to language strong and raw enough to stagger me. It struck a strange chord—or discord —in the Victorian atmosphere of his small parlor. I could not believe my ears. (A trite expression, but an admirable figure of speech.)

With roars of laughter and childish delight spurred on by my all too obvious stupefaction, Henley told me shocking stories, using a crude and astonishingly authentic slang.

I was shocked. . . . But what is more flattering than to be shocked by an Englishman in England?

Then my curiosity prompted me to ask my host where he had picked up his knowledge of obscene words and all this highly colored vocabulary. Having sufficiently enjoyed my surprise, he made no mystery of the circumstances that had given him so thorough an education. After the Commune he had associated with a number of more or less compromised refugees who had fled to London. He had known Verlaine, Rimbaud, and various others who spoke *abssomphe*, etcetera.

It must be confessed that poets' ordinary speech is often unrestrained in its freedom. The whole realm of images and words belongs to them. The two I mentioned ranged over it with their genius and did not stint themselves in enriching it in its most expressive regions. All this is well known, but here is something that is less so and may perhaps be surprising: tradition has it that Lamartine sometimes let shocking remarks fall from his golden mouth. ...

I told Henley this, and it delighted him.

Then two ladies came in.

When dinner was over they left us to ourselves, and a quite different conversation began between Henley's pipe and my innumerable cigarettes.

He spoke of a periodical he was editing, *The New Review*, in which he occasionally published articles in French. These last words gave me the sense that he was approaching the subject of me, but I did not guess that this conversation was to set me off on reflections and commit me to an application of my mind far from my concerns and usual problems.

The New Review, he explained, had just published a series of articles in English that had at first caused surprise in England, then considerable excitement and a certain indignation.

The author, Mr. Williams, had made a close study of British commerce and industry and found it dangerously threatened by German competition. In every economic field, thanks to the scientific organization of production, consumption, means of transportation, and publicity, and to very precise and searching procedures centralizing innumerable bits of information, this enterprise was systematically evicting British products from world markets, even taking over the markets in the British colonies themselves. Williams had noted all the details of this vast and methodical operation one by one, describing them with the greatest care, and had presented them in the English manner: with the fewest ideas possible and the most facts.

Even the title that Williams gave to his series of articles was becoming a catchword; a famous bill was about to incorporate it in legislation, and the three words "Made in Germany"* were immediately fixed in every English mind.

"Have you read them?" Henley asked me.

"No I haven't, sir."

"Of course.† Tomorrow I will send them to you. You can read all Williams' findings."

"And then?"

"Then you can write a good article for me on the whole series, a kind of philosophical summary, in the French manner. *Shall we say ten pages (4500 words)? And you can let me have the copy very soon? Say, within ten days?*"†

I simply laughed at him, as sure as anyone can be that he will not do something when he has neither the desire, nor the means, nor the obligation to do it. I was not even going to think of risking myself in an assignment so foreign to my tastes and for which I had not a single idea in my head.

Consequently, I was hardly back in Paris (bearing cordial greetings *for the good Stéphane*)† when I set to work, that is to say, to think. As a consequence, since the most probable consequence of an immediate and inevitable decision is the contrary decision: evidence arouses doubt, affirmation is aroused by negation; and the impossible, at first clearly perceived, soon stirs up all the resources of the imagination which work against it in the lavish production of the most varied solutions. . . .

One of these interested me. I had read something about military subjects because methods themselves interested me, and because at that time there were scarcely any examples of large scale organizations with separate functions and hierarchies except in European armies of the first rank. It seemed possible to generalize this type. Economic warfare is only one of the forms of natural warfare among creatures; I do not say "among men," for we can wonder whether man is not still in the planning stage. ...

I observed also that it was natural for science of the modern type to resemble such organized activities for which it had furnished the model. It divides, specializes, exacts discipline, etc. And finally, I deduced some gloomy prognostications from my comparison. Permit me to quote myself:

Now, all peoples who reach the estate of great nations or who resume that status in an era when there are already great nations enough, more ancient and more civilized than they, tend to imitate in a short time what has required centuries of experience for older nations; and to this end they organize themselves entirely by deliberate method, just as every city deliberately constructed is always built to a geometrical plan. Germany, Italy, and Japan are examples of nations that have made a new beginning very late, based on a scientific concept as accurate as it could be made by studying contemporary progress and the prosperity of their neighbors. Russia would offer the same example if her immense territory were not an obstacle to the rapid execution of such an overall scheme. ...

...Japan must think that Europe was made for her. ...

This article appeared on January 1, 1897, in *The New Review*. It is forty-eight years old. Yet the conjunction of the names of nations and some of the ideas found there seem not to have lost all meaning. What is now going on in the Far East and even elsewhere makes me feel that I am remembering.

Valéry–Fourment Correspondence

a selection

From a card I learn of the death of Gustave Fourment on September 26, my oldest friend, and for me one of the most important between 1887 and 1892. At first, he alone (and then Charles Auz ...) [Auzillion] were my confidants of that time. At the lycée I copied my lessons from his on the Esplanade, five minutes before the class hour. And our walks in the moonlight. We ended by knowing each other to the point that we could no longer say what we absolutely did not want to say to one another, and we spent hours together, walking without a word.

From a letter of December 8, 1940.

[Valéry to Fourment, first letter]

[Genoa] August 28, 1887

My dear friend,

I am a bit late in writing to you, but all there is to do and see leaves me little time to write to my friends in "doulce France." Finally I have some leisure today, and I get down to it.[*]

[*] Valéry had just finished his year of rhetoric at the lycée of Montpellier. He had successfully passed the first part of the bacca-laureate. In the early spring of this same year he lost his father, Barthélémy Valéry. On August 9 he embarked with his mother and older brother, Jules Valéry, at Marseille; arriving on August 11 at

Genoa is rich in monuments and I spend my time visiting them. The cathedral is beautiful, *gothico-moresque*, with statues from former times and inscriptions which I try to translate with the dregs of Latin remaining with me. Speaking of cathedrals, I will tell you my opinion of the local clergy. I think they are worth even less than ours. They are strong in Latin, barbarous in matters of taste. They spoil the churches with their mania for tawdry decoration and gilt; organs which have such a splendid effect at home are replaced by orchestras that play bits from operas; they (the clergy, not the organs) encourage superstition in the people, which is frightening. In short, I prefer ours and our ceremonies, less theatrical but much more Christian. (Please note that I am not speaking in the role of a Catholic!—but simply from the point of view of taste.)

I have visited many palaces filled with paintings. Among others, the palace of the famous Andrea Doria, Admiral of the Galleys, allied turn about with France and Austria. There I saw a complete salon from the fourteenth century!— with paintings from that period. I sat in the chair where first Charles V sat, and then Napoleon.

(Same letter) August 29, 1887

Much activity here with respect to the military. Bersaglieri, infantry, and artillery fill the streets; the whole coast bristles with great cannons which fire all day long; officers swarm. In this respect I have never seen such activity in France. I spent a day at La Spezia where I visited the battleships, among them the largest in Italy, the *Italia*, with its six

Genoa, he stayed with his maternal uncle, Gaetano Cabella, and his aunt Vittoria Cabella, who with their daughter Gaeta were then living *dietro il coro di San Luca*. [The notes to this correspondence are by Octave Nadal, 1957.]

smokestacks, and its four cannons of a hundred tons, each firing at a cost of 1,800 francs. It is something to see. A few years ago Italy was nothing, no navy, no armies; today it has the latest thing in battleships, soldiers, cannons, etc.!

The king is generally liked and respected, as well as Queen Marguerite.

Here I am at the bottom of the page (a very rambling page wouldn't you say?). When I return, I will tell you about many other things that don't come to my mind right now.

Good-bye, write to me, tell me what our friends are doing, what you are doing.

I am waiting impatiently for your news and for something new. Good-bye, reply quickly and at length to this letter that R—* would have marked with red pencil from top to bottom.

I shake your hand.

My address: Monsieur *Paul* Valéry

In care of Monsieur Gaetano Cabella†

Dietro il Coro di San Luca

Genova

P. Valéry

* Rogery, professor at the lycée of Montpellier.

† Gaetano Cabella, the poet's maternal uncle, had married Vittoria de Grassi, the second daughter of Giulio de Grassi, head of the customs office of Genoa (1850), consul at Sardinia (1885), and then Italian consul at Sète at the time of the unification of Italy. Gaetano Cabella died in April 1899.

[Fourment to Valéry]

Montpellier, September 5, 1887

Dearest,

> *Quemadmodum desiderat cervus*
> *ad fontes aquarum, ita desiderat*
> *anima mea ad te.* (Psalm 41).*

Without lying, could you ever address a letter to me with that superscription? I dare not hope so, seeing the time it took you to write me two pages. It is not that I am unaware of the lack of seriousness in the promises of friends who are traveling... But look! Friendship has the right to be demanding, since there is friendship (at least I think so) more demanding than love; because love has compensations that friendship does not. I realize also that your enthusiasm for Gothic cathedrals, your rage against those who plaster them and cover them with gilt, your apprehension in seeing the military works of Genoa and the battleships of La Spezia, leave you scarcely the leisure to think of those who are in— "doulce France." Not so much warmth, my friend, for those stones which will never be grateful for the worship you bring to them; a bit more friendship for one who isn't yet able to thank you for the pleasure he felt while reading your letter, too short and too dry.

I am preaching to you, my friend; excuse my bad nature. I am a preacher and a boring one. Anyway, that is enough for today. If I go on, you will accuse me of having learned too well the lessons of a professor whose initials I don't need to write down, as you did.† You smile! Good-bye. ...

G. FOURMENT

* The quotation is actually from Psalm 42. [See notes p. 396.]
† Rogery.

[Valéry to Fourment]

Genoa [September 9 or 10] 1887

My dear friend,

Excuse the faults of the author.
Calderón.

Your letter is here on my table, near my books and pencils; I have read it and reread it each time with new pleasure. It seems to me that I have just received a breath of air from France, and ... you will laugh perhaps, this country breeze makes me quite content. You wouldn't imagine how patriotic you feel when you are not in your own country, when you don't see the brilliant red trousers of our soldiers in the streets, and our tricolor on the buildings. I would never have believed that I am so attached to France. The childish rages that overtake me when I read the local newspapers, swarming with attacks and slander, surprise even me. Pranzini, Boulanger, and mobilization are so many themes for gibing at our Country. I truly suffer from all this. But I take comfort in opening the dignified *Petit Marseillais* which maybe you still buy. ...

A story to show you how far my chauvinism goes when I am in a foreign country: it is really stupid and you are going to laugh, but here it is! Almost every day on the streetcar I pass in front of an old house with this written on the wall (you are beginning to smile!): *General Pharmacy for the Hospitals of the French Army* (laugh as much as you like, that is it!)—all this under a coat of whitewash. Now that you have laughed, think about it, and you will understand that hidden under these banal and empty words is a whole world of memories, a complete vision of conquest, of renown, of regiments marching, colors flying, bayonets drawn, a fanfare at the head, and then, some breath of glory filling the flag!... Mobilize!... Mobilize!...

2 hours later

I have reread your letter. That superscription pleases me.* It is twilight. The sun is setting behind the mountains, an old monument stands out black against the sky. Two friends walk in the Peyrou, on the crunching gravel. They talk about the examination, they tremble ... they argue!... and the greatest questions of art, literature, and even politics are broached, defended, attacked, resolved ... and *vani, vana*. One friend annoys the other with his romantico, rococo, archaeologico-boring manias. ... They go to the library to work hard and dig into the *Contes drôlatiques*.... So goes the world! Oh happy times! Oh pleasant walks, friendly talks always too short.... You see, I don't forget. If I don't write often, *scripta volant verba, jucundissima verba manent*. I don't deserve any of the scolding you address to me, and no one is more a friend of yours than I. You accuse me of loving old stones, but I don't love old stones; I love the memories I find in them, the reveries.

> *J'aime un fier chevalier qui etc., etc.*

Enough, wouldn't you say?

. . . .

Good-bye, I hope to see you soon. Write to me, *answer*

* The quotation from Psalm 42 [at head of previous letter]: Valéry recalled this passage in *Fragments du Narcisse* (*Charmes*):

> Ce soir, comme d'un cerf, la fuite vers la source
> Ne cesse qu'il ne tombe au milieu des roseaux,
> Ma soif me vient abattre au bord même des eaux.
> Mais pour désaltérer cette amour curieuse,
> Je ne troublerai pas l'onde mystérieuse ...

my questions, and don't doubt the friendship of one who dares call himself

Monseigneur
Of Your Most Reverend Excellence
The most faithful friend and most devoted servant
P. VALÉRY

[Fourment to Valéry]

[Montpellier] Friday, September 16, 1887

Dear one,

It is me, me again, since it gives you pleasure to read my *prattle....* I seem to see you smile when you have in your hand those poor pages devoid of *wit*—as you were frank enough to tell me at the end of your letter—but where the accent of the heart is not lacking; at least I tried to put it there.... I say that you are smiling because I am smiling. Something inside me laughed, Monday morning, when I opened the envelope containing your sweet, your skipping prose. I was still in bed, I didn't sleep....

> *Un Séraphin pensif courbé sur mon chevet*
> *Secouait des lilas dans sa robe légère...*

I dreamed. I often dream since I no longer have anyone to whom I can confide my ideas and feelings every day!... Your letter, which I have read two or three times, made me think even more....

... It was in the month of October 1884. A young man, a child, entered the third form at the lycée in M. Bonnel's class. It was a new pupil, but a new one who soon attracted the good will of the students and the confidence ... of the professor. Quickly you became what, in 1830, would have been called the head monitor. Don't pretend to protest!

You *were* the monitor. Y E S ! M O N I T O R ! Happily for us, you didn't know the rights and prerogatives of your job. Totting up the sum of the fortnightly notes, you painlessly dispersed favors whose source was endless, which was good. But what was better, you didn't impose punishments. You allowed the authority of your censoring predecessors to crumble... *hebescere aciem horum auctoritatis....* So it was in the third form that I had the pleasure of meeting you. I still see you with your hood in winter, looking here and there, vaguely, lazily, witnessing (perhaps) the ruin of your illusions, your hopes, your ambitions of a thirteen-year-old student. You were my comrade, I was only your comrade, and the year went by. . . .

. . . In the second form we were separated. A few favors given and received with pleasure by one and the other. That was the time of the Garigaire. . . we laughed about . . . *le bachot qui n'est à personne.** A bit later and we didn't laugh about it quite so much!

Yes, we laughed about everything, we joked, we loved to talk, to note our likes, our impressions, we wrote verse. . . . You are a poet, my friend; not the *divus vates* of Virgil (the poet is a light thing, κοῦφον κτῆμα), a gentle likeable poet who perhaps does not feel deeply, but who feels nevertheless. . . .

The free life becomes you. "Down with the bourgeois," as Théophile proclaims. You are of those who claim that to be Raphael, one needs a Fornarina . . . several Fornarinas. . . .

---

* The allusion is to a verse taken from an unpublished poem of Valéry, a parody of Victor Hugo's poem, "Non, l'avenir n'est à personne," written in March 1884 in a student notebook while he was attending the collège of Sète, and continued at Montpellier. [See *Collected Works*, Vol. 1, p. 477: The baccalaureate, which is for no one.]

(Hé! Fortunio Valéry ! ! !) Yes, my friend, even if no one knew it, he would guess: you have Corsican and Italian blood in your veins !... I annoy you, don't I? Perhaps you think it strange, bold, that I take the liberty of probing your depths? Pardon, pardon, good friend; I am leading up to psychological studies. ... I am analyzing your mind, my friend. ... Alas, if only I could reach the depths of your heart !...

. . . .

I wanted to tell you in this letter how from a comrade you became my friend. I dare not. I dare not revive so sweet a memory; all the more since, to do it, I would have to touch on certain of your wounds, my friend, which are perhaps not yet healed.* All I can tell you is that, on a Tuesday at the beginning of that year, I saw you dressed in black, your eyes red with crying, so bereaved, so reduced that I had to bite my lips not to do like you !... Do you remember? I saw you the next day; I spent Thursday afternoon with you, at your house. Each time I came with the intention of saying something !—and I said nothing. ... And perhaps today I am saying too much !...

(Same letter) Saturday evening, 5 o'clock
Should I rewrite my letter? Should I burn it? You will

* Barthélémy Valéry, born at Bastia in 1825, died on March 13, 1887 at Montpellier. In 1861 he had married Fanny de Grassi, the youngest of Giulio de Grassi's daughters, by whom he had two sons, Jules and Paul Valéry. At the time of his death he was the head clerk of the *Douanes impériales* at Sète, where Giulio de Grassi had performed the functions of consul of Sardinia from 1855, and then consul of Italy after the unification. At the death of his father-in-law, in 1874, Barthélémy Valéry performed for several months the functions of consul. The king of Italy decorated him with the cross of Knight of the Crown of Italy.

shrug your shoulders, laugh at my naïveté, my stupidity. . . . Laugh if you want to . . . at least my letter will have been good for something!

I hasten to finish. . . . Again I am rereading your letter. . . . I excuse the faults of the author, for I love the author.

. . . .

I will stop, my dear friend, asking you not to forget me, to write me again . . . soon and at length

Ex intimo corde
Tuus, semper tuus
G. FOURMENT

[Valéry to Fourment]

[August 7, 1888]
Cette, Beyond time and space
Caro-Carissimo,

This letter would be the finest day of my life if you would forgive me the ease with which I wrote it.

I am bored, you are bored, we are bored, etc. You are annoyed. They don't give a damn.

Sh! Sh! I forgot that I was writing to one of our most distinguished professors of philosophy.* Let's be correct. The fact is that I'm not amused here, among the bourgeois and the brutes. Only the sea and a few books keep me interested in life. I live in the library, and the rest of the time I am bored. . . .

I have read:

Masques et visages	Gavarni
La Fille Élisa (! ! ? ! !)	Goncourt
Belle Jenny	Gautier
Mme Vénus !	Richard ! O Mon Roy

* Paul Valéry and Gustave Fourment had just finished their class in philosophy under Professor Bernard, and had passed the second part of the baccalaureate.

I am so congealed in the gelatine of boredom that I am writing to you without wanting to, tired of holding a pen in my hand. . . . I am empty of thoughts, almost of feelings—even of sensations.

I have but one real pleasure—bathing in the green sea under a sun heated to any number of degrees. I feel priceless shivers in plunging my tired limbs, wearied by my twenty-eight kilometers on the sun-struck road, where the water sucks and licks into the skin to the point of the fascia. Then I live! Yes, that is to live—and what ideas obsess me!

O Petrarque, Virgil, Boccaccio, Sade, all of you, Gods of the Body and the Flesh, intelligent Meats at your pleasure! You who on the pinpoint of Enjoyment pile up all your forces, nerves, muscles, bones, power, genius! You are in yourselves the greatest and you hold this elusive Truth and that Pure Reason which the Kants, the Renouviers, and others seek in their distorted, crotchety noumena.

Write to me at my address in Montpellier—your letter will find me more quickly. Write to me at length and promptly. . . . Good-bye.

Your P.

[Fourment to Valéry]

Montpellier, August 18, 1888

My dear Paul,

I am writing to you from the Library where I came to study M. Clay's theory of consciousness. Don't laugh. It is not my intention to give you a lesson in philosophy, although the mistakes you made in your last letter on Kant and the theory of noumena give me the right to clarify your enormous ignorance. . . . I am writing to you from the Library with my sheet of paper resting on the *Journal des Savants*;

may the perfume rising from this paper inspire you, inoculate you with the taste for serious and speculative study!

It is likely that I won't come to the Library again during the whole vacation. I told you that I was planning to leave towards the beginning of September, and (to my great regret) I am obliged, excepting unforeseen circumstances, to leave next Tuesday. So I shall not have the pleasure of seeing you before September 5 or 6. . . . This pains me. I received a letter from Daillan last Monday, a few hours after yours. I assure you that if friendship were measured by the length of one's letters, he is the one who would show most affection. It seems to me, however, that I ought to expect as much from you as from him, or even more. I won't heap reproaches on you; what is the use? Those things are felt, and if you don't feel them, it is not you I am sorry for—it is *me*. I am terribly sorry that my attachment turned into passion. But I don't regret it.

My dear Paul, I am so sick that everything frightens me. What for others would be a mere sting becomes for me a laceration, an excoriation. My susceptibility makes me suffer horribly, and all the more since I am not putting it to a severe test. My friend, I have come to the point of calling on the municipal counselors. . . . I am still concealing my situation from you, since it would be disgusting for me to know that others are aware of the vile acts my misery has reduced me to. . . . I have written to M. Bernard* and he replied with a letter full of kindness. I am surprised that anyone should be willing to show me a bit of friendship. I am so little used to it that I am still quite surprised. That man is the first who has done me a kindness; now I have just told

* Professor of philosophy to Valéry and Fourment during the school year 1887–1888 at the lycée of Montpellier.

you that I admire him, that is true, but I am so ill-natured that I sometimes laugh at his stupidity. For I confess that it takes a tremendous amount of it not to banish me.

My dear Paul, this week has been the week of platitudes and humiliations and disgust. . . . I am dying of shame. And to say that everything I do is done in order to sneak away later to a place repugnant to me. I ask M. Bernard for his support and the stick he offers me is meant only to plunge me deeper into the muck. But at least when the muck has covered my head, I am sure of something to eat. I wish myself a good appetite! I was telling you a moment ago that I am sick. . . . My friend, I am more than ever so, I am hiding from my family and especially from my mother, who would suffer too much; but in fact I no longer know what to do. I haven't closed my eyes for the past four nights. At moments I want nothing more than to close them forever; I have coals of fire in me. I spend days without leaving my room, where I can assure you that I don't see things in a rosy light. Since you went away, I have come to the Library only twice.

I am doing a bit of philosophy but with no taste for it, at moments of no suffering but in profound boredom. I work only out of need, in order not to think about other things.

You will easily believe me if I tell you that I miss you and suffer in your absence. Faced with a hopeless future, in a present filled with an ignoble bitterness, I need to know that you love me a bit and show it. For me, I prefer not to say what I feel towards you; to write it would be to profane it, to blaspheme. I won't write you at length today; I feel too sad and don't want to give you things to read that would give me too much pain to write.

Write to me as soon as possible, at home; if I have gone, the letter will always find me. . . . May it bring me what I so much need!

Adieu, my dear Paul, I leave you, but wishing to embrace you.

Please do write to me soon.

G.F.

[Valéry to Fourment]

Sète, August 22, 1888

My very dear friend,

Your letter made me suffer, and suffer terribly.

Your physical ailment and your moral ailment, twin brothers who help each other perhaps more than you realize, brought me to dark thoughts.

The most complete boredom favored the development in me of this melancholy, and if I waited long to answer you it is not because of indifference, but to avoid adding to your spleen.

Today the sky has cleared (God be willing that the same be true for you!). Some relatives have come to me from England and have brought a bit of distraction to my sadness. . . .

I have just reread your letter. Listen to me. You are doubtless traveling through Provence under a blue sky among violet hills. . . . Leave in the dark Montpellier, your insomnia, and all the absurdities that harass you.

Imagine for once that all the platitudes in the world last only for a moment, that the truly philosophical man endures them like a black but salutary medicine, that this supposed rot in which you breathe is only pig manure (*res cupienda*) or better (and I hope so for you) a simple step. You can go far once you are mounted on the *mule*. I know you well enough to understand and be certain that you are made for something other than "pedagoguing" all your life, but you have to begin with that.

And now think of something else; look, look with all your eyes at the country you have crossed; walk across the fields, without a rest, without reading, from evening to morning, and you will sleep. . . .

I call down on your head the rosiest of dreams; I beseech you to come back, rid of the slough of stupidity that surrounds you because you do nothing to throw it off. I beg you to find amusement in travel, *hic est salus*.

A thousand thanks for the friendship you give me. I don't deserve it, I am a poor brute who have only my five senses . . . which doesn't keep me from loving you.

I am obliged to stop. I am being called: "My dear Paul! Come here, please!"* I come running!†

I shake your hand. Good-bye. May all go well.

PAUL

[Valéry to Fourment]

Le Vigan, Hôtel Parguel‡
[August 1889]

My dear friend,

I am beginning to be tired of these eternal mountains,

---

* Valéry's English.

† A reference to one of his maternal aunts, Pauline de Rin, and her daughter Pinetta. Pauline de Grassi, third daughter of Giulio de Grassi and Jeanne Lugnani, married Angelo de Rin at Trieste. They lived in London.

‡ Valéry had just finished his first year of law at the University of Montpellier. He interrupted his studies to do his military service; demobilized in November 1890, he at once began his second year of law.

the springs and the chestnut groves of the Cévennes. They are beautiful but not sublime. I am beginning to regret my old Peyrou and my old curiosity shop and my friends. Friends! You are like the old familiar books, the dictionaries thumbed through every day, and we like to feel them there beneath the hand to open when we wish, to the well-known page.

My dear Fourment, I have chatted a lot with you this summer in a quiet wood where the smoke from my tobacco was rising in the sun. An unseen stream was running—here the water flows from every side and never stops. . . . I had gone to bed thinking I was with you near Lez, my eye lost on a charming hill in front of me, which, being completely cone-shaped and formed of wooded tiers, seemed borrowed from one of those old engravings which represent pagan sacrifices. Nothing was missing but the incense, the victims, and the priests robed in linen. From a spinning mill nearby arose a song of machines deep and rumbling like an organ. . . .

I am repaying myself here with sensations. The odors, the colors, the unusual sounds that surround me, and I gather and classify them and decompose them in myself and again attach them to others seen elsewhere, thus resuscitating treasures of souvenirs.

Yesterday, in prowling through the old streets that smell of the antique and the victuals, where the copper basins dry in the sun, there awoke in my brain the gamut of the sensations of Italy.* It is impossible to tell you how far this

* During this year, 1889, Valéry read at length the work of Huysmans, which he must have discovered two years before if we think of the poem "Solitude," written in 1887; the words and the expression itself are evident testimony to a page in *A Rebours*. The prose poem, "Les Vieilles Ruelles," which Valéry wrote in September

led me. I saw again suddenly the populous and colorful quarters down there, the blasts of light on bare walls, then the churches, the cool shadows with spots of gold, a vague smell of incense and wax and again (I am citing myself):

> La Vierge byzantine et de massif argent
> Demeure hiératique en sa chape orfroisie
> Fixant ses yeux de perle aux Cieux, comme songeant
> Aux Azurs lumineux et lointains de l'Asie.*

You see, that's all I am, me, there is no use in your talking and blaming me. In me there is a predominant atavism. I am descended from one of those curious families of the Italian republics of the fifteenth century (the Galeazzo Visconti of Milan),† and I live in that period. I care nothing for politics and jurisprudence and am not a republican, except in those republics where the senators are living *Titians*, where the Boulangers dress in damascene armor, on the marble terraces at the foot of which in the blue water sleep the gilded and painted galleys. Bells ring in my head—not those in the bell towers of France but more silvery and gaily chiming. They are those of the pink bell towers, emerging from the greenery towards the blue . . . for these you reproach me. . . .

My dream has fled again! These machines, plashing, carry me to England in the cold mist, pierced with flashes of fire and the whistling of boats. There a warm interior, very

1889 is dedicated to J.-K.H. (Joris-Karl Huysmans). [See *Poems in the Rough, Collected Works*, Vol. 2, p. 216.]

* The end of the poem "L'Église" which Valéry, after revising it, dated October 3, 1889. [See Notes, p. 398, and *Collected Works*, Vol. 1, pp. 326–327.]

† Through his maternal ancestor, Charles-Joseph de Grassi, father of Giulio de Grassi, a relative of whom had married a Visconti, niece of Cardinal Federico Visconti, archbishop of Milan. It is thus that Valéry, tracing his genealogy, could speak of the illustrious family of Galeazzo Visconti, Duke of Milano who vanquished Bayard.

comfortable, very bright, in the rain trickling down over the windowpanes, the carriages fleeing at a gallop, a good pipe, a good armchair and coins enough to fill the sea.

England makes me dream of the *Indes*, of the bizarre cosmogonies of impenetrable temples, and all of mysterious and theocratic Asia surrounds me.

Ah! How I despise the Flahaults and the Meynials, digging in the meadows for polyptichs!* In the meadows I go looking for mushrooms [*blavets*] and rhymes,† at 500 leagues from the campylotropous ovules—in the polyptichs I find endless suggestions, evocations, disguised in barbarous Latin from vague and puzzling epochs ... the naïve charms of the early Middle Ages ... refined barbarisms, Byzantine jewels imitated by the Burgundians, a whole universe of rare and artistic vibrations. ...

. . . .

This letter, which for you will be an incomprehensible puzzle, is for me a basin where I vomit up all that I dreamed this morning in the Bois. Too bad for you, dear man, you will lose nothing in the way of insanity by my absence.

Everything I touch disputes me ... still less, however, than everything I produce.

* Valéry was given the assignment as a student in the Faculty of Law (first year, Professor Meynial) on *La Polyptique d'Irminon*, the work of Abbé Irminon on the polyptich or enumeration of manors, serfs and revenues of the Abbaye de Saint-Germain-des-Prés, under the reign of Charlemagne, etc. And also, under the direction of Flahault, professor in the Faculty of Science, Valéry, with his brother Jules and friends, went on numerous and regular botanical excursions from 1886 until 1892.

† Pun on *blavet* (mushroom) and the name of the poet Alcide Blavet, active in the Félibrige movement.

To hell with it—no matter where, out of the World.
I feel that I am going mad—luckily. I am mad already.
Good-bye,
PAUL

[Fourment to Valéry]

[Montpellier, 12] September 1889
10 o'clock in the evening

My dear Paul,

I am distressed to think that I have been here for nearly
two hours thinking of you and have not yet begun this
letter. . . . Vague thoughts, memories, desires that won't
allow themselves to be imprisoned in sentences. If I were a
musician, instead of lining up words that cannot express
my feelings of the present moment, I would play you a
melody, something rising from the depth of my soul that
could echo deeply in yours. The Creator blundered in
depriving me of the ability to express my most intimate
thoughts. I would like to believe that He has shown himself
less unjust toward you.

. . . .

And now that we would wish to express in our verse
the vision of that ideal statue, which we carry in our minds,
and when the vision is gone, are you not frightened, even
disheartened, to have been able to say no more than such flat
and banal things! The language of the gods has been pro-
faned, and if the Muses exist I see them taking flight, weeping
and veiling their faces.

My dear Paul, it is bad to make the Muses weep . . .
especially it is not allowed to make them weep too long.
As for me, I hope they will finally smile upon you and love
you. You deserve it so much! And surely, at this end of a

positive and money-adoring century, is there anything more deserving than to love Poetry ... or Philosophy? (It is true that *Philosophy* and *Poetry* are one and the same thing and we both hear the same voices.) The crowd passes, laughing at the man who, despite his talent, lives in poverty. Who reads the verses of our poets ... I mean those who deserve to be read? Would anyone read novels if he did not find in some the ignoble or at least the racy, in others bourgeois sentimentality ... enough to bring laughter or tears. ... It is never because a work is beautiful that it is admired by the crowd, it is because there is always something adequate to vile tastes or base passions ... or indeed simply because the author is in the fashion. Ah! My dear Paul:

> ...*Ces choses-là sont rudes*
> *Il faut pour les comprendre avoir fait ses études.*

and we are quite right to feel desolate.

Yet we would be wrong to be discouraged. As for me, I feel sure that I shall always prefer even bad verse to an *elegant* experiment in chemistry, and that I shall always prefer the one who analyzes his soul, even if the latter analysis were badly done, to the one who analyzes the products of his body. I have no doubt that you are not of my opinion. Besides, you have *personal* reasons for putting entirely above any demonstration in geometry the worst verses in the world.

I am cruel, don't you think, my very dear friend; and I am perhaps unjust? I speak too frankly to you; I am even sure of not telling the truth in saying that your verse is "bad." Don't believe that to tell the whole truth you must call them "abominable." ...

I am on the way to being much amused; I am teasing you, I don't mean to hurt you. Besides, you know too well how passionately my soul is attached to yours, to take umbrage at what is for me merely a game, a prank. I see you here before my eyes trying to read this gibberish: you smile as you read those places where I smiled as I wrote. Pay no attention to the stings, and let each of my sentences be a caress for you. ... Ah! My dear Paul, if I were not afraid of being too ridiculous, if I were quite sure that you would understand, I would tell you that. ... No, I prefer to say nothing. Love me always and much.

I am weaving this letter out of the purest and sincerest part of myself. Perhaps it won't please you? What do you expect? It's impossible for me to talk about "the fifteenth-century Italian Republics." ... I prefer another world to that "universe of rare and artistic sensations."

My dear Paul, you are living a life that is far too artificial. Don't imagine that you are obliged to keep in step with Théophile Gautier and Baudelaire. The least you could lose is your *originality*. Let us be sincere, and because some have been pleased by the refinements ... let us not believe that this is poetry. The external world came and shattered itself against their senses. They felt! ... Let us feel in our turn and may the memory of their sensations not come to interpose themselves between the world and our soul. Let us not forget, on the other hand, that *their* sensations have as little objective reality as ours.

. . . .

For myself, I would suffer greatly to see the talent, with which I believe you are firmly endowed, lost in slavish imitation. If you imitate (and we all begin with that) never let that imitation become an *aim*, but a means; let me explain. In every art there is the craft, the know-how. It is learned in the school of others. Gautier will teach you to find the exact words; at least he will make you feel its importance and even its necessity. That marvel called the *Emaux et Camées* will inspire you with a taste for the word-image. You can learn a great deal from that study. I would like to believe that it offers no danger. . . . I don't wish to let myself repeat what I have already told you several times on this subject, more-over without convincing you; Delille is a great describer. . . . However that may be, you can use the tools made by others, you must begin by *training your hand*; but don't forget that the search for the method must not be the artist's aim; that *the work of art has no aim*, but spouts from the bottom of the soul; that true poets are not virtuosos, but the inspired.

I beg your pardon for talking at such length about aesthetics. . . . Yesterday I was reading *The Second Faust* of Goethe. After the death of her son, Euphorion, Helen vanished. Everything material in her disappears. Faust now has in his arms only her garment and her veil. . . . Work to acquire that garment, which clothed a divine form, that robe in which, later on, you will clothe the wife that your desire will create. If ever you hear the "inner voice," then you will have less difficulty in revealing to us the new things with which she will fill your mind. Your intimate feelings will be expressed in a harmonious language, which you will have learned in studying the best. The correspondence will be established between your hand and your brain.

Do not believe, my dear Paul, that after finding Helen's garment you will be condemned never to possess anything else. You shall have Helen; the love you feel for her will bring her to life. I was mistaken a while ago to complain of the injustice of God; we complain because we do not see far enough. Our desires will be realized inevitably—in this world or in another. If it is not given to you in this life to write a verse poem that for others than you is a masterpiece, my dear Paul, I am consoled in thinking that your impotence is not eternal, that a day will come when I shall enjoy hearing you speak in perfect verse, a bit less than Byzantine trinkets. . . . I count, however, on not having to wait for the life reserved for us "no matter where out of the world," to test that enjoyment. In any case, God is good and . . . I am a bad prophet.

You must be saying: that character *bores* me! Once more, I'll never pardon myself for discouraging you. I only want to make you more difficult toward yourself; if need be, to transform your taste for the bizarre, for extravagant fantasies, into passion for the *real* and *eternal* things. When you come I'll explain all that to you. You greatly need to beware of words; when you describe, I strongly believe that instead of having before your eyes the representation of the thing to be described, you imagine a dozen terms which you want to combine in the most Baudelairian fashion. I shall explain this to you at length. . . . Come as soon as possible; I ask you to reflect a great deal. We shall talk about literary works. . . and even about your poems (is it literature?). Oh! Pardon! Pardon, my dear Paul; love me anyhow. Be more indulgent with me.

Do you know what time it is? Two-thirty in the morning. I haven't seen Daillan since before you left.

Ex altissimo corde,
PANLOPHILE

[Fourment to Valéry]

[Montpellier] February 17, 1890
Evening

My dear Paul,

I have much to say to you, and if I bring myself to say it, it is almost in doing violence to myself. Ah! If I had not promised, I would not write to you. The *Conte vraisemblable*,★ which you gave to me last Sunday, I have read, certainly, and with an attention I have not given to better works.

. . . .

I beg you, my Paul, to disassociate yourself from this *Conte*, no longer consider it to be yours, and judge it objectively as I have forced myself to do. . . .

I end, dear Paul, in imploring you to give me a less imperfect work than this *Conte*. I would wish for more care, more study. . . .

G.F.

[Valéry to Fourment]

[Montpellier, September 26, 1890]

My dear friend,

In the first place, I beg you not to make fun of me as you do at the end of your letter. In the second place, I would have preferred less history and more description and, as you say, catalogue.

These days, something enormous just missed happening in my life, and . . . it may still happen, soon.† I shall naturally not tell you about it. You will have the *pleasure* of guessing. Be it known that it is due to Pierre Louis, with whom I am corresponding more than ever. I am still writing a few verses . . . when the Barracks releases me.

Fernand arrived the day before yesterday from the island. This pleased me. . . .

★ *Le Conte vraisemblable* [A Likely Story], unpublished in Valéry's lifetime and left in a drawer, was written in September and revised in October 1889. A first draft, unfinished, carries the title *La Folle Journée* [The Crazy Day]. [See Notes, p. 398.]

† A reference to the proposal Pierre Louÿs had made to him to publish a collection of his poems.

These days I have made plans. You know that this happens to me. I have built up in my head two superb novels and a short story. I may possibly stop there. You must know that I relax by writing to you; for me you serve as a mental canapé. I have just written to Pierre Louÿs and I laboured over the epithet; so I am taking my repose by wallowing in short-sleeved sentences! It's good enough for you!—still happy if you don't get an avalanche of Sardinoux's litanies before the end. So I don't give a damn.

. . . .

I don't know anything further to tell you. It is true that all this parroting tells you a bit about me. . . . So I am going to copy some lines of verse for you . . . and the choice is not easy, to satisfy a cold piss like you.

If you have written to me before Sunday you will get a fine letter—perhaps!

Good-bye,
PAUL

[Valéry to Fourment]

[Montpellier, September 28, 1890]
Dear friend,

I am copying the beginning of my letter to Pierre Louis for you, since it is for two hearers:

"My friend, such is the magic of written characters on paper, so great is the power of the invisible forces that couple and enchain our minds, that I feel some unknown spasm of sympathy in receiving your letter together with *another* coming from *Provence*, both seeming to bring souls in their folds. Two letters from the two friends still alone in my shrine of friends! What a delightful hour of remembrance and true spiritual love.

"The one, the writing straight and thin, austerely neat, emanates from a metaphysical spirit that dreams of Reason.

"The other, wide and high, in an episcopal ink, seems taken from one of those manuscripts where the Ecstasies are written!..."

84

Yes, dear friend, an hour truly virile and delightful, an afternoon of blue sky, at the back of the presbytery garden, which you know, leaning on the dear angelic notebooks, "Où de pudiques lys grandissent en silence,"* if I am permitted to cite myself!

And after responding to the one, I repeat my antistrophe to the other, but how much more intimate, nearer to the secret chalice that flowers in Us.

I thank you for the vivisection performed on Alc...,† but this is not yet all I wanted to know. Your sentences are not precise—say, for once, all your thought or rather all of his.

Very suggestive, the details on Mme X... I am still perplexed. Could there be a mania for maternity?

I love you very much when you sleep beside the dull pond of Berre, vaguely dazzled by that amethyst glimpsed among the fluid and troubled azures of smoke.

The incredible thing due to Pierre Louis is not a leading article, but much more and a great deal less—though I don't yet want to condescend to it for fear of a sudden madness. *Vedremo* as the Italians say.

I no longer read anything. I am ruminating on my finds. It is true that I have just now sent back to Louis the rare and beautiful manuscript of *Hérodiade*, a poem in precious fragments like precious stones. . . .

These poems always make me dream of those pearls disdained by the chickens!... What makes their emerald green splendor, their perfection and their lure as of gems is this: they are at the same time like them, polished and

* The conclusion of a sonnet written in 1889. [Where modest lilies grow in silence.]

† Alcide Blavet. The allusion to Alcide Blavet and the details on Mme X seem to indicate a letter from Fourment which is missing.

brilliant, and yet with no bottom, unfathomable, with mysterious undersides of dreams and correspondences. Underneath these verses there are levels of associated ideas, multiple evocations—the whole beneath a hard, shining surface, obscure for anyone seeking by his power of reasoning instead of finding reveries in his dreams! The difficulty overcome is enormous, embracing so closely those confusedly sad visions, to conserve beneath the precise and luminous clothing the vagueness needed so that the apparition may circulate—this is enormous!—enormous!

Go and tell Blavet these things. He is too well educated to understand anything at all.

Good-bye! Write to me.

I am not sending you any poems—you don't even tell me whether you received the others!

P. A. Valéry

[Valéry to Fourment]

[Paris, September 23, 1891]*

This is the unreal city where for me no thought can stir ...where so many marvels hidden in palaces are well guarded against dreams by the rivers of noise and flashing lights that are the streets. .... And a moment ago we looked at *La Joconda* and now—if you had seen us, under the light rain whose drops carried the electric light as they fell, carried off under the umbrella across a boulevard by two foolish unsheltered girls whose drunken and rosy dance gave wings to our fine top hat, grave and shining, quite compromised, one on the right, one on the left, in front of the white cafés on the black mirror of the sidewalk.

* Valéry arrived in Paris on September 19, 1891; he remained there until October 24. His brother Jules had arrived a few days earlier to pass his law examinations.

And there—the Sainte Chapelle, and there, Notre Dame and don't look at us, ladies!

Oh, I won't tell you what I saw, since as yet I have seen nothing at all.... Oh? Some beautiful things—but I am bored rather. When I left you on the quai, that hurt me a great deal; then I began looking at the moon through the window. Instead of seeing the countryside, there was an almost obscure reflection—a nose appeared, with eyes. I recognized a bit of myself. "Poor Poet," I said—then a bit more face, "Poor little Corporal!"—and then "Poor Narcissus!" And all my beings made me weep. The night, blue with incense, evaporated the appearances. And I became new. That is why I shall not recount this or that for you. I know Paris already like my dresser drawers. I am drunk on Gothic and the Renaissance and the rest. I shall know this only in memory.

Again, I have seen *nobody*. Louÿs is not here; he will arrive soon. I entered his *cabinet de poète* to write his address. Everything in the room disappears before the enormous effigy of Wagner. Saw Mazel, Masson *le fumiste à la Willy*. All of them bore me. I won't see them again. It is better to see "the girls."

. . . .

Perhaps I will go to London. Write me a long letter. Talk to me like a serious man who *still* sees the world in its general being, without disturbance from the vagabonds and the trollops. Good-bye,

P. VALÉRY

[Valéry to Fourment]

Paris, October 1, 1891

Your letter didn't surprise me.* If I don't care for close embraces, I love the distant ones, since our phantoms are more handsome than ourselves. Mine haunted your lines and seemed to lower its eyelids slowly—and I had the always cherished sensation of a mirrored soul which you, dear friend, held out to me. We had many secrets, that is true, but we would not dare to see each other again if all was said. It is good to wander still toward one of those majestic evenings, where each one talks as if alone in those intimate lands, where the Other guesses beneath the *obscure words* the accompaniment of Truth.

As for the fine gesture, let it show itself always without exhaustion, let us leave the *Letter* in the drawer, leave the lips separate—human.

Then a great reproach, a dissonance that struck me cruelly: "About two years ago a certain awareness of . . ." This is bad. Some childish demon misled your pen—and you know very well that it is not true? . . . *My old accomplice?* Ah! Haven't you told me all—and I, all? Didn't you over hear my confused wishes? DIDN'T I UNDERSTAND the scattered words?

The good Sardinoux,† the excellent, thinking that I had long since and forever fled, wrote me the most beautiful of letters, a solid and mountainous letter from a definitive friend. He is one of those who make me most proud, he is the rock of kindness, completely bare, who takes hold on me to the point that I often regret leaving them.

* Fourment's letter has not been preserved.
† Comrade from the lycée of Montpellier.

I shall close by giving you several quick pointers to what I have seen.

Let's not talk about the quick Dubus, Merrill, Morice, *Meunier*, Bérenger, Mauclair, De Guerne, Dierx, etc., hardly glimpsed.

Before approaching Louÿs—since I was panting with boredom, in short—I wrote to Joris-Karl,* whose thin calligraphy drew on a grey card the granted rendezvous.

I chatted with him for an hour and a half, about priests and Magi—and abominations and literature. The man is already grey, quite bristling, with bulging eyes, and the snoring speech of the Flemish, sprinkled with barracks language—suddenly a wide flash of benevolence. We spoke Provençal! And you should have heard it! He is about to launch into pure mysticism, as I understood. In short, we'll talk about it again.

But I am not finishing with him. Yesterday I managed to slip into the Library without a card. I was leafing through the manuscripts of da Vinci, Albert Dürer and Mallarmé, when Louÿs took hold of my arm: "Yonder! Look. It's Monsieur de Montesquiou—the prototype of Des Esseintes!" I saw nothing else. Everything disappeared. Alone, this meagre Seigneur, thinly clothed, and on his hat those extraordinary light-yellow gloves, his cruel mouth and electric eyes, interested me. He is the one who had the enormous tortoise paved in gold, and created for himself this subjective refuge—precisely issued from his soul. He was so nervous that he felt my constant eye, and often lifted his own. I cannot tell you the effect, the trance, the uneasiness, and the sensual delight that I felt. I am not trying to describe—that is

* Valéry kept the scratched-out draft of this letter to the author of *A Rebours*. [See Notes, p. 402.]

still impossible. But I believe that I have seen the most exquisite, the most treacherous, the most delicate of the devils. . . .

Good-bye, I am leaving in haste. Excuse this horrible letter scarcely written.

Tell Auzillion that I still don't have the time to write to him—I will try. Poor old Féline is stuck.*

PAUL VALÉRY

[Valéry to Fourment]

[Genoa, September 23, 1892†]

If I respond to an invitation of empty, dampened phrases, if I wish to complain and put into words here the possibility of being moved, of being for an hour on your left in the too luminous air, vast and accustomed to a walk toward the west—no! The ghost of such a life, ours yesterday, would be no more than indolent discomfort. Tell me, isn't it a thousand times better that, for each of us, nothing more should arise from the Other than . . . the "pure notion"—the only *true* one?

Thus the future skeleton, which is all we are, seen close on, ripens, detaches itself, and falls, with the disappearance of its constitutive uselessness, so. . .ELEGANTLY, shall I say, that a single minute is useful to this consummation, the

* Féline had just failed his entrance examination for the École polytechnique. He passed it the following year. It was Féline who introduced Valéry to mathematics: the theory of groups of transformations, Cantor's theory, etc. See herein, pp. 359ff.

† On August 16 and 21, Fourment and Valéry had dinner together at Palavas. Valéry left for Genoa on September 14, arriving the fifteenth. He had received his law degree on June 28. Fourment, with his degree in philosophy, thought for a moment of becoming tutor to the son of the French consul at Barcelona; but finally was appointed in early November as *maître répétiteur* at Béziers.

almost zero of time to clasp the hands being squeezed—then the curve of a slippery flight and the recovery, after the natural slowness of the beginning, with its primitive rhythm (as it used to be, at ten o'clock, under my reflector where you used to come).

Yet, let's change nothing—and, for example, let's roll with the special tactile delight that this is vain, a subtle cigarette, just as under the trees along the roads, near the water, or elsewhere. And if all that precedes a writing of any kind is a brother-silence to the habitual silence between us— for long hours and before speaking—now let the dialogue take its place, and spread, or rather both of the two vague and almost useless monologues which we were.

I scarcely see so many museums, nor the thousand dancing girls, nor the famous countryside, if not indolently. The shattering of calm moments always favors a vertigo of mine, an absurd delirium which is the painful contretemps of my inner measures.

.   .   .   .

I was going to put an initial as if to satisfy my fatigue, but I still have to tell *you* a word, the important one.

I know that you haven't forgotten a certain weakness that was mine, last summer, this winter, and this summer (the *last word* remaining with me, and my pride as well, with which I had to be nobly provided to persevere knowingly in Stupidity). The object, the sign and seal of these variations disappeared, completely, like a candle blown out on a certain date in the month of July.

Nothing is more authentically natural, plausible, almost *agreed*. But—it is here that the odd, the exceptional, and the unique take place, with finally the trace of a plan, with a *willed* connection, an expected solution—exactly on the evening of my departure, as I was walking in a street where I often saw HER and thinking about her for the first time in months—at the corner, there was her parasol showing her to me in a diminished and well known light, leaving me speechless, blind to the grace, to the beauty of her charm, and simply distracted with astonishment and the desire to understand it.

The structure of the event annulled even the person and myself who caused it. To think about it is difficult for me, as in every undecipherable situation allowing no *hypothesis*. What do you say about it? Say it at length.

P. VAL.

[Valéry to Fourment]

[Genoa, October 9, 1892]

A long letter to you is still in my drawer... faded. The astonishment that inspired it was useless—the letter also.

... the two worthwhile deaths of these last days, the Poet and the indefinable celebrity, who both disappeared, have the fate they accumulated for our reveries. A kind of justice is apparent in this—if I assume, in the midst of a brief and constructive idleness, that each man's destiny continues after his death according to the theme and the order he chose in life—which makes Renan into God knows what and places him where I can well imagine Lord Tennyson!

This pure dandy, however, was seized with a certain hesitation against skimming the supreme heaven, for having been voluntarily appeased by an elementary view of poetry, and assimilating not only the whiteness and grace of the Swan, but even the low flight itself, around a first calm pose, on the water.

If by an unforgettable theological instinct here, you will excuse me, I declare that I firmly think (among the numerous relations with particular individuals) that three qualities are the foundation of the Hero. To wit: liberty, intensity, purity.

Tennyson borrowed only the last from the lakes around his retreat. ...

Good-bye,
V.

[Valéry to Fourment]

[Early December, 1892]
12, rue Gay-Lussac, Paris*

My old Fourment,

I am astonished to have no more news of you. I need it. My friends here cannot relieve me of the more profound ones elsewhere, and if so many masks, secretly handsome or worn out, amuse me, babbling such exquisite names as Mallarmé, Whistler, Heredia...that is merely the gesture of a stamp collector who throws his wares to the wind and slumps into an armchair, bathing his eyes in the antique landscape of a window.

Yes, there I lean out in my desire for calm, and a regret for my old curiosity shop. Everything was so suddenly swallowed up. ... If you knew what happened to me here! I am keeping quiet about it, since on that *subject*, forever closed, you discouraged.

Good-bye, write to me at rue Gay-Lussac.

PAUL

* Valéry had been in Paris since November 26, 1892; he was living at 12, rue Gay-Lussac in the Hôtel Henri IV, run by M. and Mme Manton. He remained there until October 24, 1893.

[Valéry to Fourment]

[Paris, December 17, 1892]

I am sorry (so you no longer want to be the old accomplice?) to be obliged to keep quiet—and in letters to you!—the development born of an episode and a recent *predicament*, very curious, in which our friend Auzillion played the antique god next door.—And his supple genius. . . .

What are you doing? What do you smoke? Who are you in love with?

I can't manage to have a restful, easy waking. My fatigue is my life. It is quite innocent to say that I no longer sniff any but good natural things, butterfly trees, sun in the open air, and—a more subtle atmosphere, purer nature, cool surroundings—a woman's presence here and there, whose swooning poses and perfumed draperies, or glitterings among furs would light up all those hours when one is not in high tempests, would adorn the nights.

For the error is in believing that an artist tries to convince himself . . . and struggles to flee from the carnal group to the dear harmonic abstractions. In reality, he is constrained to the opposite and (a rather horrible thing) strives to plunge, drowning his pearl, to the bottom of the unbreathable common milieu.

(I continue above.) I believe, and this was the most interesting illusion in my former "perfectibility," that the human race is far from a "triumphant perfection" in the relations among its members. The more I think about it, the more TRUE it is: in friendship there are all the resources, *all*, in an élite group, for finally wearing out and replacing the notion of Love. Consider the conception of a communication between beings better than merely illusory, as the limit or circumference of the problem, and see how far the friendly approach surpasses the erotic. Alas, the difficulty lies, practically, in the advantage itself. For this fatal unity, the friend can be more easily entered than the woman's belly. The difference, in a crushing number of cases, remains. . . .

P. VA.

[Valéry to Fourment]

[Paris, February, 1893*]

Suppose a hypothetical day, imagined by you, when you would think of me with the indifference of a horizon coming to remind itself of the sun, this letter. Above, diving, my face is *writing*. Below the whiteness where the fingering is lightly spread by the ink—yours to whom I'm writing. The whole in you, on the chance of a tepid thought that assembles and undoes itself without clatter, according to the beginning of spring, the calm.

Then, what would you imagine I might write to you?

Well, here is what I *must* write to you, and the only things that I *can* write to you.

Leave with me, simply, the antique belief that I am *not*, among people or when the door is entirely closed and the work of the moment finished, *alone*.

It is true that the confidence that I once was must today take leave of the living ! . . . All have deceived me, and I return that confidence to several of the dead in my mind, on my table!—as in their final heartbeats, around me and amid the space of night that I inhabit with them . . . like a room under the influence of mirrors.

But my joy also is to believe in what I have believed at times. Joy soon put to sleep by the giddy sense of having

* Fourment did not answer this letter. The correspondence was not taken up again until November 1896.

been ... (let us say the ridiculous word) misunderstood. I have visited all my friends with the purpose of offering them, some day, a supreme betrothal, an experience of apotheosis. No one saw in it one of the summits of humanity, nor perceived the radiance of condensed friendship and that this held a new beginning of the World and the flowers. Alas! There is no longer Anyone willing fixedly to face the Impossible, to devote himself to the divine pleasure, making the sun—otherwise than by monkey tricks and vague literary writing, as little detached, naked, and clean as the vulgar "andante" of the majority and the deformed human beings by the millions, who are made fun of among the young who have read Verlaine.

This may be the good catch, but for Me, who am in the fire where people really burn and to ashes, I prefer a fire of my own.

All this may be, for you, indifferent, mere words, sounds and meaningless signs—this is certain and it matters little. I am asking you neither for a response from *elsewhere*, nor a souvenir, because I do remember. And on the other hand I know the answers because of the many evenings we have spent together, when I am given merely the authorization to speak aloud, like a madman in a place with no echo, where he feels familiar and alone.

P.

12, rue Gay-Lussac, Paris

[Valéry to Fourment]

[Paris, December 1897]

My dear Gustave,

I must thank you. I am noting Auzillion's change of address, which he had not given me. I shall write to him soon; time is lacking now—and almost the desire. I would pay a high price for time if it could be bought. You wouldn't believe how I debate with myself between my three or four different existences piled up into a single day. Paris, hard and full as an egg, is exhausting, but where else could I find a day like last Sunday: three levels of different conversations with perfect interlocutors; then the concert, sitting beside Mallarmé. In the evening, the other sex.

Afterwards, two days with a cloudy mind, asleep standing up, at the office, etc.

You want to learn some English? "All right!"* Except for technical works, I suggest that you read reviews and the newspapers rather than other things. For example, every morning, read the English newspapers, the political rather than literary ones. In short, use me as you wish.

I am always working away at my psychomania. It is impossible for me to consider it as absolutely nothing. I have made every effort without success. I would come back to it again and again. It seems to me moreover that I could, pen in hand, sufficiently justify my point of view. At bottom it is a method and not a system. It doesn't explain, it shamelessly replaces certain things by others; they are representations and their value is not to be looked for anywhere but in its applications. From this point of view, I can be discontented with it. I would like to make for you a more lucid sort of exposé than it was, in my fragmentary writings and in our necessarily defective conversations. If you agreed to this traffic, I could send you the plan, which it would be useful, moreover, for me to be *obliged* to make. . . .

The best to you,

P.V.

* Valery's English.

[Valéry to Fourment]

Paris, January [4], 1898*

My dear friend,

I saw Auzillion a few days ago. He was not without curses in plenty. . . . He pretended to have been sick and he seemed deflated. On looking him over, I decided that he was unhappy not to have, I fear, the resources for research or inner occupation. That doesn't hinder trouble. That's the wire on which everything limp in life flutters. Without that, I would have killed myself or decomposed a thousand times, since at every moment the relief map of the world becomes so harsh or so flat that no one can move ahead nor breathe again. So I am now extremely worried and I am going to talk with you and I shall be obliged to think about it while doing it.

Your letter fought me sharply. Your objections, rigid and written down, enlighten me and don't seem to me insurmountable. What seems to me more difficult is to explain myself. I don't know by which end to catch you.

You reproach me for wanting clear ideas, for sacrificing accuracy to precision, reducing a complex (obscure or clear, involved, etc.) to a few abstract notions combined—in short, the use of quantity. And all this requires explanations. The easiest way is to expose yourself—how these objections seemed to me unfounded.

I do not propose to make a system. The time for systems seems to me past or to come. I do not wish, then, to replace the world by a certain group of clear ideas. I mean, on the contrary, to see more completely what it is. The details of stars shown by telescopes, the curve which observation

* Written on the stationery of the Ministère de la Guerre. Valéry was appointed to the War Ministry in May 1897.

shows that they describe, the conditions of a very fast object, etc., are not directly given, but certain instruments make it possible to know them and to add them quite validly to a knowledge of the world. The same is true here. First of all, I make my instruments.

But let us go on to the important point of view. That is the *Arithmetica universalis.* I do not consider mental states in themselves; they are infinite, discontinuous, etc. But it is possible to believe that their variations or their fate may be better known. So Euclidean geometry does not describe real forms. It is part of the observation of real forms, and, in considering for example all the movements that the most *irregular* body, the least that an "object of science" can take, geometry has noticed that for some of these movements a line has to remain fixed. That line can only be a straight line and the movement is that of rotation. Whence definition. . . .

P. VALÉRY

[Valéry to Fourment]

[Paris, March 9, 1900]

My dear Gustave,

Excuse this piece of administrative paper: it is made, in short, to announce to you that for the past few days I have been engaged to Mlle Gobillard. This young person is related to the family of the painter Manet.*

To unite me to this milieu has been one of S. Mallarmé's projects, and it has been done. . . .

Another great artist (along with Huysmans the last one

* Jeannie Gobillard, the niece of Berthe Morisot. They were married on May 31, 1900. His wife was connected with Édouard Manet through Eugène Manet, the brother of the painter, who had married Berthe Morisot.

still living that I admire), Degas, rushed things at the last and the definitive words were said in his studio.

I am dazed, stunned, charmed, absurd, etc. I dined last week, as a result of these circumstances, with Mercier, who made an excellent impression on me.

A propos of these stories, here is a good one: yesterday I received from Kolbassine* a registered letter—of insults. It had been two years since I had heard from him. Now he has seen my name, with my few words, in the lists recently published of the supporters of Mme Henry. You can imagine the rest. . . . You remember "Fourmies." I replied with three lines which were calm but firm:

> I regret this affair. For me it spoils a fairly pleasant memory, after all!

What has become of you? Don't be so lazy, and think sometimes of

P. VALÉRY

3, rue de Beaune†

[Valéry to Fourment]

[Paris, April 6, 1900]

My dear Gustave,

I intended to answer your letter—a thousand worries have suspended that answer.

---

* Eugène Kolbassine, professor of philosophy, was on the faculty of the University of Montpellier. In 1896, Valéry dedicated *La Soirée avec Monsieur Teste* to him. The Dreyfus affair caused them to fall out.

† In a letter to his brother Jules, December 1899, Valéry told him that Mme Manton had "kicked him out for he didn't know where" from the Hôtel Henry IV. He went to live then at 3, rue de Beaune until his marriage (May 31, 1900), then at 57, Avenue Victor-Hugo; finally (summer 1902) in the house that Berthe Morisot had had built at 40, rue de Villejust (now rue Paul-Valéry). He remained there until his death on July 20, 1945.

I am happy about your plans for a trip to Paris since, I hope, we will see each other—less often no doubt than if I were still a bachelor, but as often as possible.

I am planning to marry about May 31. I am coming to know the worries of organization—and the difficulties now imposed by limited finances.

But you have to see a bit of everything.

Naturally, no news of Auzillion. There is no more reason why I should have any now than before.

So I have inscribed him among the "lost." Moreover, I felt when we saw each other again (here) that we had scarcely anything in common ... except memories. Sardinoux wrote me an affectionate letter and announced the birth of a son. This old Sardine is close to my heart—and with you, the best part of my past. Little by little I have had to renounce cultivating friendships which, until these last three or four years, took up a third of my life—and for which I still congratulate myself. I often tell myself: how many good companions I have met—what luck—thanks to such spirits as you I knew immediately or very soon to look for the real values, and not to have confidence in those who are published, are read, or are known.

Looking at the other side, I clearly saw the fault of writing —its falsity—(addressing a *vague* public). I felt that it was a degradation, an abasement of the fine and always profound thing, constituted between oneself, *ad amicum*, supreme elegance. But I confess that I have not succeeded—in a single case—of pushing this spiritual nearness *extremely far*.

I remember being shunned sometimes—sometimes having been reluctant myself—I would have wished to find someone who would have been with me as I am with myself.

All this is foolishness or, if you like, the irrational limit of a tendency.

Now—besides the conditions of life—I am too much enclosed in the most special of circles; I have elaborated tastes so particular to me, a manner of thinking so elementary or peculiar that I see the world in my own way, having given up all communicable particulars: *when there is someone else* I stick to the ordinary.

That is to say that I make no more friends

I am marrying.

Your,

P.V.

[Valéry to Fourment]

[Paris, January 12, 1901]

57, Avenue Victor-Hugo, Paris 16ᵉ

My dear Gustave,

Your scrap of a letter gave me an old pleasure. I was waiting, not having been able for lack of time, to notify you.

I send you my best wishes and wish for us that we may meet. But when and where? Have you given up your trip to Paris?

My news: since August I have been on leave—and have a situation with the president of the Conseil d'Administration de l'Agence Havas, under very agreeable conditions.* There, I am instructing myself in many contingent things, and talk with that excellent employer or read what interests

---

* Valéry left the War Ministry definitively in June 1901. He became private secretary to Édouard Lebey, director of the Agence Havas. Valéry had known his nephew, the poet André Lebey, at the time of the publication of *Le Centaure*. It was not until Édouard Lebey's death, in 1922, that this "employment" with this "excellent employer," afflicted with Parkinson's disease, came to an end.

him. That has forced me to digest Kant's *Critique of Pure Reason*, among other things. A black piece! In exchange I make him digest more than one work of that admirable de Maistre, etc.

But this state isn't durable! Must I return to the War Ministry? Boredom. And besides the work, I write—an extravagant thing.* I say, besides the work, because I have always reserved that word for the pure operations of my mind.†

My future story is almost entirely written in the simplest language, and the most abstract, which will make it seem obscure when it is merely unusual. I have been stuck there for three months, and it has taken only its first steps—or pages. But go out and introduce rigor and novelty, together, in a literary country; introduce continuity in a moment of incoherence and inattention. It is a project so absurd that I end by loving this often mortal and unmoving writing.

You, what do you do outside your classes? I take it that you don't go in for cards, nor much for newspapers. From where I am, I contemplate the back side of these noble organs. I see their noble inspirers come—their directors—and I listen, mute, to their oracles. They are dirty powers. I have known times when these confidences would have amused me. But, now and close on, they are mediocre pleasures. I run, now, to my wife and to sit down again at that table where I bore myself in my own way.

The best to you,

P.V.

* *Agathe* or *La Sainte du Sommeil*, a prose poem begun in 1898. It was not published until 1956. [See *Collected Works*, Vol. 2, p. 205.]
† A reference to his *Cahiers*, which he had begun to keep in 1894.

[Valéry to Fourment]

[Paris, January 11, 1903]
40, rue de Villejust

My dear Gustave

I have been too tired and taken up to write to you at the proper time. I have so little time—and so often feel at the end of my strength—that I must be forgiven my tardiness, and even the performance.

Auzillion, seen again, quite often since we have been able to break the stupid and inert charm, refreshes me; and, with surprise, we gab, outlandishly, I think—different or changed —but each of us against our will—and the intentions remain identical, still discriminating and just.

In fact, the first thing we did was to reunderstand each other in half a word.

What a distinction! It is enough to divide men: I place on the right those who communicate through the slightest things. The devil take the rest!

I have changed myself profoundly. And I am changed, also. In short, there would be tomes of stupidities, ideas, worries, desires, and suffering—all the material of being to enumerate for these last ten years. . . . Then, with Auzillion here, everything is changed chronologically. I begin to joke again. Again I find this reciprocal, instantaneous well-being and this interpretation or mutual reading so fast, which I liked so much, as you certainly remember.

That is in the realm of the gods because it forces one to be profound when one wishes—and allows a shared weakness when one feels it.

I know that friendship would have been my great passion. I hate the public, the crowd, and humanity in proportion to the liking I feel for coteries and the few. I have no reason to complain. I have been happy in my friends—only—that was long ago. Today the depths of the *heart of my mind* are deserted. That absurd expression is good. I use it inwardly with clarity enough and find no other. At the death of Mallarmé this heart was stricken. Therefore it is.

In sum, I live with the immense regret not to have carried this passion for the closeness of mind to the almost visible zenith. . . . Here, one is obliged to fall into nonsense. . . . But that matters little. I wager you have understood me.

Have you found anyone at Draguignan of the exquisite or overwhelming sort? There, no doubt, they have taken refuge in these hard times when we are witnessing the final defeat of the individual. The time of misery for the "human plant" has come. I judge by testing myself, and I verify it in every one I see. All the best of them withdraw or deteriorate. I could draw up a list of names here and show you, by enumerating them, a singular destruction of desire, of study, of sure talents—or of pride. The taste for the grand manner is lost. There is no longer any *parti pris*. Originality was killed by the ease that someone discovered in adopting it, only to abandon it.

Moreover, this entire country has no North. It has a monopoly on nothing, and that more futile than ever, not even envying the rich, not realizing that each minute lost at this moment in the world, degrades it in power, in number, in influence and drive—it contemplates itself, and votes.

What do you think? How tiresome it is not to be able to exchange words quickly and without so many pages!

Your P. VALÉRY

[Valéry to Fourment]

[Paris, January 14, 1903]
Wednesday

If I were free, my dear friend, I would be at Draguignan. How many times, even when you were at La Rochefoucauld, have I dreamed of taking a train, to appear without warning between you and your shadow. You are singularly a part of my horizon. You cannot guess the number of times I have questioned you. Now, I am stuck here, to the point that I left Paris last year only long enough to do my military service with the reserves.

What exhausts me is the endless interruption of my occupations. I begin, I stop—I suffer stupidly, my days all broken up.

In the end, I have myself alone, I guard my thought ferociously. No one at leisure can understand it nor, above all, contradict it. And as a bizarre compensation—because of that division of my day into so many separate efforts—myself is my own contradictor.

How I would like to pour my troubles into your ears. To have another hour with you, and not even take up our old life again to melt away the time.

Is it possible? Would you recognize me?

. . . .

Listen. In a few days write me again. Tell me whatever you like. That would do me more good than you can imagine. Tell me about your life—your real life—not your public life.

This is a service I demand of you. And then, you will see, I shall demand another of you. . . .

Your P.V. who runs to his job.

[Valéry to Fourment]

[Paris] rue de Villejust, 40
August 14, 1903

My dear Gustave,

On the stroke of midnight I had a son.* His birth was hard; a rough and infinite day preceded it.

Now I don't know what I must think, and hence I will not think.

Doubtless I should do as he is doing: wail.

Your PAUL V.

* Claude Valéry.

Valéry–Gide Correspondence

a selection

[Gide to Valéry, first letter]

Montpellier [December 21, 1890]
Sunday

Dear friend,

I am absolutely crushed not to keep our appointment, but I hadn't thought of our morning church service which I must attend with my relatives. I cannot excuse myself from going with them. I have only time enough to apologize to you and ask you for another rendezvous. Tomorrow is impossible. I will be at Nîmes. But Tuesday, if you can come to the rue Castillon either at 10 o'clock or at two, I will await you impatiently. If you are not free in the morning or in the afternoon, please leave a note at the hotel, proposing another time.

Your devoted A. GIDE

[Valéry to Gide]

Sunday [December 21, 1890]

Don't feel sorry, dearest friend, not to keep our appointment, but if you go to Nîmes do visit the old cathedral for my sake. I have just written to the rue Vineuse* and now

---

* The address of Pierre Louÿs whom Valéry met at Palavas in May 1890, during the ceremonies of the sixth centenary of the University of Montpellier. Valéry had just finished his year of military service, his *volontariat*, with the 122nd infantry regiment stationed at Montpellier. [The notes to this correspondence are by Robert Mallet.]

I will *work* a bit, under your invocation, O industrious one. I have a bit more courage, but how far I feel from what is needed. Men scarcely suspect how painful it is for the *child* to ask for the moon and stretch its little hands, its empty hands, toward the unattainable star!

Good-by until Tuesday. I will intrude on you in the rue Castillon.

P.

[Valéry to Gide]

[Beginning of January 1891]

Dear friend, would you have the goodness—the kindness —to bring with you tomorrow when you come to see me the book of verse from which I can copy the *Chercheuses de poux*?* Also, when I have you at my house, in my power, it is certain that you will be obliged to read to me those modestly half-veiled verses you have noted for André Walter, which I love from afar, as those Moslem ladies, whose eyes only, one sees under the veil.

Until tomorrow.

PAUL VALÉRY

[Gide to Valéry]

[January 16, 1891]
Friday evening

I hope, dear friend, that you will have supposed every-thing as the cause of my silence rather than negligence or forgetting, and you will certainly be right, since everything is more true than that. The causes are many, moreover, for the delay of this first letter: to begin with, I have been back

* By Rimbaud.

in Paris only less than a week, and, as I had told you in advance, I could not actually write to you before my return, having lived such full days since I saw you last that no other occupation could take its place. Days that you will perhaps know later on, days that synthesize in a few hours the whole past of a life, like those poems of Poe that we were talking about, a whole poem in one supreme refrain. Then, once in Paris, so many absorbing tasks took hold of me that, though filled with annoyance, I saw the dear moment drifting away when I might take care of the growing intimacy of the friend I found in you.

That moment having finally come, I felt so timid and so awkward facing this new affection that here I am at my fourth effort to write you a letter, and last evening I went to bed at 1 o'clock so weary and unhappy that I tossed the first three into the fire before going to bed.

Truly, this first letter (you will excuse me), I still don't dare make it very long: I have childish fears of going against your wishes and risking I don't know what that might displease you.

I shall wait for you to give me courage, to tell me a bit of this or that to encourage me to write to you: it is this great desire I have that makes me so awkward. I am afraid that this first letter may serve as a model for those to follow and that out of awkwardness I may launch our future correspondence, all of it, on the wrong track. I am afraid that you may model yourself on this manner, and I would prefer to be guided by you.

I would like (if that correspondence is meant to have no other conclusion than your happy arrival in Paris)—I would like it to have a certain unity, a certain fixed color, a certain stable originality, giving it a very special taste; I would like finally to say to you what I cannot say to others, and that for you the same should be true.

. . . .

And now, I await your letter, which will be the *first* of *our* letters, for this is only a prelude: write me at length, I know you have the time to do it. . . .

ANDRÉ GIDE
(alias Walter, alias Bernard Durval)

[Valéry to Gide]

February 15, 1891

I am very happy for your happiness, my friend, which is the sense of strength and the radiance of inner light. Something joyous and of easy clarity rises in you like the stalk of a lily lifting itself to the lips of the sun. But you are wicked to make me desire for so long a time the full profession of your soul through your book. This saddens me almost, to know that it is known before I knew it. However that may be, I understand your wholesome pride in knowing the high approval that welcomed it. Life that is real, the life made of happy and fulfilled creativity and victories of choice, is open before you; the free road flowers beneath your magnificent strides. What do you feel? Tell me all. . . . A piano sounds beside me, vaguely tormenting and boring me with delights. Why?

Louis sent me his portrait. He is very handsome, like a priest of some fabulous religion where prayers would be the most beautiful poems in the world. When shall we have our effigy?

I am sending you then, since you want it, this *Narcissus* weeping in the blue woods . . . as far as one can think from the sad and handsome young man that I dreamed. I wrote this poem in two days or six hours of time, on demand, as you know, and I repent it. He will open *La Conque* in a miserable way, and will blush with confusion. ... Tell me as frankly as you talked under the cypress and the turpentine trees of this country beneath the moon that I have not forgotten—tell me what it seems to you.

I am sending you the only copy of it that I have, since I burned my rough draft so as not to see it until it is printed.

Good-bye, friend.

Your uncle had the kindness to invite me to the students' evening which he gave a few days ago. Your remembrance inevitably haunted my mind among so many strangers that I didn't wish to know. Again I saw on a table the horrible *Princesse Maleine* whose escape from terror gripped me slightly again.

Once more, farewell. "Twilight is here."

P. VALÉRY

[Gide to Valéry]

[Paris, March 2, 1891]
Monday morning

... I live in waiting, just as before I wrote *André Walter*. I live in the anxious expectation of a new moment of work. I have great fears of never recovering that power of production, which I had when I was younger, and which astonishes me now, it was so violent—and what frightens me about myself is to admire others too much and without that prideful desire always "to do better," which an artist should never lose. I admire too easily, almost lazily, and I admire *André Walter* in this way, with the retrospective laziness of having been the one who produced such a dream. You know that I had, at that time, admirable confidence—I was credulous of the future. Later on, I shall recount those times, because things then seemed to me beautiful. And now I want to attempt even more difficult victories, for I fear that in repose my strength may turn sluggish. Then the daily elbowing of brutal realities (beautiful dreams, the magic faith, the "proof" of things unseen, as the apostle says). My poor soul, which at first believed itself the only living being and was drunk on its solitude with visions born of herself—she now shivers with sensual pleasures, for they also are joyful; she shivers and seeks refuge in vain, in I know not what Solitude against the violator's assault from outside—and which encircles her, the poor girl!

Ah! If it were possible, I would love the clear faith of my childhood—still!

I would wish that between us there might be [word missing]—and I have said this to you—above literature, and that is why—and for frail coquetry—I do not send you my book, and also, perhaps, for fear that in you the book may deflower the dream of the book—let us say for pride, if you will. And then also for desire of the strange—and I love you no less for that—but I am still somewhat afraid that you might love me less when you have read the book. Meanwhile, if you should come across a copy of the book, I consent that you should buy it, but as a book by someone else, a stranger that one need not encounter, like a work beyond the tomb of some now dead André Walter. Then in Paris, when you come, I shall write you a beautiful dedication in a delicate copy of the most "tribal" edition.

Farewell, my sweet friend, write to me as I wrote to you —at length; and tell me about you and me, as I talk to you about you and me, unless even more intimately still, for be sure that I shall increase our intimacy as time goes on.

Don't hold this too much against me, for it distresses me even to think that I displease you.

Your true friend,
ANDRÉ GIDE

[Valéry to Gide]

[March 24, 1891]

I am waiting for you impatiently, although May will *already* be dim for me because of my July exam, which *I must* pass.* But still, all evenings will be yours, and other hours also.

. . . .

I imagine you at Rouen for *Lohengrin,* and envy you not at all moderately. A piano friend has, alone, somewhat revealed that music to me and hence Music itself. . . .

You ask of me an article for *L'Ermitage.* Shall I confess that I don't dare write it, cannot write it? . . .

But why don't you ask Barrès for a *real* plug. One good line in an article sets you going suddenly and a hundred times better than a thousand "notices" on cabbage leaves.

. . . .

I am working on a great fresco supposed to evoke antiquity, *Hélène,*† but you know that I am a poet of the fourth order and "paved with good intentions." I also want to do something for you alone. It is ripening.

And there you are! The hours turn somersaults and I still find time too long! I am impatient for Nothingness which

---

* Examination in law at the University of Montpellier.

† This poem became the sonnet *Hélène, la Reine triste,* first published in *La Chimère* (1891), then by *La Conque* (October 1891), and later as *Hélène* in *Album de vers anciens* (1920). [See *Collected Works,* Vol. 1, p. 6.]

is cruel, and I would want life to be an hour long, to have finished quickly—and lost nothing.

I want to thank you, before signing, for the mystical gift that you announce. Your gifts are constant and all the friendship of the poor man I am hardly deserves them. But farewell.

P.-A. VALÉRY

[Valéry to Gide]

Good Friday [March 27] 1891

My dear André,

... I am in *Lohengrin* up to the eyes. I am ignorant of the first word about music, but I listen and imagine, when one of my friends at the piano, in the evening, plays for me the "Prelude" or the "Duet", or "The Mystic March" in the second act.

That music will lead me (it is already preparing me) to write no more. Already too many difficulties were stopping me. Narcissus spoke in the desert. When I saw it again in print, I was so horrified that I immediately locked it away. To be so far from one's dream! And it is bad! That stuff can't even be read.

After all, what written page reaches the height of the few notes that *are* the theme of the *Graal*? *Hérodiade* alone in French poetry can be read without too much disgust and torture. And this is still not high enough, still not diamond enough! You see that I am difficult.

We shall talk about the rest. Sirius will burn for centuries yet and the extinct moon also will be beside us, like a book.

PAUL VALÉRY

[Valéry to Gide]

[July 4, 1891]

Dominus, illuminatio mea.

This is a new friend talking to you, dear André: the other soul is almost dead.

Keep the memory of that vanished one; I don't know what is going to happen to my poor and turbulent entity.

For a long time I had accumulated my being. The substance of my thoughts was devotedly chosen amid the chaos of things. I had created myself incomplete but harmonious, weak but moderate. Now unknown days are upon us.

One glance has made me so stupid that I no longer exist; I have lost my beautiful crystalline vision of the World, I am an ancient king; I am an exile from myself.

Ah! Do you know what a gown is—even beyond, especially beyond, all simplistic desire of the flesh?

But only the dress and the eye. The idealist agonizes. The world, could it exist?...

And how I do thank you for your great kindnesses. You are the best.

P.-A. VALÉRY

[Valéry to Gide]

[July 1891]

My dear friend,

I must write to you to calm myself a bit. I am frenetic—such a sea breeze is blowing that my hair is wet from it and I breathe the sea air!

If you knew how she penetrates me and what love it is! It transports me and would make me howl foolish things;

t is the triumph of an indomitable trollop, trumpeted abroad by the vast winds that leap and roll and play truant on the waves. My brain is full of those winds and glittering waves that whinny; against the furiously spurted foam, the black vessel is frightened.

The sun—down there—must irritate the tempests and the growling horn announces formidable combat. ...

P.-A.V.

[Valéry to Gide]

[July 13, 1891]

O salutaris!

Although your letter seems to disdain what attracts me in friendship as in all things—the absolute—it is entirely of an ineffable truth.

I would like to recount to you, dear one, all that I have felt and guessed, and the spider web balances on which I have weighed a few tears, if to dream again of the days past were not as painful for me as the gesture of a wounded man with curiosity who lightly strokes sensitive and clotted bandages, beneath which there is suffering still.

If you knew how much I was suffering and how much my transfigured stupidity seemed admirable to me!

What is most illustrious in these novelties, is that the whole Drama was mine. I gave myself the spectacle of Love. ... But this time everything screamed. The *pure mind*, familiar with *meditations*, ran away badly bitten. ...

The Enigma proposed by the mouth of the cruel virgin.
(Pindar, fragment 35.)

P. VALÉRY

[Valéry to Gide]

[July 1891]

Dear André,

... My examination ended poorly but well enough. My books are open again, but I am still the wakened sleeper.

As for other things, I could say nothing at all, knowing nothing more. ... "What would I seek in love?" Myself!— that self which escapes and flows between avid fingers, that is the *man* who breaks away at every step of the soul, at every hurt, and which would appear suddenly, at certain stormy moments, growing perhaps, or defiling the whole being and the grieving spectator who is there.

I would seek, I have sought there a manifestation of the external mystery, an occult correspondence, a harmony of wills.

I would wish these lines could tell you more than the signs that compose them. I have thought for a long time after writing this, and I add this thought, of a mysterious sort, to my letter. I hope that you will find it.

Good-bye.

P.-A. VALÉRY

[Valéry to Gide]

August 10 [1891]

...Only the vague sound of money made by water on limp leaves consoles me. ... Nothing consoles me like that. Art is a plaything. Science is crude. The esoteric is the most beautiful of lies. Nothing is complex, far away, really secret and subtle—except this pale noise of water. Water. This world is ridiculous as a clock; those stars turn around and round stupidly, very few in number (3,500), not much, in short, nor curious. And what are brains to me, so simple!

People whose hair is getting longer strike poses against the sky, posing as Orpheus—because they can break an alexandrine into 8, 4 or 3, 9, or they repeat a letter in verse! Horrible!

Our flowers are as stupid as women! The reciprocal is true. Temples are useful only in imagination. Books!... are what one is. They are remade—therefore, no use. Women as lovers are filthy or stupid, mothers are inferior. There is nothing to drink that isn't cheap and barbarous. Only one artistic *scent*, salt—perhaps coal. Incense stinks. Death is comically small. One should finish only by explosion!—or sink, nose down, straight to the bottom on a five-master that would founder like lead with all her sails!

Everything is false! The dissonance splits the ears of my understanding. Language is poor as a widow. Nature is ugly as if a second rate artist had made it. The other world doesn't exist, for not one soul would come back. ... Now nothing is created. ... The pagans are stupid. The Christians ugly enough to give fright; nirvana is the paradise of beasts. Hamlet would be fine if there were no drama around him. Mystery doesn't exist, alas! Poe is the only one...even *he* has a few false notes. Barrès is on the point of turning out his pickets and hanging himself. The scholars made the newly rich stink. Causes and effects don't exist! We create them, Gentlemen! So what does that prove?

Style? Go and watch them fabricate it if you want to vomit! Artists, you will go mad! Bourgeois, you are stupid! ... Who made the universe? I did! God is an atom that radiates. God is principle. God is the Good. God is the Beautiful. God is three; no He is two! God is an Idea. God is! ... So God is a few words. That is not much. ... Movement begets number. Force engenders movement. Will engenders force. What engenders will? Engenders? Who? Why the moon?—and why the minor mode? What is the essence of the sad? Who is being mourned here? The devil sleeps after his meals. He is getting old. Ah! All is the desolation of boredom. Nothing is strange, nothing ... !

This is a sleepless night. Good-bye.

P.-A. VALÉRY

[Valéry to Gide]

[Montpellier, August 1891]

Dear André,

You whom I created, you who created me, you who gave me a new image of myself and who have transmuted me into your being, do not trouble your soul for me. You *must* remain near to the rare and radiant É.* (since I must not write any other letter with this name); may you be happy with this real apparition and talking to the phantom. You understood, with some pity, what such cares were for me, yesterday, and how much I venerated from a distance the one whose hazardous meeting troubled me on certain days. Having gone away, I do not know where, she leaves me confined with my letters useless in a drawer. And I remain here. Winter will come down. ... Moreover, it is especially in October that I shall be in Paris. (Unless I go to London.) So, perhaps you will be able to meet me there. I shall write to you, besides, from up there. I fear being a bit lost. I shall not go to any literary public house, but I should very much like to see Mallarmé and Régnier. I hope Louis will show me these phenomena—happy if he doesn't make some pompous, Orphic presentation. I am glad to see him. We are going to say many bad things about you!—especially if you are

* Émmanuèle, that is, Madeleine Rondeaux [later Mme Gide].

present. He will cry out for Bayreuth and the "solemn morning awakening of the trombones of Parsifal"! I want very much to carry away all his letters so that we may be mutually embarrassed! What contradictions already. I would very much like to see Joris-Karl also, but I don't know where he is living, nor with what right? It would be best for someone to point him out to me in the street. . . . I am sure that Louis will find me *weak* and a *one-stringed* instrument. What chatter! You are beginning to grit your teeth. Let me caper and browze on the new bark—I am ordinarily too gloomy and almost stupefied.

Do you remember? You told me one evening that you loved... farce! I never believed it. ...

P. VALÉRY

[Valéry to Gide]

[September 1891]

... ME, I *never* forget. I don't share myself, being too nearly nothing, but each of the truly *mine* has me WHOLE! Yet you are the only one to whom I have said certain things. Certain people, many people define me as slightly or not at all *sentimental*, not much as a *philosopher*, but a bit of an abstracter of aesthetic quintessences. I admire them for knowing me so well. I pass for gentle; I am violent—but absent-minded! I am taken as light-hearted, merry—I am boredom and despair in person! But I smile inevitably. I never tell an intruder my thought, but what I suppose pleases him, or gibe at him, under the circumstances. I never speak my soul in verse nor in any other literature (except this which is not one) since to write is not to make oneself blush, nor to affront indifference—but indeed the ambition first to lay hold of an ideal reader and to draw him after you, without being moved oneself, or perhaps to dazzle him, stun him, reduce him by superior Truth and the magic strength—yes, marvelous!—to create all that one wants by little signs like these.

. . . .

I have galloped on all roads, and cried the call on all horizons! One corner of my past life—unknown forever to All—has enlightened me on the pulsation of the little beast which is exasperated sensibility. Science bored me, the mystic forest led me to nothing, I visited the ship and the cathedral, I have read the most marvelous of poets—Poe, Rimbaud, Mallarmé—analyzed their means, alas, and always I encountered the most beautiful *illusions*, at their point of origin and birth. Where shall I find a newer magic? A secret of being and creating that surprises me? You will smile, here, dreaming of my poor efforts. If you knew how much—really—I detest them! My great future poems are seeking their form and—this is insane! No, you see, in passive art as in the active, I have found only motives for rage and disgust! First of all, those who study man in himself make me vomit! Only the Church has art. It is she alone who can give a little comfort, and who can detach us from the World. I don't want to allow myself to talk about it— you already find me long—but this would have to be told, cried out: we are all little boys compared to the liturgists and theologians, since the most inspired of our own— Wagner, Mallarmé—bow, and *imitate*.

...You see that you must not be jealous. Friendship, your clear word is still the only thing that filters down to the depths in me. Friend, your manifestations toward me are the purest sign of a Truth, if there is one. And your letters are still bells from the little country of my birth. So, I remember! Your jealousy tinkles delightfully, the bad dream dies away...yes, it is just that! Long ago, when I was a man, before there was literature, before there was stupidity— before the cloud. ...

P.-A. VALÉRY

[Valéry to Gide]

[September 11, 1891]

The existence of my body is the least beautiful of dreams. Then, silence.

But a woman, with a few years since her youth, passes and does not know me. I hardly know her name. Most likely she is not beautiful. Yet her image remains with me. I am aware of her, around my table. What notions have I not woven for her. Have I understood a single possibility of distress or tenderness? Have I not even written to her! The letter is in my drawer.

What angel with fingers of disdain protects this prose from living? Do I know whether tomorrow I may not speak to her? More resolute than yesterday?—unless disdain be the strength of the feeble.

And You, who come to add this epilogue of a vast Thought, the Imitation clothed in milk, at the memory of the snow-like goodness which you embody, a writer who succeeded in writing to you, tell me if there is still *balm* in *Judaea* and if you think I am unpardonably stupid.

To You who deserve boats filled with bouquets and the salutes of liberated slaves, to you always "I offer my empty cup where a monster of gold is suffering." *

P.V.

---

* From a line of Mallarmé's *Toast funèbre*.

[Gide to Valéry]

De La Roque, encore
[November 3, 1891]

I am exhausted, I no longer dare to come back. Pari
frightens me. I am beginning to understand you and you
fright of the city. It shakes so many thoughts ready to enter
the brain, that we are distracted from the profound ones.
We want to live too fast, which is worth nothing. Then I
distrust myself; I know that an old desire to succeed is half
asleep in my depths. ... Here, I am pure mind. Day and
night I roll in abysses of transcendences. I have just read eight
volumes of George Sand.

That gave me a disgust for love (I had it already, in part)
and for all sentimentality. And for myself as an individual.

I want very much to talk to you; I think I understand
you better. I understand that intimacy is desirable and
possible only with a very small number. (I wanted it with
everyone!) Is intimacy even desirable? What is it?

Doesn't the sense of a Presence suffice? To know that the
other is there, that there is someone else.

Up to that point I wanted to *make friends* as one "makes
love." That is ridiculous. It comes from my not wanting to
make love.

. . . .

Pure Mind!—"in the upper air." All passion, all emotion
is despicable if it is not transcendental. Empathy itself is
something rather contemptible. Sympathy is the recognized
weakness of the creature who is not self-sufficient. One must
be self-sufficient—with God.

Poe made his. I have read him every day, and every day
he grows greater. Today, I find him colossal; and if it is not
he, it is at least his kind.

124

Schopenhauer now. I find him too bright, too clever. He is not well balanced, he wants to persuade too often. I would prefer Kant. But Schopenhauer will have been for me the initiator.

My *Narcissus* is finished. I don't know what to think of it. It's too polished and I could change nothing about it but the whole—yet I believe it is skimpy.

Will that please you?

In any case, the effort to write it is not lost, because it cleared up the whole of my esthetics, my ethics, and my philosophy. And no one shall keep me from believing that every *author must* have a philosophy, an ethics, and an esthetic which are characteristic. Without that, one can create nothing. The work is only a manifestation of that.

Have you read Balzac's *Louis Lambert*? I reread it every year. For me, it is enormous. I even find that it is written. Nothing has staggered me like that vision of Louis Lambert in the dark room, nothing —not even Poe, I believe—and yet!...

What else? I read all day, and I meditate beside the fire.

We are on the best terms, Louÿs and I: he writes me fine letters. I am delighted at this, since we can be only on the best or the very worst of terms.

With a few mutual concessions, how well we get on—the three of us! I wrote badly to you, with frozen fingers in a huge salon badly heated by a country fire.

Farewell.

These are the thoughts of one day that I am writing to you. Tomorrow, in Paris, I shall again be the vain and ambitious gambler that I fear I am.

Good-bye,

A. W.

[Valéry to Gide]

Montpellier [November 16, 1891]

Illusion for Illusion, I keep this one...

I thank you for a dedication* that inclines your beautiful work toward my distant hours like a flower attentive to those familiar with its beauty.

Dedication is a blank gesture which says, "This is to You, work of my fingers; eat and drink, this is our communion." And I dream of that admirable literature which someone might invent: to write each of his books entirely for one Person ... but is that not the magic and fragile virtue of Correspondence? The letter, which forces us to give the friendly perfume of present minutes, without omitting the intention of waking, when we were seeing each other, is it not an ornamental and charming work of art, a delight consented to by two and with Time, a true essence of the hour's emotion, and which goes a bit flat in the drawer, just enough to gain in refinement.

Next, I beg you not to call me *poet* any more, great or small. I am not a Poet. Nor any other title. Must I repeat to you the same talk as to Louÿs? That I am not a Poet, but the Gentleman who is bored. That any normal, cubic, affirmative Beauty turns me away. I scorn phrases and their rhythm and all those mechanics scarcely unforeseen, which *do not amuse* me. Expression alone wins me. Final symptom: I reflect on the inevitable vulgarity of writing the word Soul, for example, in verse.

In the end I miss you more than ever. You must be curious, seen through the Coat of Arms. I offer you:

"D'azur au dextrochère d'or tenant une coupe vuyde du même, où souffre un monstre."

* No doubt Gide's dedication written on a copy of *Traité du Narcisse*.

126

My dear friend, you accuse me of joking. That is possible. Is it because I said something bad about the "most holy Sympathy"?... Wait, this reminds me of a fantastic tale that I will write *tomorrow*: a man who searches the world for a perfect friend and who forms friendships with various ones. Finally he manages to meet himself one day, and makes his own acquaintance. So...

Good-bye.

P.-A. VALÉRY

[Valéry to Gide]

[December 3, 1891]

My friend,

...I would be very long in this letter, if you were not tired already of the torments so often recounted; I would be long on complaints and black with boredom. But what's the use? You know the monotony of antireligious lines from my previous authentic ones. And to talk to you I am forcing myself to disguise even the stagnation beneath the stupid effort of an arabesque style of writing. Reread (if you have any desire to guess a part of this moment), reread my letters of July and August, add the rest which I am dropping, out of a peculiar laziness, and you will have me present, rainy, inert, sour.

But I promise you to be good—if you come. And if I desire anything, it is yourself. How annoyed I am with most of my friends! All the more one dislikes to insult oneself.

Our little family was so good, last May: "And what do you think of...?" Those children were playing with the stars! Doesn't it seem to you that, almost without seeking each other since, we know one another much better? First, "nous nous tutoyons" each other (isn't it funny, that

verb), that is to say, we talk beyond these times like handsome Antiques, or early Christians. To say *tu* is already a free
and purer gesture. In English we say *tu* only to God: "Thou,
God, Thou, Lord!" When we are very intimate, and there
is darkness, the murmured *tu* gives the illusion of a word
spoken to oneself and a response from oneself. True, isn't it?
—Are you coming?

P.-A. VALÉRY

[Gide to Valéry]

Saturday [February 1892]

My friend,

There it is, finished. Thursday I saw Régnier; when I
talked about the *Entretiens*, he told me that this was Griffin's
business. So it was to Griffin that I sent your manuscript.*

It was quite imperfectly that I understood the *intention* of
the opening passage underlined (I am waiting to see it again,
in print). But the ornamental motifs that follow amused and
stunned me. They are perfect, new—ravishing. Do that then,
as maritime decorations for your *Naval Esthetics*.

Régnier, without having read it (we were at Louÿs's
house with Hérold and others) advised me against your
dedication, at the same time thanking you greatly; but "not
in *Entretiens*," he said.

Did you receive Vielé-Griffin's *Les Cygnes*?

For myself, I should like a bit of calm. I am exasperated
the whole day; it is a matter of absurd tasks on every hand.
Books bewilder me—these libraries where one would have
to read everything. I am doing Greek again with delight.
But how much time it all takes—and for what?

---

* "Purs drames." [See *Collected Works*, Vol. 2, p. 213.]

Balzac again and my piano; a bit of writing, but I am not very lucid since I left you.

Ah! Some Rimbaud again; I work endlessly at *Les Illuminations*. *L'Antique*, certain "phrases" are clarified now in a fantastic light. It is amusing to work at it.

Good-bye, this letter frightens me. I am afraid of signing it Mauclair—but the truth is—I am too dull today and if it were not for your "pure dramas," I would have been silent. One should not write, if not delightfully. Good-bye.

Your friend,

A.G.

P.S. Write me as quickly as possible a clear and luminous explanation of Verlaine's *Beams* which close *Les Romances sans paroles*. Everybody talks about it, no two have yet agreed.

A.G.

[Valéry to Gide]

[February 15, 1892]

Friend,

Thanks for the delicious words about my *Dramas*. Yet I had the feeling of an incomparable fiasco.

That is why I had not written you a line with it. The end is absurd, impenetrable—it annoyed me very much. But I still had too much remorse. . . . Your little passage here is a very bad memory for me. I was so stupid as to make you run away?—and not one good hour of absolute communion. Not one intimate hour of those cool nudities of the soul, not a single friendly Galatéism. Perhaps we missed some star in the sky. . . .

Now I have a bit of fever. I am in a "club" of friends where we evoke the spirits of the furniture. These evenings are rather surprising.

And poor C! He had an interview with Péladan lately, at Nîmes—yesterday I found him flopped into an armchair with a sinister bottle on the pedestal table and the hypodermic syringe—so I had trouble. People die of it very quickly, they say.

Then there are other songs, as you guess. This changes the light. There were one or two scenes of the Mass, quite stirring, and at the "Elevation," a concentration of will on a certain head of hair!

But let us be quiet. I am awaiting Astarte—where all will be beautiful. *Vivat*!

P. A. VALÉRY

[Gide to Valéry]

[March 2, 1892]

My friend,

I remember ancient questions, which I forgot to answer. I have five volumes of Banville (six even) and in none of them do I find *La Grève des Forgerons*. As for Mallarmé and his Tuesdays. I am diligent, always more and more, despite the cruel snows soon to come, or the drunken masks of yesterday. Mallarmé told us about Banville, one evening when there were only three of us, Régnier, Hérold, and your friend, while Louÿs was tasting Yvette Guilbert, I think.

I would have exquisite things to recount from that conversation. Mallarmé moreover was preparing a lecture on Banville who, according to him, realized (but scarcely) the ultimate and most lightly divine gesture of the poet, the one who dances like a flame above the heavy humus brought in by others—flower of light floating above the rubbish. . . . But all that, he must tell it.

I believe Lazare is powerfully disconcerted by your prose

in the *Entretiens*; immediately I begin screaming around that they are marvelous. Decidedly, the staff and the administration have no more changed than the format of that review, and if I am part of it, it's because I am invited, like you.

Now tell me: if you come to Paris, will it be at Easter? That is very important to me, because my good Drouin is planning to come up and spend the three days he will have for vacation (he is doing his military service at Nancy). Mockel also is coming to settle here, I think, at this season— he is charming. In fact I shall spend some time there myself, between two visits to Munich and with the excuse, perhaps, of *La Conque* I will invite you to dinner with Henri de Régnier and Walcknaër, and naturally Louÿs. There you are.

I am leaving in a few days—less than a week. I am terrified about it, and what a fever!—and the question of a travel library. I must give up the whole business.

If I were a bit less demented I would have copied for you, from the first *Vogue*, Rimbaud's *Les Communiantes*, but that would have made you ill.

. . . .

What more? I am on my sixteenth novel of Balzac. You judge whether I have the time to write. But you, and your famous letter, the one that no one writes. Well, is it written? And that anxiety?

Ah! My little elegist, you can at least leave Montpellier? And without being too sad?

Yes, we both talked poorly at Montpellier; to talk at agreed and arbitrary times, that is good when we have only a few things to say. But we had everything, and time avenges itself for being violated.

Good-bye; I am awaiting your *Naval Esthetics* or some new verses. One must do admirable things; I assure you that it is an obligation.

Your faithful ANDRÉ G.

[Valéry to Gide]

[March 3, 1892]

Dear friend,

... I am deep into *Eureka* and the *Illuminations*—I cannot work positively—and Louÿs no longer writes to me and you not often. ... I am writing to you with the right ear (the one that opens on the garden) filled with the *Twilight of the Gods*, where what is admirable pullulates. But *Siegfried* also, the son of the Bird! One of my musical revelations. (And it is, I think, very ordinary, technically.)

There it is. Ah! I have reread *King Lear*, which is famous Maeterlinck, a bit better. One scene is extraordinary—it is the pure triumph of all literature—perhaps! We must talk about it again.

As for Narcissus, he wrote one more letter to his drawer and regularized an emotion by stupidity.

Moreover, Lent is beginning; I am going to be reborn to dogma, to the good rhythm of ceremonies—green leaves in the cathedral, profound Jeremiads on the organ—and the grey weather in the colored glass panes turns the heart as the sea is turned by the porthole—all vacillates. ...

P. VALÉRY

[Valéry to Gide]

[March 18, 1892]

Dear far one,

Louÿs also shames me for not working. Do you believe it? I shall answer him soon in the way that *I must* answer him.

To you, who know me the most often, I don't wish to repeat my frequent absolute words. You know very well that it is not worth while to write and be silent, and to recount one myth or another. (I am still awaiting your *Narcisse*, of which this is almost the conclusion. ...) I meditate, and try to refine myself, so that death may be less *physical* and less hard. One must not give birth to the conventional, don't you think, and we are all so much menaced by it.

Thanks (as an interlude) for your dedication in *La Wallonie*. You are, Louÿs and you, incomparable friends. I have done nothing to deserve you, and that is why you must not be surprised if, myself, I have dedicated nothing to you yet. Your affection, and two or three others, is the only one of my works that I like. Except for you, I am scarcely the Poet's "charming timid one"—unfortunately.

I am very conscious—too much perhaps! But I like artists only for that. Nothing would be more painful to me than to pass only for "an occasional" rhymer and writer. Art is a second life to me, the work is the family or night games.

. . . .

What a fine number of *La Wallonie*, exclaims Louÿs. These Belgians reproduce *La Fileuse* by the echoes, it becomes a spinning wheel!* And with that *L'Arion*, prettily wicked, experimental sonnet!

* The same number of *La Wallonie* contained Valéry's sonnet, *Arion*, and two months later, *La Syrinx*. In the bibliographical notes, his *La Fileuse* was cited.

From you, the exquisite rainy dawn, from him a poly-chrome marble,* from Régnier a long allegory. It is a true fugue in four parts that we are pursuing.

Will you be going to Bayreuth?

P.-A. VALÉRY

[Valéry to Gide]

[April 4, 1892]

Dear friend,

Your muttered letter had a singular meaning, an admir-able esoterism, and not willed, I believe. There was exhaled from it, that morning when I received it, a strange unfor-mulated *kindness*, which I had so much emotion in grasping! —as if we were twin mirrors each of a different metal, and that a gesture might have taken place in the one—then, after an exquisite moment—might have bathed in the other, the same and yet *elsewhere.*

I am furious that the army should keep you, and that this bitch should embrace you by force. . . . Your letter made me relive the grey religious months that once were mine—before I knew you and even Louÿs, and the throbbings of the heart, the transports, the palpitations felt there, and which will be spared you, since you are no longer the child always weeping, ignorant of himself and restless as quicksilver—the child I was at eighteen years.

I am studying law, up to my ears and bored! I don't have the courage to chat with you and talk about art or some emotion—that would put me in a rage, and even you hardly want that!

* Pierre Louÿs's *Astarté.* The January–February issue of *La Wallonie* was dedicated to Gide and contained two of his poems: *Lagunes,* dedicated to Valéry, and *Octobre.*

I am waiting for the little books and the manuscript, with natural impatience.★ Good-bye

P. VALÉRY

[Valéry to Gide]

[End of April 1892]

Your very impatient letter makes me want to copy it again for you with delicious idleness so that you will understand that it is the same thing here. . . .

And: "Each day one thing more annoys me with which I amused myself the previous day: that is how we grow older. . . ." tempts me. And yet I have a few Ideas these days —or shades of Ideas—but the time is failing with patience, and July comes on with its cudgels.

I felt, last night, that if I had had the friend at my hand, I would have committed a few follies. I have been so disagreeable these weeks that yesterday I would have wept over the flies—but they are very sceptical, knowing that they are worth nothing.

Then I was brilliant for two whole hours: nothing but the quite spiritual sea, a sky sways, and with little sparkling steps a Saint Victory of Samothrace approaches on her marble galley, brandished by the clearest of waves.

Then a rage for every kind of analysis, a perversion of conscience, an aura of extra-lucid somnambulism. Finally, a yawn. . . .

I am a bit tired of adorning everything but my boredom, and after having thrown ocean drops on the sun, I turned to the right to come back.

★ *Les Poésies d'André Walter* and *Le Traité du Narcisse*. The manuscript is the "*Narcisse secret*" mentioned by Gide in his previous letter.

As for *that story*, I detest it: because of Her, a certain poem broke my fingers a while ago, and now it's finished! One must be very wise and study his law. "The Medusa" disappeared recently at noon, for some bluish dwelling where her Odyssean marine hair will find the good armchair of summer, rocked by someone without knowing that I exist, while the child plays (and now I am truly interested in his child although he is ill-formed). We would have been happy! Romance and hazy moonlight. Ah! Stupid! All that, André, is the unconscious; it is the misfortune of not understanding acutely enough or rather not *feeling* what one understands—almost.

In this whole affair, I deserve whistles and rotten apples, except in the second act where my guardian angel dictated to me some of those beautiful lucid words of which the writing, carefully preserved, will be for me tomorrow's intimate glory and a kind of future encouragement to gesticulate better and speak my role.

I very reasonably failed to destroy myself two or three times (perhaps I shall dream of it again tomorrow) for simple motives: first, to satisfy nothing; next and contradictorily to be as stupid, identical, and entirely human, which is the height of bad taste. An acknowledgment whose existence redeemed my own, having precipitated me into the analysis of that in which I was supposed to differentiate myself, as regards those minutes, from other people. Whence *theory*, that is to say life for fifteen days.

At her future return, I studied some law (not sure!). I am still afraid of a certain fatal interview—the first to take place at a *Charity* ball, or perhaps we shall have to make pretty speeches, an alms-purse in hand. I am quite capable of fainting or some physical stupidity, a detail which almost happened several times—at simple encounters in the streets, henceforth frightening. . . .

Here's a page that ends with your own yawn, and I am stopping it. Tell me your advice and what happened. You talk to me about my verse—and I can't remember which ones?

My mother sees very little, and I dread Paris even more with her. It is sad—without another word—to see her saddened, and sadder if she plays some obscure gaiety—feeling her way, to pacify us.

Good-bye. I await you in violet words.

P.-A. Valéry

[Valéry to Gide]

[September 5, 1892]

André,

What are you doing, you incessant traveller, to whom this letter designated for La Roque will arrive some day or other to be read by the unusual light of a strange beach of stars, of those where three suns, green, yellow, and red pour out their fires? Where must you be adored now, and in what book do you allow me to dream (like the *other*—Sappho) of the title and the bed left empty in what country?

I am leaving for Italy in about ten nights (write to me first) and I want, absolutely, to know from you a thousand horrible things—before: if Louÿs is in Paris (I acknowledge here that, furious at last for his brevity, I did not answer his card from Bayreuth a month ago). Next tell me all about your service—where you are going and under what conditions and whether I shall see you in Paris, in a month approximately. I confess to you that I am going *down there* or *up there* in a distrustful and cloudy mood. It is just as alone as I wish myself! And should I not be delivered to all the fogs, to the giddiness of a child and of October. What do I know?

You, in the regiment, I am sorry for you for a few days, perhaps a few months. But if you knew the G O O D it does— the red hot iron in the naïve water! It is only there and in the struggle that a man becomes *tough*. At each vacant minute, millions of electric *reactions*, sad and pure, sublimate you, and summarize you to a geometric point—nothing, solitary, where everything *is*, where one is, absolutely and as never again, his sole and singular "self."

I am now master of a few supreme esthetics. I shall not speak for fear of a thousand written errors.

. . . .

Lazare, who makes us celebrated young people, inhales me with a laugh. Small wind in the printed leaves. (Besides I don't know where he could praise us this way, by threes!)

But even so it is quite fine, our trinacria, three points where a good circle of gold and friendship passes. . . .

P.V.

[Valéry to Gide]

At Genoa for the past week
[Chez M. Gaetano Cabella]
[September 21, 1892]

Dear André,

I envy your quiet work. I am caught up in the madness here, feasts and festivals without a brain, costume balls on board the ships, arts to be eaten all day. I spend my evenings with an extraordinary collector, the Englishman Mr. Mylius, smoking in his house, which is a Cluny opening directly on the sky and the sea. This man has marvels that would make

Goncourt die of jealousy, and which are used for living, for sleeping, quite stupidly in a habitual dandyism, handsome with indifference.

Here I look at nothing, in short. Italy touches me so close that I cannot even give you its general tone. I enjoyed one ballet particularly—an entirely Italian feast—a few paintings vaguely bowed to, the *Saint John* by Vinci (brother to the Parisian) etc., some Van Dycks, but all this annoys me *here* as banal. Even in my uncle's house, if I go out, there in the stairway is a twelfth-century chapel and the walls covered with creatures in marble—angels and bulls.

I go down the little streets, to the gardens, to the flowing waters—to live alone!

I admire your fecundity, you already have complete Works. I am still reserving myself and by force. My sonnet, *La Syrinx*, dates from February; it has been greatly crippled. Example: *bouche* for *boucle*. Good-bye. I shall be in Paris about October 15. Where will you be stationed?

P.V.

[Gide to Valéry]

Montpellier [March 1893]

Dear friend,

A kind of disquiet came over me: why didn't I, before leaving, take back all your letters which—alas!—I had loaned to you. If I hadn't such rare confidence in you, I would fear never seeing that correspondence again; I know very well that you will return it to me one day, but I should have liked to be able to bring it here; for me it would have taken the place of yourself. The most exquisite of habits, the sentimental habit, makes me expect you at every moment, and I talk only with those who have known you and talk to me about you. The first evenings, I would walk up to the Peyrou to see from the top of the terraces with their black swans, their calm basins, the sun setting and the sea smiling in the distance. Then I would tire of this too solitary walk.

I didn't see the museum again, I didn't look back at the gravestone where we used to chew enchanted roses. I didn't walk again as we used to do in the evening under the trees. I didn't see Coste again and I am afraid of seeing him. I live expecting to leave and go bathing in the sea. In three days, at Cette or Marseille, I shall embark for Spain where I await my joy in the sun.

Is Paris still just as unbearable? What does one do there? What are you doing there? Are you publishing masses of things? How shall I see you when I come back? I imagine Louÿs vilifies me while chatting: out of negligence I wrote him such a friendly letter that he was confused by it. For him to be all right, I must beat him as I have never beaten women. There are certain days when that is tiring; one would willingly shake his hand, but the moment one turns it loose, he gives you a thrashing. "But after all, it doesn't matter."

Write to me while I am still far away; here I haven't the time to do anything, but how I would like to read a letter written by you.

I am your

ANDRÉ GIDE

[Valéry to Gide]

[July 24, 1893]

Dear friend,

Your first letter to me is that cold glass of water the most truly *wet* to be found on earth, in the country, in a hole, folded with grasses.

I was in the midst of an unhealthy season—that is, when I think I am alone.

I am very lonely! When my head is working, I enjoy it generally, and thanks partly to that isolation. But when the wind subsides there is nothing around me. Communications have been cut. Terribly alone. You know too well (alas for you!) how my experiments in expansion failed, narrowly— in all senses. The fact that this guided me elsewhere and electrified me—this is true. But to say that, in short, I have never known Satisfaction, plenitude, even the slightest form of spreading out and settling in. . . . Around me I beg the stones. They are rocks! (All this vertigo—which full day-light gallantly dissipates, but full daylight is not continual.) I feel that a favorable being would make me live, would draw out my existence for several centuries, as if I were exchanging the old conscience for a new one. Notice the point: to dream of these communions is scarcely more interesting than dreaming about a boot. But to live that dream and, mean-while, dream something else, illuminates.

If, for example, I had held Rimbaud between my hands, within reach of all my spiritual mechanics, machines of savage delicacy and enormous strength, to weigh, decompose, and construct to move, I would have mocked the con-querors and the aeronauts, the learned and the architects. . . . The error, I wager, of many people in my regard is to imagine in me—in spite of all—an ulterior motive that is *literary*, to believe that I tend, in short, despite the restriction that I profess and the renunciation of some *new genre*. I can easily guess those sophisms, many of them because I knew they *must* be formed. But these people are excusable, knowing neither Me nor Rimbaud.

Beside these dear insulations, I indulge vaguely in grammatical speculations. Schwob forced me to read Paul Claudel's *La Ville*. A book in which the description and the statics would be very amusing, and . . . urgent. Good-bye, dear friend. You are lucky to nest. God knows when I shall see trees!—and seas, especially!

P. VALÉRY

[Valéry to Gide]

[August 26, 1893]

Paris is beginning again. I am alone here, sometimes, and often the Clignancourt, the Saint-Denis that I like, the little boats where I go and stretch out in the bottom against a glass pane at water levels that seem bottled, to smoke, to go over to the Alma to smoke again with Régnier, amusingly.

Yesterday evening (most discursively) I recognized on the boulevard an old and dear acquaintance, the Russian Kolbassine, one of the rare men *comme il faut*, a true thinker whom I brought down here, to sit down and talk, talk, talk until tomorrow—a debauchery of everything, our travels, a scene of astonishing comedy where the speakers seem to know everything and in a single allusion to jump leagues of the spirit.

There are centuries since we saw you. Or Louis (who is in Paris, I know, suddenly brought by the news that his brother had been named minister plenipotentiary and one of the international commissioners for the Egyptian debt, in Cairo).

While awaiting a departure of some sort, I live more or less this way—with the current. . . . So as not to think, I spend days at mad calculations, mechanically—or at atrocious fantasies. Then hours in the streets, fixed in front of a jeweler's shop in the rue de la Paix, or modifier of the comforts in rich hotels, or of the galleries of steel.

Induced like a metal by noticing all those troubles over the terrestrial basin, who from Paris go to India, kill again in the "Midi," then over Italy, bleeding the whole length of the year like a serpent of horrible energies over the world, bound to what completely new whirlwinds? Who knows? I feel in my being the influence of certain comets, and my "dominant visions" of the moment follow the great incline of immense numbers, the obvious movements of nations and individuals, deformed by some procession of the equinoxes.

There are *à peu près* a plenty. What? The *à peu près* of a galvanometer. Fine title.

And if I told you that I admire—as a literary man—pages of the geometers that no one, neither Rimbaud nor . . . the reality has given me the *view*, the sea swallowing—like opening a volume by Laplace by chance, the other day, at the page of the flow of the tides. At the moment, the gurgle and the sway came to me, the tone of steel, the swelling, the sudden leakage to the West. The word: syzygy!—the smell of that gadget that moves and shines between azimuths, coordinates, parallaxes, etc., the height of the sun—every-thing.

For extraordinary reading, I had Poe's *Love Letters*, something that you understand is dizzying for me. But we shall talk about it again.

All my respects to Madame Gide, to whom my mother asks you to send her greetings. Good-bye. Write soon to your

P. VALÉRY

[Valéry to Gide]

[September 28, 1893]

I see Louÿs often, as you have perceived by the elementary jokes at his command. This leads me to make a remark: Louÿs has a kind of ascendancy over me—an extraordinary power of irresistibility, half that of a woman, who endures by her presence—and enough when he is not there for me not even to want to exercise, in this connection and with this gift, any method at all of arrangements, permutations or analysis—which is indeed most astonishing.

I haven't told you about his discovery of a barman who is almost a genius, nor how, one beautiful night about a month ago, we were brought together by him in the rue Rembrandt, Henri de Régnier, Robert de Bonnières and me, delightfully and then abominably drunk from a thousand American drinks, which the Man in the white vest had been bringing to us since midnight. A true chemist, come to mix champagne and muscadet with the eggs, or finally to present that unheard-of "Last Drink," * made of all the liquors imaginable but having the taste of clear water—the strength to fell an ox.

Et cetera.

I live in the vague as never before. My situation is becoming grotesque. And I am unfitted, besides, even to dream of it.

I am watching over the dissolution of a friend who is dying of a little known syphilis, and the ruin of that man suffering a number of the most intense sensations and actions magnetically induced, all rather chilling. Every day—however—the anaesthetic libraries give me a few hours of peace, where the reading of formulas of uneasiness precipi-

* Valéry's English.

tated into dizzying states of mind turn beneath my eyes for a long time. Finally, I grind in the piston.

I have received nothing from you for many weeks. When are you coming? And with what manuscript? By the way, a rather curious coincidence is to be seen in the last Poictevin,* where certain pages (except the senseless words dear to him) have the tone of being written by you. Or rather, perhaps the resemblance of atmosphere. . . .

Your P.V.

[Gide to Valéry]

[Biskra, November 27, 1893]

Dear friend,

What silence! I am at Biskra; aren't you at Montpellier? I have just been very ill, and I am now living at Biskra, not as a "tourist" but as a convalescent. I regret the great desert of the Souf and the Djérid, which I was not able to cross. My chest went out of order even before I could reach Gabès, and it was by way of Constantine, not by the South, that I was able to get to Biskra where I am sadly vegetating. At least I have made two marvelous crossings, unforgettable, and where I wished you were alongside me in the other desert bunk. Portholes are marvelous eyes through which nature looks at you.

I won't tell you anything about my trip because I believe you don't approve of it, but I think traveling is also an art and that it can be amusing. I have tasted kinds of distress unknown to me before; I amused myself by living only with officers and I now have the memory of truly brutal feasts. I have often longed for Paris. Because of you now,

* Francis Poictevin (1854–1904), a friend of Villiers de L'Isle-Adam, Mallarmé and Verlaine, author of collections of short stories.

I regret Montpellier a bit. I am anxious to know that you are there, because of what is happening? It isn't possible that nothing is happening there and you owe me a thousand details. Write me something long, then, and complicated like your life, sad and learned. Tell me what is coming of all that, all that we have talked about so much. At Montpellier, someone is looking for you, one of my most charming friends, you will recognize him by his build—"a Lily and one of you all, etc.," and by his hair, which seems made by Monet. A silk scarf about his neck, bent, awkward, and exquisite. His name is Eugène Rouart,* and he lodges at present with Miss Twight, boulevard Case-Neuve.

You can talk about many things with him; he is very *au courant*. For me, I am no longer so, and I am uneasy, in vain, to know what is happening. When I know what you are doing, I shall already be greatly satisfied.

Good-bye. Write to me. I am

ANDRÉ GIDE

[Valéry to Gide]

[December 8, 1893]

Did you find my letter at the post office?

You say: "very ill," I don't know what to think of it. Where are you ill? Why? Yet you are in the sun and you have been in the sea.

Yes, the sleeping-car with compartments is indeed freedom. In a bedroom, the best, one must try to put into it everything needed for thinking. There, all is. Your words

* Eugène Rouart (1872–1935), son of Henri Rouart, collector of modern painting and friend of Degas and Manet. He also was the friend of painters and poets, and later was elected senator from Tarn-et-Garonne. Author of a novel, *La Ville sans maîtres* (1898).

revive it for me. You know that I almost no longer have more than a "vision," a delirium. That after having played with landscapes of readings and engravings, only one *hectare* of the Pacific, moving, came to me, a desire for the little wave that wakes and dies and does what it can to the equinoxes. It takes a clipper to go there. Yet Kolbassine insists that we must go to Batavia. He recalls the Island as if he had made it or simply as if he had been there. All the details. I let myself be tempted. I really believe that, out there one is nearer, not to nature (or stupidities), but to the cosmos, than anywhere else. There are earthquakes, cyclones, the sky, etc. The misfortune is that we haven't a penny.

My life, dear André, is neither "sad nor learned." It is saddened these days by the sudden insanity and suicide of one of my best friends—who was somebody. A young lieutenant of the marine artillery (the one to whom I *showed* Mallarmé at Fontainebleau), the most balanced fellow in the world, went mad suddenly, carried away by the dream of infancy among the mountains and marches, to kill himself at Annecy. I went to bury him at Nîmes the day before yesterday, etc. How ignoble are the solemn customs of modern life! A barbarism, a disgusing idolatry!

As for me, I am doing nothing. I have a glimpse of something rather new, I believe, to arrange—but first, to find. You would call it a (little) Treatise on Complexity or Theory of the Instrument giving the manner of resolving . . . etc., with an appendix on generalizing the notion of the three analytical quantities in constructive operations. The whole in a single German word. But I cannot work at it. At moments I dream of having an army of workers who would be made to think and purify what I catch a glimpse of. To refresh us and put our Sundays to good use, we would give those days to constructing buildings on ground or water.

Good-bye, Wanderer, pardon such an ineffective letter. I see M. Rouart rather often. I believe that he will be something *good*. But when shall I manage to lose that stupid mania for showing people that I do not think as they do? Another pardon that I owe you and how many!

P.V.

[Gide to Valéry]

Maison des Pères Blancs, Biskra
[December 1893]

My great Enigma,

Our two letters crossed. That makes a false pass, and all is to be done again. There was no use trying to surround my illness with mystery—my mother could not ignore it; her anxiety was even too great, I am already much better but just escaped being gravely ill. Nevertheless, I am going to remain in Biskra all winter and I must take good care of myself. I have never been less bored. I am reading a lot of German; I amuse myself with Darwin; I write to you when I dare and go for a walk while rereading. Palm trees bore me, but I amuse myself around them. I am awaiting a piano. I have no news from Paris, which makes me lose interest in it. I don't think of going back there for a long time. I am glad no longer to like the tumult, and I shall have aged very little this time.

Don't attach too much importance to my little plaquette,* I beg you, you see that I have not dedicated it to you. But shall I ever again dedicate something to you? And wouldn't that, then, be a sad sign?

* *La Tentative amoureuse*, Librairie de l'Art indépendent, 1893.

At least we can write and read to each other through others, and that is exactly what we shall do. But don't you, then, have anything published? Will you never attain the C-sharp? Imagine that I have nothing here of yours that is printed, to be reread!!

Good-bye. My other letter asked you for another sort of news. I am asking still.

And remember me, respectfully, won't you, to your mother.

ANDRÉ GIDE

[Valéry to Gide]

Montpellier [December 14, 1893]

I see you with the shadow of a palm on Darwin's stationery—photographed. In such reading matter, at the sun's foot, the principle must be to jump paragraphs. To read, down there, can only be to plunge into those beautiful studies by General Daumas on the Arab proverbs concerning horsemanship. All this is a kind of revenge—since you tell me that you have nothing of mine, printed, to be reread. You know that this is injury, entirely Arab-horseman, in short: as if you were cutting off the ear of my mare, etc.

Besides, I am at the Coast, in the roads, downstream. In the midst of moving out. In the midst of a cold, in the midst of a cloud, in the midst of Montpellier, full of mucus and at very short intervals.

This town is complicated with various annoyances: in the end, I combine the pots.

The news you ask for, which refers to a special obstacle, is capable of a conjecture. You know the past. Combine one year of absence plus the enigma of the beginning, the curious anxiety, etc., minus Paris and the thousand pre-occupations of the mind that I once had, the research, etc., plus an arbitrary coefficient of time. This gives us the situation at zero, beginning with my arrival here. But I notice now that the old *tension* contributed strongly to the development of consciousness, that is to say, the freedom of seeing and judging. And in fact, there is a weakening of influence, also an increase of curiosity fairly free and perky. Nevertheless, a few words from a fat-head have at times made me spend a detestable day. Finally the curve would be: yesterday/Italy/Paris/today.

Today, then, a tendency to periodicity and balance. I have often noticed that all progressions of this kind (friendship, etc.) tended in me to periodicity. But this is not general. So, it seems that between Louÿs and you it cannot settle down. The most *useful* meaning of this *obvious* regularity seems to me to be this: that to its arrival corresponds the possibility of . . . leading parallel-wise one or several other similars—no less than to undertake another still blunt and irregular . . . , etc. But all this is verbiage that will seem idiotic to you. The *scientific* appearance is purely metaphorical. Nevertheless, this fantasy can *make* one think.

About your little book, I haven't yet had the time to give it a good reading. I confess that the notes seemed to me a bit of "parody." Is that what it is? I would lose countenance, all surveying and the metrical system, if I didn't remind you that the word polarization has two meanings as distinct as those in the word *vol* for example, and which you fail to make precise—whether *souls* have magnetic or optical polarizations. You can, of course, attribute both with no grave inconvenience, but it is well to give warning. More than that, the *heaviness* of bodies only augments their attractions, the distances being equal. . . .

. . . .

But when you say that the unity makes the rectitude of the line, I can only approve you. *In fact*, the equation of degree *one* is that of a straight right line. But how many people in whom the function is lacunar (with holes) or shows a closed curve!

Good-bye. I pass the babble to you.

V.

[Valéry to Gide]

[February 26, 1894]

My dear friend,

The mail is chaos. I understand nothing about your letters. You talk about yours in terms that remain obscure to me— so I have not received it. And I am unaware which is the last that you yourself had from me.

But had I seen nothing come, be sure that I would have regularly written if . . . if my situation had been better. Let it suffice me to tell you the present hitch.

First, I am leaving for Paris Saturday next. After four quite useless months at Montpellier, where the desire to return to Paris, the local *pneumatisme* and a thousand stupidities, putrified me.

Second, my mother is unreasonably affected by it—and although I have never allowed anything to appear to anyone —that is a heavy load, it is hard.

Third, if I leave, you will guess why. My life is an apple, bad luck, but so long as I have it, I must satisfy it, I must look for paid employment—to *establish* myself, and I am very uneasy in leaving—I know the difficulties, those that are latent in my mind and those that circumstances construct. The Paris that I desired wisely comes to me with struggles of no interest, but sure disappointments, things that entangle your legs. I have only what I deserve, may I say—and that is just—*publicly*. Imagine, my poor André, that only rest and forgetting pursue me, that I need *security*—brutally, in all senses—and of a certain company—a nonisolation. It was long ago that I killed all ambition, all paradises, all tomorrow. I long ago accepted everything, but I have come to the limit of my ability to endure uncertainty. A petty example: I need books. I would like to have a few indispensable works in mathematics—not only can I not buy them, never asking for money at home (and besides, they are very expensive books)—but even if I could have them, I would not know where to get them, having no real home.

And if I dare to give to my preoccupation its whole extent, despite the bad effect, I say that even with things at their best, even lodged in Paris and not poorly, I shall still have many a rheumatism in my destiny.

A convalescent like you will laugh at my lack of prudence, and from his point of view he will be right. But from mine, I cannot keep myself from not being wrong. Goodness! I really believe that an ordinary observer would judge me severely. He would read my letters and what would he see in them? Continual complaints, a man of twenty-two already a grumbler long since—who nevertheless prides himself at times on his *reason*. The same gentleman, so richly endowed with discontent, denigrates 999 out of a thousand over every thing in creation. An irresistible argument—a peremptory tone—*he* has created nothing, hasn't he? He complains that he doesn't compare his lot with so many . . .

etc. He talks about his research, his *ideas*, and he can't find the conclusion of a not very difficult situation, in short, etc.

Well, my friend, you will be the one to judge. It is because I believe you will not think this way about me that I have again filled this paper with my stories. And indeed if I feel strongly about that, could I talk to you about anything else? Truly also our written or spoken encounters are not, then, very gay! You must at times find my judgments irritating, my letters smothering. You know, or rather must know it, nevertheless, that behind the iconoclast that I am at times, the vague isolated engineer that I also find in me, there is especially the . . . or rather a sense of existence, a very sensitive conscience, before which *all is equal*. I mean to say: who does not divide himself, who suffers or rises, undivided. Strange base: at all the moments of trouble, when the general wave of life comes back to that geometric point which, as a child, I wanted to be, the images in my mind are always of the sea, where I wear out the last minutes of a life or a vigil. I confound my existence, then, with all that country of the open sea, and I feel myself dissolve. What is called feeling, is that for me . . . and I follow, across the abstract itself, of enlightenment or analyses, the influence and the deformation of that dream. And it is still there, that in their moments of exaltation and possession in me, the forms of friendship or love bathe themselves also, finish bathing themselves also.

At Montpellier, 9, rue Vieille-Intendance.
In Paris, 12, rue Gay-Lussac.

P.V.

[Valéry to Gide]

Paris, 12, rue Gay-Lussac
[March 19, 1894]

You see, dear friend, I am here, and your letter, your dear letter will have my response at once. . . .

I am writing to you between two errands so as to arrive on time at Tunis . . . and this can only be an acknowledgment and a word from people whose lines cross each other.

I am expecting a vague job here, in the Exposition of 1900. I am not counting on it at all. Heredia gave me a good welcome and *talks* of busying himself about it. Since my arrival, you see the time lost, the relations: when I come back, I have a minute, before going to sleep completely under the eiderdown, devoted to a rage. Again I see in a spasm of time my things, my true race. I know that I am not from here, that I shall finish perhaps quietly by lasting, by carelessness. At moments I feel that my life has not begun, that the events described in my favorite moments are on the way, will wing —uuless thev have been here already for a very long time.

Then all that is worth nothing. I know too well that I am, as you say, incommensurable with too many people and things. I wonder if all of them have such bizarre motives for development as I have.

Now, in writing to you I rediscover the saltiness of vigorous old mornings, I remember.

I believe you can go to Italy—rather to Florence than Rome, to Genoa rather than Naples.

If you go to Genoa, write to me. I will introduce you to my family down there.

One word: I am witnessing the arrest of what is called literature. Half unconscious, this momentary end. People feel that nothing justifies continuing. You remember that I seemed to exaggerate by mimicking Cassandra. Well, beyond the inanity of what is done, disappearances literally do take place. The existence of persons as typical as Mauclair, for example, are signs staring you in the face. If that man can show himself (and others besides), the mechanics of the century must be in profound transformation. But I don't have the time today to search hypothetically for its function. And then, afterward!...

Kolbassine is right: Batavia and a chessboard.

When will we see each other, my friend?

P.V.

[Valéry to Gide]

12, rue Gay-Lussac
[May 1, 1894]

Your memory comes in here where I am smoking. We look at each other on the sly. I sense that he reads my character at one of those moments when he has lost his tongue....

Game of cards!

And you think, seeing only your own, and me mine (both of whom, in ten minutes together, would touch each other).

You know, the quiet!—the "Gulf," well! I didn't find it, nor the puddle, nor the lobster pot itself.

Up to now, the bread and the tobacco are there. Also the insipid public libraries (the browsing can be heard, dispersed over the space of the rooms, the clock, mentally, the reading). At certain corners, I encounter things known in the past, kinds of knowledge and deliriums, drained into cesspools, become excrement.

I chat with Mallarmé, no longer knowing what he has written: he was a gentleman, very kind, and offering his cigarette. One talks to be talking, as one does to the family cat. And no one interests me directly. There's no use talking. When I am awake, the face, the gesture, the word rolling over the cravat, the logic, and the law of the individual's discourse, I see them at times.

At my house, I no longer talk to myself. So, this evening, I am writing to you in the stinking smoke without looking at the vague room above the paper.

What does that mean to you—works of art? (On the stage, this last word must be pronounced with an accent of UNTRANSLATABLE CONTEMPT.) You are lucky to be a Protestant. You can go to the churches, see the Pope, etc. Good-bye. Write—and above all, come back.

P.-A.V.

[Valéry to Gide]

[May 25, 1894]

You write to me as you would to Z, or better to X, and I deserve it—probably.

I tell you that I am tired of the people here; you see them—they haven't changed—and yet I pretend to frequent them, since after all, once a week I need the man and I go to talk with him, in a kind of brothel.

I am thinking of going to London. My confused day invented this and I shall go presently. This is obviously stupid: it would be better to come back *in advance* to the research on the nature of space and directions, to the architectural dreams of constructing immense cities and parks, to the movements and numbers of a sandy and mechanical Strait: besides, today my eiderdown is my passion, *primo*, because the weather is as cold as winter, *quarto*, because it is "very nice" like people on the sidewalk and lets itself go, sculpting living people, giving enormous pleasures to the fingers of physicians and artists, of a fine model of solid elastic: the light.

In London, if I go in June, it will be for a short month. There I shall write a play in which the elements will be student-oarsmen of Oxford or Cambridge. They will love each other there on the river, smoke a great deal and show bare arms, savagery, boxing that will capsize their boat too much loaded with jealousy, beautiful youth, and sport.

Do you want a Holland or a Japan?

What has become of that fastidious and beautiful Italy?— and you in it? I order you to write a little less to everybody and more to me, who know nothing. Speak of the Medusa at least—and roundly, if not, I shall forget you at London Bridge.

V.

[Valéry to Gide]

Paris, July 14, 1894

Here I am again in Paris, dear André, and in an incomparable gloom. Minutes that I won't recount to you have passed, and now I regret London like a fool; the French annoy me. If I had the slipshod habit of writing a journal I would put down: "This evening, dined in ten minutes, went up again to smoke, stifled with boredom, with a slight flavor of rage later on." *That* is beginning to be all my days.

Yesterday, I vomited all my papers onto the table, hesitating between two propositions: (1) reduce them to pellets, (2) classify them. I discussed this seriously. I wanted to classify them! I was sure to stop at once—which happened.

Then, I set myself to thinking politics.

Among the books really indispensable and which no one will write, I often leaf through in my mind *The History and Philosophy of Ingenuity*.

The remarkable nullity of English literature surprised and charmed me. France has two little doors, which in passing through, one may still make a bit of the new. The misfortune is that no one distinguishes them nor cares about them. The true misfortune is that there is only one reader in ten million who judges by himself. Besides, the unhappy young man who wants to be that reader and who lives in the provinces is constrained by his age, mechanically, to take the opinion contrary to those around him. . . . Ten years afterwards, when he could reason, he is disgusted forever to read anything other than his journal and the twenty volumes which he wedded at the age of 19 years. This is history, but seen.

Two days ago I wrote a rather long letter to Mazel to compliment him for an article on Education. Note that to be stupid literarily and even in discourse keeps no one from writing a good article. This after all is not the first that he has done outside of Art, and which does not displease me. *Naturally*, I don't follow his advice. Nevertheless, all our Remy de Gourmonts and our Bernard Lazares, who are such great philosophers seen from below the crowd and such high *littérateurs* with anyone who reasons a bit, would not have made much of a theme. For me, who am as far from being a literary man as a philosopher, and even to be no matter what—even, alas, a clerk somewhere—the two important points are the only two a pedagogue never dreamed of. Education of the senses. Preparation for puberty. This is not to be found at Sorèze, nor at Henri IV, nor at

Eton. Whence in part, the strange world we live in, and a great proportion of the number of stupidities and idolatries everywhere, in the intimacy of oneself, in the customs, the writings and the laws.

Painting. In 1894, there are still people of taste to find an interest of some sort in Rosetti as a painter, and ... in Burne-Jones. Which leads naturally to announce to you the marriage of our *friend* Coste.

I don't know whether I wrote to you from London. I believe not. In any case, I have some enthusiasms there, or rather the sense of enthusiasm possible at a certain moment, which would be good. It is the City, above all, the commerce, which beckoned to me and which I have not had the time to study. Here, there is an atmosphere of room for machines or the interior of a heart. Our heroes are there. And while someone refers to Loyola, to Tristan, to Persius, in order to see the passionate and the calculated more easily than in the *Cour d'assises*—this corner is making ready to efface from the effect of our time all other glory and all other movement.

Verification: in the recent period when I was reading, studying, and writing verse, I would have cut off my tongue and my head rather than think and say that. Remember our walks at Montpellier, all the stupidities that I would say and the immense pleasure of walking together (for me, at least). It has remained with me that I cannot imagine seeing you without emotion. But when? It seems to me that we have known each other for twenty years.

Pierre must be with you and I envy him. I admit that I cannot think of our relation without astonishment. I have known him for four years. And I know him no better than on the first day. He has conducted himself with me in a manner to make me blush with generosity. One of my secret embarrassments is not to know how to recompense him for it. To such a point that by spoken words I have never pleased him and I never congratulate him and I approve very little. I am difficult to the point *that I require my friends implicitly to act against their nature.* It is a misfortune that comes from my torments—you have known them—you are almost the only one, and one other person who took care of me and still cares for me from a distance.

I must add that, for three years, I have had neither correspondence nor conversation with Pierre. Each encounter makes him, for me, shy of mercury. At those moments I admire several other friends of mine who are decidedly very patient and charitable. This can be read by him as well as by you.

Let us reflect. . . . Someone who knew me several years ago saw me again recently and found me greatly changed—like a seed which hasn't produced its own plant, but another. I answered her: "Dear, I was then an attractive young man, careful to avoid any friction with people, and I am becoming exactly the contrary rather quickly. I was enthusiastic and a believer in certain words—I nourished myself largely on books and the ideas prevalent among my fellows. Today everything *must* come from me. I admit nothing that I don't understand and I translate the word *travail* by *trouvaille*. To learn, read, labor by the piece is not work for me. I would think I was lazy to write encyclopedias, since to write in itself, or leaf through, is a pretext for *finding nothing.*"

And now I have already burned up half of the July 14th. *All right!*

P.V.

[Valéry to Gide]

[August 25, 1894]

I believe the Orient would want me. Not that Quillard has responded to me, but a gentleman wrote to me yesterday that a place as professor in Cairo is at my disposal. I declined. Constantinople not being open, it would not please me to take the vassal's place. And then, all that doesn't mean positions!—but oriental postures.

If I were rich—*today*—do you know what I would do? The physical life. I would take up the discipline of rowing and riding horseback. And I would do nothing but that, and swim from morning to night. Today, no one but the rich can have muscles. I had the intention—spoken, not thought —of *writing* the little drama of a few muscles, on leaving for London. This ended in an unexpected boxing match on a canoe in the middle of the river. The canoe capsized, everybody escaped by swimming toward the white reeds and the lilies on the banks. Curtain. Rouart was pleased with the little play that I related to him. The interest of the *thing* was to make three male carnations. There were no women. Only a skiff circulating through the play, loaded with three or four silent females. This was part of the décor and, like the rest, served merely to nourish the conversation.

I reread the *Discourse on Method* recently. It is certainly the modern novel, as it could be written. Notice that later philosophy rejected the autobiographical part. Yet this is the point to take up again, and then we shall have to write the life of a theory, just as we have too often written that of passion (*couchage*). But this is a bit less convenient—since, puritan that I am, I require the theory to be better than mere faking, as in *Louis Lambert*.

Do you know Wronski? I leaf through him—this madman with enormous genius, but mad. Head ringing with bells!

Good-bye, old friend, and write to me; I need that, and will reply.

P.V.

[Valéry to Gide]

[September 7, 1894]

I am reading your letter on my return from a week with the Hérold family at Lapras. Everyone was reading the whole time. I held this record: three Balzacs in one day, etc. Quillard writes me to think no more about Péra. So much the better—or worse. That is the way with serious affairs.

Rimbaud is the only engineer of this century who is not the son of the preceding. In fact, the others are Poe, Balzac, Stendhal. We see immediately that the individuals, Goethe or Laforgue, Hugo, Villiers, etc., are aside, and change nothing "at bottom." To look for similar figures in the sciences, the group Poe–Balzac is like the group Laplace–Ampère–Poisson, etc. Rimbaud himself is allied to Faraday–Maxwell–Thompson. Especially if we isolate what he has written that is completely new—from the soiled memories, the tough meat for the dogs—the rest. The volume to be written on him would reduce him to *uselessness*. That should be called "Prolegomena to the new analysis." My work has been, to seek what that *could be*.

Unconsciousness in Rimbaud seems to end with the time when he wrote. Already in the *Illuminations*, there are traces of duplicity in his work, etc.

I have reflected a great deal these days on the young people I have known, and among whom I have known many types, not of the lesser ones certainly. The society of today offers them nothing but getting rich—honors being beneath everything. Glory, unbearable to consciousness. I have seen many ambitious men born to rot. Some by seeking the complement of the verb *to desire*. The others lacked seriousness. The man who most succeeded called himself Hugo. He had not even the power not to repent of a stupid remark he had launched.

The world is full of intelligent softness. And whoever has the courage must waste his best years in remaking his brain entirely. Put everything in question again and you can't manage to do it. Who will write this great Drama: "Mutual Concessions in Perpetuity."

I shall tell you one day about the *serious* with its applications to literature.

Rouart is a charming friend. I have rarely been so quickly at ease—that is, understood in the measure to which it pleased me to be so. But he floats a bit. He needs to learn how to do himself violence, to evaluate himself. What a difference with Walckenaër, whose successive impressions on me turn to the worst. I talk to you about it without tact— but you know me. He is an envious man without depth, imitating common distress. He had himself presented to Princess Mathilde. All that so I may enjoy the account he gave me and to think that he thought about it for three months.

Finally Meryem ravaged Louÿs. Poor Meryem.*

P.

* Meryem was a young Arab, of the tribe of the Ouled-Naïl "who exploited their girls reputed for their beauty." Paul-Albert Laurens and André Gide knew her at Biskra and shared her favors in 1893. "I can compare her only to some *Bacchante*, she of the *Vase de Gaète*," said Gide in speaking of her in *Si le grain ne meurt*, where he tells of

[Valéry to Gide]

Paris, 12 rue Gay-Lussac
[November 10, 1894]

Dear André,

You decree me accused—and in my turn you give me this thermidorian title which, silently, I so often give to others: "Enemy of the human race." My only astonishment is that you waited so long at least to say it. . . .

I have been in Paris about a month. I am very nervous here, and ill three days out of six. Thereupon come a thousand tales of the maddening kind. The last from yesterday: Régnier, with a kindness and nobility that pierced me through, having learned that the secretary's place at the *Revue de Paris* was vacant, solicited it for me. A slight delay made everything misfire. I had the most stupid impulse of rage that can be imagined. It increased as it recognized itself. The misfortune was the coincidence of this anecdote with a physical condition of which I have had enough, enough, enough. The imaginative continuation of that in me (headache, etc., disappointments)—this becomes immediately a first-rate bombardment of London—liquor washes of Englishmen in the Strand flowing even into the Thames. But judgment goes to bed meanwhile.

Let us come back to our diplomacies—in no order. So, I take up your letter, and having read it:

(1) Confidential question—in numerals. Didn't you receive a letter from Rouart a while back, and mentioning me?

how Pierre Louÿs suddenly decided to leave for Biskra in order to know Meryem in his turn. On August 10, 1893, he received these lines from his friend: "Meryem is the prettiest, the most gracious, the most delicate one that I have seen. She is astonishingly small, Javanese. Unfortunately, she is not to be had." He was to take her as a model in *Les Chansons de Bilitis.*

(2) As an abortionist or an *emménagogue* of books and letters, or *antimaïeutique*! I reply with no constraint that I have always beseeched my interlocutors not to take any account of my sentiments—which is very easy—next, to accept none of my theories without testing them logically; moreover, I have always repeated that I could not conceive a *general* theory: a non-personal theory is a non-function of the theoretician.

(3) That is enough for the *quia corrumperet juventutem.*★ Let's come to the individual:

I know how I can be judged, because I know what I have shown. The fact is that if my friends or groups of my friends were locked in a room, and a question was put to them about me, the variety of responses, even their contradictions, I believe, would be curious. I could put at least one name beneath each of the following opinions: I pass for a poet, crazy, rational, mystic, heartless, disparager, too distrustful, too confident, too open, secretive, amusing, pedant, etc. I forget light and heavy. And all that shows me to be a pretty bad reasoner, fairly general and clear as day.

What I know is that I feel myself really too different— not perhaps that I am more so, but that I feel it and *tend* to feel it more than anybody else. Do you recall: I told you to give up the ideas that I held as soon as others seemed to me to hold them. It is still true. I want to be the master in my house.

... But in what way am I distressing and for you, my friend, who seems to say that your letters are scorned, that I don't understand you, and that the primary motives of my acts escape you?

Remember that you have been almost my only confidant —*always*—that I have often had nothing but the repose of

★ Because he would corrupt youth.

writing to you and reading to you in the distressing weeks when the difficulty was to go from minute to minute—and at this very moment!

The reproach that you must feel against me is that I have tired you by a useless continual complaint, but isn't it somewhat softened by the fact that you were the only one to whom I allowed myself to make it. I have suffered enormously from loneliness. If you knew how I regretted your absence, if you recalled your former remarks, old moments!

Dear friend, I have lived for a long time under the morality of death. That shining limit brings to my mind movement and life. I believe that few men since the fanatics have chosen that charming, intoxicating and liberal base. All that I have really wished, I wished by fixing my eyes on the word *End*. I have always acted to make myself a potential individual. That is to say that I have preferred a strategic to a tactical life. To have at my disposal without disposing. This had an aim of intimate, imaginative equilibrium.

What has most struck me in the world is that no one ever went right to the end. In the past, before having read in a volume of Goethe, on the quais, the same sentence, I spoke this absurdity: "One must have an impossible aim." Well, I know that these are stupidities—but as feeling they exist, they command, they lie at the bottom of every poetic mind. It is not necessary to make a theory about them. They must be satisfied or explained, or both.

I have reinvented many things. Other men, for example. I have honestly destroyed notions that muddled my mind. I wanted to throw my boots in the face of words, instead of polishing them. I have made and still make systems that are absolutely *to measure*, theories where there is room for my substances, connections that for me are convenient elevators, water and gas for reverie or analysis. I have wiped my windowpanes; I have scratched the nascent pride, of which I have never had much, despite the appearances perhaps.

I have written bad verse which taught me the recipe for the good ones. And I have detested Flaubert—as a cat does a dog.

There are my crimes and my bad instincts. Judge me. I am as capable of loving as anybody else; I even know how to put in novelty and violence. But patience is not for me, mediocrity poisons me and vagueness kills me. I would adore someone that my mind had not decided after six months to suppress. Woman or man.

In the end—between us—do you know what I see, and our relation? I see, I feel that we love each other, but we both show to each what, reciprocally, frightens us most, you a sort of Paradise—and me a certainty of Hell.

Ah! Leave Switzerland where it is, and come!

VALÉRY

[Valéry to Gide]

[November 16, 1894]

Dear André,

You give me your warmth again. Again I feel this vague uneasiness of being too well—this bed where one is melted among the sheets gently. You will leave with me, then, this special familiarity that we have. I can easily guess that henceforth I shall have no further news and I guard that news as an old man guards his girl.

Likewise that same Rouart, who was charming and whom I somewhat scandalized, I was never able to do more with him than talk *in abstracto*—to everybody—by answering him.

The first winter that I spent in Paris, we were together, and sufficiently stiffened. Perhaps I talked a great deal in that large closet disturbed by my smoke. I was trying to express those ideas scarcely yet born. I had a committee of public safety in my heart, when each morning guillotined its evening. Every shelf carried its manuscript of your writing— and I circulated, becoming dangerous as one is in a glass-works.

With incomprehensible methods, you ended by syllabi-fying your Schumann, Chopin also, and as always at the tenth measure. I was beyond music, which helps me enor-mously to think, but not of *It*. . . .

The supporting beam of the schooner!—how I lived there!—floundering among the bales and things in the hold. I still admire the lamp that I watched down there, asphyxia-ting itself, its ear packed with slaps, with hiccups, the filthy water so nearby, the stiff changes in the tone of the winds, the laughing ruins of the waves against the neuralgic wood of the couples. It was beautiful to think of. And how one would dream there of immovable armchairs, of an enormous garden, yellow and blue!

All this is far and near. My mind wearies of despising what is, turns back again at times toward many an ancient and charming possession. It has loved. It stops, and then it hears the kilometric whistle, the cold and acute objection, the recall to the logical step. I have never resisted it. *Naturally*.

I am unfortunately too idle for *Paludes* to trouble me at all. If I had been a secretary, you would certainly have given it to me for the *Revue*.

Good-bye. Write me at once in your curious script of woven willow, one of those letters where again I find your monologue, your plurals (since you love plurals, don't you?)

and my old admiration for your way of talking or reading (since you revealed to me at the "Cheval-Blanc" that it existed.)

Your

P.-A. VALÉRY

[Valéry to Gide]

[December 2, 1894]

This morning I wanted to write to a little girl that I love. But I spent the evening in such a way that it is your letter only that I shall answer. I am spending my time with a young girl to whom I have promised to respect the essential. I grasped with joy this rather rare occasion and we make love not without swoons—but with her dressing gown, she, me, my clothes which don't open. Her virginity knows all. But my experience learns some things. It is curious as a Jesuit thesis: *de peccatis per approximationem, quum visus manusque unice denudantur.**

All that takes me an endless time. I had promised myself to write something for Louÿs. A colloquy. It wasn't long. The theme settled, the incidents foreseen—I put it back into the hangar of pleasures with no trouble and there was no further question.

As for metamorphoses, bah! pschtt! pshaw! It's the weather that changes. There will perhaps be metamorphosis the day when the *climate* itself will have changed. Life assured, patience possible, combats exciting, what a fine telegram to be addressed to you! But without that!

Moreover, how do you expect me to do? Personal principle.

. . . .

* Concerning sinning little by little while the eyes and hands only are bare.

During one fraction, I am entirely in *my* theories. (I don't have the time to characterise them. It is a special analysis that rather satisfied me a few times.) Another fraction is consecrated to speculations of a scientific kind. Extension of notions, the logic and psychology of sciences such as mechanics, or analysis, induction, etc. At other times, I dream only of diplomacy and practical management, strategies, or even the arts, cities, material works, or again a few literary applications, numerous trials.

Finally, a strange corner, inexplicable, which I had told you about at great length in a fragment of my letter before last, the one I didn't send. There were visions of wars on land and sea. I give way to them madly at certain moments. I am unaware of their source. I know only that from my earliest childhood they existed. Their regularity and their force astonishes me. I *feel* the weight, the delicate form, the energy of the cannon and the shot. I imagine flights of armored ducks buzzing beneath the ports. Then cartographical terrains with lives of men. (A row of men is my inductive triumph; I deduce extraordinary things from it.) Do you know Vinci's drawings of a bombardment? There they are.

So I am obliged to work!—by irregular flashes. I saw Huysmans at home yesterday, fiddling with proofs which he can't make up his mind to return. His novel, *En route*, treats the question of the Trappists. The truth about the Trappists. Blasting the fable: "Brother, we must die!" It seems that this doesn't exist.

I shall go back to Bailly's. But, I have been told, *Paludes* is a book with keys! The best to you,

P.-A.V.

Valéry to Gide]

[January 3, 1895]

My dear André,

I am working without enthusiasm on my article, and it is
snowing. Everything is flattened. That poor Vinci is going
to spend a bad quarter of an hour. It will be written without
sun and without envy. I have spread over the table all the
old notes, all the albums, notebooks, and backs of envelopes
which bear only the important word *pigé.*

I am going to write a serious page of padding that would
give me nausea to read. Luckily, I have only to write it. I am
beginning to see the trick of padding. I shall do a piece on
architecture (old loves), one on mechanics, one on the
fortification [of Paris], etc. I'll put in, somewhere, a view of
the theory which I would have loved seriously *punctually* to
make, and for which I have all the big points ready and
written.

Then some stuffing, and phrases (what I call "château-
briand with apples"), a few citations to steal some lines, and
there you are! Imagine that fifteen pages of *La Revue* equals
Le Voyage d'Urien for example, in length.

What contempt! The great Flying Man must be folded
into these formats. How many times I have seen him, from
the Peyrou, crossing from the sea to the Occident, breaking
the circles of the delicate sky. He was making his experiments
in the air, on his now inseparable machine—but in reality, on
me. Was this teaching me to read? What an alphabet! A thing
which, if it settles down in the mud, is in the summits of
trees. Farewell, I plunge again into the magma of dead
words, skins of ideas, grease of rhetoric. Keep warm. I thank
your uncle very much for his brochure. I read it, thinking
the whole time how much I would have preferred to make

a watch, or caulk a boat (at Malta) than to dilute the minutes with ink.

P.-A.V.

[Valéry to Gide]

[February 4, 1895]

My dear André,

I end by writing to you at the rue de Commaille, you so often forget to give addresses. Moreover, that is why I had not answered you. Your mother wrote to me to give me your news and I learned the beginning of the vicissitudes with which you finish the story for me.

Vinci is at its worst! I believe that everything is to be done again. It's a bore. I showed it to Drouin with pleasure (honest and charming judgment), who at page thirteen made me observe that I was not talking about Vinci. I knew it only too well. But what can be said of such a man? I don't criticize the style; it is excellent. Example: "And here we come to a remark worthy of attention." That is how *Paludes* should have been written.

I can show you a place to live, a hotel that is wholesome. It is between *rue du Bac* and *rue de la Planche*.

Let us talk, so not to obligate anyone:

I cannot accept a place in a socialist newspaper, because I have the idea of presenting myself soon to the War Ministry. This would be Fénéon II.* Moreover, to write to be writing —I see nothing in it but money. It depends on this place and these paid articles, very important things: a home, a gilded armchair, muslin curtains, a good stove, some books, and the ability to go to London twice a year.

* Félix Fénéon, who had been arrested the previous year at the time of the anarchist manifestations.

Moreover, is it necessary to deliver Kolbassine to these Apaches? I always fear his spurts of excitement. If he should take up writing, there are chances that it might be politics, and from there to being dismissed, expelled, there is only a tenth of a millimeter.

Pierre Louÿs is in Seville, 9, plaza del Pacifico, Hotel Paris.

I will do your commission but not without fear. Go and find him! Kiss Lola for him! Tell him that he was seen slipping into a brothel, Calle Molliena, etc.

I have gab sessions with Stéphane from time to time. Recently I made him rather indignant about Villier's tomb. I said that I found these concerns absurd, stupid; I stigmatized the funeral superstition of the Parisians (who are the last people on earth). Another time, I told him—and it embarrassed him sufficiently—that glory has *galette* [money] as its motive, that I put it even beneath, since anyone can be completely conscious and cast an envious eye on money, this is avowable, and even more; whereas for glory, one must truly be dazed by error to run after it, etc. He must consider me as the hen that hatched a serpent.

Good-bye, dear friend. I leave you to your heat—we are under the white *merde*, hypnotized by the roofs.

V.

[Valéry to Gide]

[May 1895]

My dear André,

I have nothing new. Ever. I am at the point of verifying in myself some rather curious variations. I know now that every two weeks I have a physical difficulty. This is my monsoon. I stop working. From time to time I do the brass, I "tripolise" the house, to watch it oxidize again. Besides,

I can work only on something difficult, and all that I can find reduces to a small number, well known, and with which I shall never finish.

You know that my mind's direction was chosen precisely according to the various difficulties of a certain number of questions. I have always run to the important. So that I am caught between what is mine and for that reason alone disgusts me, and the rest—that is, what I do not have and which discourages me. I know what I have found. I have here two or three hundred problems, resolved or not, which are always skipped over. I promise to bring in no matter who. And there, one must respond or disappear. I am the one who will disappear. There are moments when I would like to have someone to educate, to fortify (laughable and true!). I am stupid enough to regret the experience of a method and a few ideas, which I shall not have. If I had the holy peace now, perhaps I would again plunge into the great game of the mind. I recall that I became almost alcoholic. When I dream of the vigor that I had at moments, I understand to the very bottom the present infirmity.

You are begged not to be worried about me and not to lose one spark of your feelings: first, because those moments are rarer than your friend's anxiety; and second, because for these last there is nothing to be done.

Good-bye, dear old friend, read Virgil to Rouart, I am hurrying to see Hérold.

V.

[Valéry to Gide]

[August 18, 1895]

Dear Paul yourself! I am bored—bored, as if my name were Hermogène or Mélisande, I am annoyed and bored. These red breeches hypnotize me, and this article exasperates ne. His last game was to appear on the fifteenth without the dedication to Schwob. Here is another mystery. These idiotic sorceries recall to me the word, celebrated and so beautiful which is in *Rotomago*. . . . * Here there is an individual, very tired of the marvels that some sorcerer or another suggests to his furniture, and he cries out at a moment when some trap is still working, where the sofa is filling with water—no, the room—it's the sofa that is the boat, there is a sail that comes out of it, etc.; he cries out: "Allons, bon! Voilà les bêtises qui recommencent!" This word is irresistible (believe me!) and it pursues me. I tell myself at every moment!—the only verbal charm against the marvels of cardboard and back luck—or luck—that grows. You see the application of that by the importance that people, books, dirty seas, trees, and numerals, give themselves.

"That a mite offers him in the smallness of his body, parts incomparably smaller. . . .

"Well, good! There are the stupidities beginning again!"

. . . .

I am astonished with you that you understand me so well, and surprising you during your digestion, as is proper with boas (who have swallowed an ass) I howl: "Well! Tell me about it then!" I'll send you later on a copy of the offprint with its dissection in blue crayon, in parts: (1) commercial and false, (2) purely arbitrary, (3) embryonic and discussable.

There you are! (As you always say when, with hardly a glance, you are off to your business. . . .)

And now, when do you marry? Where?. . .

VALÉRY

* *Rothomago* (not Rotomago) is a fairy in the twenty-fifth tableau by Ennery, Clairville, and Albert Mounier, presented at Paris at the Théâtre Impérial du Cirque on March 1, 1862.

[Valéry to Gide]

Genoa [October 9, 1895]

Dear friend,

You must be married, you are perhaps en route? I would have liked to give you some sign of life on this occasion, but I no longer know where I am. I am completely distracted. Maneuvers, departure, so many cities traversed, all bewilder me. Finally I have been stagnating a bit in Genoa, since yesterday at Milan I found a Christ by Vinci for you, still the same. You will have it when you wish, but where? I have no news at all from the Ministry; I am vegetating before going back to Paris. My mother is with me. She regrets not being acquainted with your wife. I don't think you will be in Genoa before the end of this month. That would be the only point in common.

I went to Venice and to Trieste, scarcely sensitive on the whole, except (I shall know later on) to a few Tintorettos and the gondola, a kind of *hansom cab*, asleep, funeral, etc. Milan gave me goose-flesh as always.

The little I have thought, since my departure, was of a military nature. Rather curious phenomenon—due perhaps to my twenty-eight days. "Very zealous corporal" was entered on my grades, and, in fact, I had a man put in prison and another in the discipline squad (with much difficulty, besides).

However, look: traversing this line in this plain must infatuate one with strategy and tactics. It is the most fascinating checkerboard in the world, and with the incompetence of Bouvard, I *saw* nothing but "military crests, turning movements, danger zones." Imagine that the stations in this country are called Lonato, Verona, Peschiera, Castiglione, etc. Now, with this nonhistory that we once inhaled, with a

few memories of blank rifle shots, I fabricated for myself a
MECHANICAL or PSYCHO-MECHANICAL view, attempt-
ing to melt the *terrain*, always so interesting, the individual
and the *complex of individuals* equal the army in an organized
composition. Imagine what the algebraic or pseudoalgebraic
expression of this ensemble would be, with the values to be
taken by accidents of the ground, geological laws, the
productive countries, the very displacement of races on the
given surface relief of a Lombardo-Venetia.

You derive the esthetic instantly. And I am talking to a
young husband! My friend, you know very well that I shall
not write to you saying that I am sending wishes for ... and
for. ... I beg you to tell your fiancée that you have a friend
who is sufficiently your friend to shut off the *epithalamium*.
He reserves vague things for indispensable occasions. I shall
tell you quite plainly that I am sorry to have no hope of
seeing you for centuries, that you are quite right to becloud
yourself in the distance and to flee from US. (Don't go to
Constantinople—you'll be bored to death.) Good-bye!

P.V.

[Valéry to Gide]

Paris, rue Gay-Lussac
[November 14, 1895]

Dear Traveler,

I have put off this answer, and I am dawdling, as one goes
through his pockets on the doorstep of shops, when one is
dressed as a boy: I believe that I have told you all. And you
predicted the rest. I go out, I come back, I smoke, I see great
men, I am interested in their eruptions—I try to see if the
ground trembles; one hour a day, I pretend to be working,
and afterwards I take my umbrella and do the sidewalk

without catching a thing, alas!—except the malady of th
movement and its desires.

In Italy I was awfully bored. A kind of flair for interestin
things made me aware of the Tintorettos of Venice, th
Adriatic waters, and the slums of Genoa. "But enough!"

Music draws me like tobacco. I went to the Opera las
evening, then killed time in some beer hall or other. Nov
I want to fall in with some creature for the pleasure o
turning her head the wrong way (physically) and to look fo
a long time. I assure you that this makes one want to spit
as into a well.

The Adams, the Griffins, the Souzas, the X's and the Z'
produce. Louÿs is publishing a novel with the greates
success. I haven't read it yet. They say that it is "Very Good."
Anyone would deserve to be shot who uses such idioti
remarks. You can hear that—from over there.

I am perhaps going to have the luck to bring Kolbassine
to Paris. The poor fellow is caught in university intrigues—
he is certainly the one man in the world least capable of
getting out of trouble with our wily functionaries. He doesn't
have the gift for that. It is even curious to see how theoretical
he is in his campaign plans. Finally he has been given a
glimpse of a temporary post in a lycée here, and you know
how much I would appreciate that. I would finally have a
friend who at least thinks more than he writes, and who feels
as I do how much these two things damage each other in the
end. And then, he is lazy—completely!—and we tell him
so at times with indulgence and sympathy, with the exquisite
tenderness of accomplices. But he is a lazy one who would
teach me many things without knowing it, whereas I!...

Rouart continues to annoy the canon of I don't know
who, the one who counted twelve heads and something,

who wears ridiculous ties and has Béarnais volumes sent to me—to which I respond with somewhat brutal but sad insanities. He is always friendly, discreet, and furious.

In the end, we are still under the most curious government in the world.

Don't complain of my letter. I have already done a great deal of writing, and then it is quite enough for the post office, always a bit musty.

I was forgetting your compasses. I shall receive them one of these days, I think. While awaiting this enigma-gift, I send you my astonished thanks. Write the "Treatise on the Compass."

P.V.

Valéry to Gide]

12, rue Gay-Lussac
[May 18, 1896]

I must write to you, my friend, not to have always to repeat everything. I really like to talk only with you. The others amuse me at moments, but it is only with you that I don't have the sensation of "must" and "have." I have had two other friends like that, but there was always between them and me a bit of silent war—for reasons!—but the years have silted up friendship and all the rest with it.

I have wanted to write to you about trees. Thinking about you, I saw the green of La Roque rolling behind us, in my mental tunnel. Then I forgot you among the vegetables, I admired the plane trees, the birch, and others. I had known for some time that the tree is the one thing in the world that doesn't yet bore me. (I am speaking of what can be seen—and I am speaking also of very tall trees, with bright leaves and rather glossy—the horror of callus trees.) The sea and waters in general disgust me—by abuse. There remain the

tree and the famous "any kind whatever," which alway
leads me to those vague inventions that I express for other
by their clearest results, and for me in a language more thai
cryptographic, mixed with scientific terms and "idiosyn-
cratic" productions.

In the end, it seems to me that fine trees give me pleasure
and I find that I am happy only "together." They are, to
feelings, like a good deep breath of air exactly at the hoped
for temperature, or like a perfect bed, espousing the back
of the body and giving it the idea of quartering oneself on it.

I am ruminating. Griffin wrote me a fine letter to thank
me for my dedication. Summer! Rock of pure air! Nonsense!
I am reruminating. I want to make some experiments in
Le Centaure, a vivisection, in short. But I am lacking an
adequate subject. I have always wanted (since 18–, the great
period) to invent the history of a man who thinks—since
no one wants to try it—and I would like to make a study of
that. A histology of one part of it, with procedures in the life.
If I were sure of finding amusement, I would take it up.

Meanwhile, I am rereading *Candide*, which reminds me
of the night table at the Hôtel d'Honfleur. This evening, the
great dinner of the Centaures with the whole *lyre*, at the
d'Harcourt, and "no one will have spirit except us and our
friends"!

All my respects to your wife—and to you nothing at all.
You have already taken four pages.   P.V.

[Valéry to Gide]

[Montpellier, August 4, 1896]

Dear André,

... Ah! My old friend, I am gallantly bored. I am working
for *Le Centaure*, a nauseous bit of filth that I swallow with

isgust, without even having the courage to prepare. I write without a pause and going I don't know where.

No matter! I am furious to miss my baths, since the weather is humid and I am afraid of neuralgia. I admit that Jbu himself loses all his savor here. *Merdre* is not good. It is stupid.

I have finally found here an old friend in whom I have great *intellectual* confidence, despite the stories and ferment told you about, three or four years ago. We have talked a great deal. The people who have known me are not very sure of me. They are astonished (diplomatic style) by the fact that I do nothing *concrete*. It is known that I am interested in many things; I am said to have a devouring curiosity, but after all it would be necessary..., etc. Let's add up: this opinion is that of Louÿs, of Kolbassine and the friend in question. What would you think if someone settled your account in this way? Remember now that it is not a matter of responding with terrible things. That would be more than easy. But I am not given to indignation, because I distrust myself, being a party to a suit, of certain optical illusions that come out when personalities intervene. More than that, there is an imposing tribunal. Without counting that you think the same, no doubt, and then it is a supreme court!

Well, aside from the *contre de carte* which is easy, I repeat —aside, also, the serious value of this judgment that rests on obviously false ideas—for me there remains a very keen sadness. There is what it means to prefer friends to a public. Do friends then believe only in the public sanction? Do they feel, by chance, particularly hurt because someone prefers them to the whole world? This is strange.

So! So much the worse for me! I do my job. I live on my means. I do not know how to write a book. I know a bit

how to stir up a few things here and there. I know very we[l]
that I shall arrive at nothing, but what does someone arriv[e]
at?

I ask my friends whether I have often failed in th[e]
IMPLICIT pact. Whether I have not at times said some inter[-]
esting things, whether I have not suggested to them, whethe[r]
I have not put a certain good faith at their disposal, whethe[r]
I have not shown them my research—asking them to offe[r]
precise objections, declaring null and void any formula o[f]
blame or praise, while exposing myself to the point of doing
for them, at the risk of friendship, what I would have wishe[d]
they might do for me. Not one responded to me. . . .

What makes me sad is this—that it will be necessary t[o]
go on, still more alone, and wall up the rest of the windows[.]

This is very hard, when one works with enough disgus[t]
already, and one's only remaining pleasures—or rather a singl[e]
anaesthesia: frequenting a few persons.

They will make me *really* ferocious. Good-bye.

P.

[Valéry to Gide]

[Montpellier, September 1896]

Dear friend,

I wanted to write to you immediately after your excellent
letter, which did me the greatest good, and I could not. I am
not at all well. I am having neuralgia, insomnia, and the
whole bag of tricks. I have spent atrocious nights. I don't
know whether it is the weather or something else, but this
whole month has been very hard for me. I believe we are all
going to Paris in short stages—by way of Bordeaux, etc.—
about September 20. My family will spend a month up
there, I think.

Your letter is extremely accurate in all that concerns me. There is not one of its terms that I haven't thought of a great deal at various times. I am very happy for it because I find myself at times with no defense and exposed to all the fantasies so troublesome in friendship, for this reason, that *the more I think and the more I clearly conceive myself*, the less I can explain, and explain myself clearly. I do not know why you have put a "blind confidence" in me; you seem to be a connoisseur of melons! And notice—this is rather droll—if I do honor to your penetration of that confidence, I become immediately ipso facto an individual of unadulterated vanity! This is extraordinary.

I stammer more and more with Monsieur Teste. I am as disarmed as possible. The *Centaure* torments me; the good man bores me—I don't know what to stuff into him—at times when neuralgia leaves me the leisure to be simply a beast. Yet, beyond style, composition, and bricks and mortar, which are missing, I believe I have put into them two or three curious things—but to look at it closely, nothing less than *literary*.

You will recall that this is my first effort to make a *bonhomme*, etc. A kind of novel (without intrigue). Moreover, disgust or lack of time or lack of talent, the *effects* that I wanted to make were finally either suppressed or were nothing. So my *mechanical* effort expires, is stranded.

Write soon. What is Rouart doing? And Drouin? I dedicate you to the infernal gods for having let go your piano. That is insane! Quite simply that! I predict to you that you are going to be exhausted. If someone took away from me everything that is not a fundamental preoccupation, I would explode!

I read the "Fondement de l'Induction"* coming from Paris, on the train. I haven't opened it again: I don't know at all what is in it. I shall reread that this winter. I have letter from a bit of everywhere, scarcely thrilling. You see it from here.

P. V.

[Valéry to Gide]

[Montpellier, September 19, 1896]

Dear André,

I received your little *sun stroke* quite well. I don't have the time to talk about it with all the . . . and the . . . necessaries. I need at least five minutes to unpack my baskets of metaphors and I don't have five minutes—especially moral ones.

I leave Monday *for* Paris where I shall arrive Saturday, making the trip in short steps. Before leaving, I shoot the habitual glance over the balance sheet for the month gone by. (A nasty habit that one evening, four years ago, made one of my friends almost weep, as I was putting before him the question of the year gone by.) That lost month is doubly lost:

(1) No sea bathing, or very little.
(2) Not a minute given to the Great Work.
    Illusory gain—writes *Monsieur Teste*.
    Mediocre gain—read two or three serious books.

I hope to see you soon. In any case, we are again approaching one another. Pierre Louÿs on the worst terms with the *Mercure*, dismissed, etc. Fifteen hundred victims, no details.

Fist blows to Rouart.

* "*Du Fondement de l'Induction*," by J. Lachelier, a thesis, 1871.

The following is a copy of a letter to Eugène Rouart.]

EXTREMELY CONFIDENTIAL.

My dear Rouart,

I thank you greatly for, etc. If Degas says yes, please have the supreme kindness to write (legibly) to the *Centaure*, rue des Beaux-Arts, the following note:

Monsieur,

Valéry asks me to tell you that Monsieur Degas has accepted the dedication of the little gadget entitled *Evening with Monsieur Teste*. He asks you to sign and date this dedication thus: " *To Monsieur Edgar Degas.*" (To be written in italics and in *capital* letters.)

You will sign this note or, if you remain in the dark, have it signed by Gide. If Gide refuses, imitate his signature. You will end, young man, in continuing this little business by acquiring a legible but fraudulent handwriting. To hesitate is not permitted.

Fist blows to Gide.

N.B. If Degas refuses, then write me and tell me about it.*

P.V.

[Valéry to Gide]

[Paris, October 5, 1896]

Dear friend,

I don't know how to make *ziboux*! I am sending you some rough animals, but don't forget that these specimens would be photographed and that the bigger and coarser they are the more they are worth. I am at the point of regretting even the necessary smallness of the mark, since by stirring

---

* Degas refused the dedication.

the theme of snails, I have seen some very amusing possibl
combinations. For example a grey of this kind:

[A drawing of four snails, in line]

Or again this subject (better treated):

[Drawing of a single snail twice the size]

The snail delights me for he has his mineral shell, or the
regular thing, and his remarkable mucous flesh, quite
shapeless, quite distinct. It is a very simple complex—almost
ridiculous. And then he has such astonishing horns, in which
the visual and tactile sensations seem mixed and the length
of which is a sort of function of the sensation.

[Drawing of a snail's horns]

I can also make you a hippocampus. But in fact the
thinness of the final *seal* forbids any combining.

Your letter about *Teste* came in the nick of time. I admit
that the rereading of these ten pages had left me an annoying
impression. That of a thing done with elements that I find
rather good, but sufficiently riddled, and on the whole
deplorable. I am aware that I wrote one after another and
without any other overall view than an effort to fill twenty
pages of my writing with the help of notes linked together.
But finally a real impression of discouragement and *political*
uselessness (understand me) had come over me. Accentuated
further by a day spent with Pierre Louÿs, during which
time I recognized that I had written *nothing literary* in four
years. And yet, to write, I cannot now do anything else!
You know why. And yet, also, to write I must do something
else, precisely that which can serve me for something.

Your observations on the sentence (page 37) is radiant!
But I recognize that I understand nothing about syntax!

: would be necessary at least to put "everything" in the
plural. I am not entirely of your opinion about Teste's words
to somebody or other. Given the *extent* of the new, it seems
to me that nothing should break the sphere of complete
intellectuality in which the narrator himself moves.

What is annoying to me is not to have disposed the same
elements following a satisfying psychological order.

And truly the conversation is too much *cut*, and somewhat
stupid. Enough of that!

I am dining this evening at Rouart's (who will not know
how to take me, and to whom I shall at once make an
enthusiastic and sincere eulogy of the last Degas to be
exhibited). Read in the last number of the *Nouvelle Revue*
a dazzling article by General Dragomirof on the *arme
blanche*. It is truly of a rare intelligence, and he is a general
who doesn't hesitate to insert four pages on logic in a subject
of this kind.

My mother sends her salutations to you both, I was about
to forget to insert it, out of " *Testisme*."

V.

[Valéry to Gide]

Montpellier [February 22, 1897]

My dear André,

I have finally received a letter from Pierre, in con-
valescence. He tells me that he seriously believed that he
would die and that his telegram was, to his mind, a farewell.
He foresaw the speech of Mendès and Bauër, etc. His letter
is truly gripping.

I am myself feeling better. With no illusion moreover
concerning the true nature of this "better." I now know
perfectly well that I am constantly watched over by the
symptoms. In other words, I have the right to be well,

within strict limits. Work has not yet come back. I sit down religiously at my table but only to annoy myself.

However, I had the small satisfaction yesterday of explaining to a judge, for whom I have high consideration and from whom I am sure to draw more objections and a more eager competence than from anyone in Paris, literary theories, which I shall use in my thingamajig on Mallarmé (if I do it).

This scrupulously careful interview has almost given me the desire to finish precisely by writing and publishing *The System*. I have long feared I don't know what absurdities are hidden in my work (and besides, there *are* such things), but I have not yet, with the best faith in the world, encountered a fact or an idea that might torpedo my affair to the point of sending it to the bottom. Yet I have still not found the exact order of succession of particular theses. More than that, there are complete buildings to be constructed for which the plan is made, but—work and patience?

If I knew that a certain publication would reach the target, that is to say, would raise discussions, I would do it. But this is improbable. A curious objection that I often make to myself is this: I find the thing that I attempted *so natural* that I am astonished, dumbfounded that no one dreamed of it centuries ago. From that to telling oneself that there is some monster at the bottom of it, there is only one step.

VALÉRY

[Valéry to Gide]

[Paris, January 11, 1898]

Dear friend,

I thank your wife greatly for your letter; I had asked Mme Drouin to remind her sister that it was hoped that you would write to me! I am happy not to have to detest these ladies, even in giving the greatest attention to doing so.

My friend, I am—by chance—extremely annoyed. I believe that my mother is coming to live in Paris with my aunt, and I don't look without some apprehension at this double change. What will they do here all day? What shall I do with them? I don't know; and if I don't live with them, this will mean their almost complete solitude; if I do live with them, how shall I manage, accustomed as I have been for so long a time to the use of time at random (especially now, on leaving the office)? In need, in any case, during the few hours of freedom that remain to me, to be as unstable as possible, as ready to catch flies—or miss them—as possible.

This is complicated by a question or two, both delicate. You guess the first. The other is that, once again in the family, I would be better cared for, a bit richer, probably more comfortable—perhaps too much so. I camped here for so long a time in the most simplifying disorder, encumbered with books, smoke, dirty linen, scattered belongings, papers, etc. . . . that I could no longer see the end of this mixture, nevermore—otherwise, the impromptu marriage, *tabula rasa*, a completely new existence. I am very hesitating, very surprised at the transformation to be undergone now, although I foresaw it long ago. I consider this a very important thing as regards the rest of my life. It is as when the nomads sat down to determine the future villages.

I am continuing to talk about myself.

My Semantics thing has appeared.* I am quite positively displeased with it, but *zut*! I shall probably do the *compte-*

* Published in *Le Mercure de France*, January 1898, under the title *Méthodes*, an article on the latest book of the grammarian Michel Bréal: *La Sémantique, science des Significations*.

rendu for Huysmans' book for the *Mercure*, in February.[*]
It is all right with him. Having had the pleasure of bringing
him closer to Mallarmé some time ago and to disperse a few
vapors, this latter (S.M.) brought us together last Thursday
in a tavern with extreme English beers. The duet was
curious.

Sunday, I spent the afternoon in Laurens' atelier. I
preached him the TRUTH. You know what that means
(someone thinks he hears the barber's footsteps on the stairs).
Besides, here is a sufficient though not a necessary definition:
the *Truth* is everything *qui emmerde*. He certainly saw it.
I believed he is well endowed, but lacks a bit of audacity.
Besides, he offered me the familiar spectacle of all the talented
and honest young fellows that I have met. *They are all afraid
to give themselves extreme pleasure.* And those who are aware
of this say to themselves and cry out: "We are all finally
going to give ourselves pleasure." But they won't go along.
I give you this impression for what it is worth.

You have made me a very good Mallarmé. I beg you to
give him my affections (not in his hat).

Pierre is in Cairo. *Bilitis*, a fine success underneath, not
yet thundering but very serious, a success *one to one*, which
is perfect. I would have—in spite of such probable reserves!—
written almost willingly three or four pages on that book,
if I had known where to put them. Now the desire is gone.

Signoret wrote to Mallarmé that "Valéry gracious and
modest is silent, etc." I am delighted with this virginity that
distance gives me. It's nice.

I don't want, in the end, to talk to you about myself,
that is, recount what I was thinking yesterday, or the day

[*] The article on Huysmans appeared in *Le Mercure de France*,
March 1898, with the title *Durtal*.

before. That gripped me strongly, and today the ennui above and others paralyze me.

Your old P.

[Valéry to Gide]

Saturday (tout de suite)

[Paris, January 15, 1898]

My friend, thanks for an excellent letter! Your Signoret amused me greatly, so much that I saw him once without speaking to him, besides. I am very nervous. I wrote to Montpellier—a long letter, very *reasonable*, excessively defensive. I don't yet have an answer. . . . Then yesterday I went with Moreno to the puppet theater to see *Ubu* played by themselves. Between two acts (if I dare express myself thus) I went to the bar, a small ordinary place filled to the brim. There, belly to belly with Quillard and Hérold, those gentlemen talked about a vast proclamation to be inserted in the next *Hermès* against the army, the government, the generals, etc. A very lively discussion had taken place between Gourmont and Hérold, the first being on the right side of opinions. You know that the opinions of our excellent revolutionary comrades and friends have the gift of annoying and exasperating me. So I did not utter a word. But no doubt my features, still poorly educated, have *marked the hour*, since Quillard had the kindness to notify me that he was taking the responsibility for the factum to intervene and that *that would not compromise me in the least*. To which I replied with a dull grunt. You can imagine my internal cocktail. Then, my feeling was clarified on a clear point. I promised J.-K. Huysmans an article on *La Cathédrale* as soon as it appears (the thirty-first of this month). I have quite decided not to insert a line in the *Mercure* if this pamphlet "sees daylight"—now, he would see it either in February or in March—then? And I insist on writing the article which certainly will not amuse me—but it is due and promised— and I want to do it *solely* to try to give pleasure to the author alone. As low satisfaction, I had a diabolical idea, I took two steps, right up to Fénéon's flat belly—reciprocal politeness— and I told him that I shall probably come to *La Revue Blanche* to bring him a copy. If all this happens, I am going to change my name. To what point the "vaguery" of all this disgusts me, you see very well. These revolutionaries who never start a revolution, can they make fun of the military who never make war? And there are protests against violated justice, humanity misunderstood *et patati et patata*. We see individualists who are not even individuals and all these eternal *cocos* who want to make omelets without breaking the inevitable eggs! The least Jesuit knows a thousand times more than they; the least wine merchant sees more clearly, all that being no more complicated, at bottom, than bookkeeping. To see a country turned loose in this way, at random, disgusts me. Among other things, we must not be mistaken, we are going toward an acute anti-Semitism, which can become a cause of extraordinary trouble. The excitement of all the Jews is remarkable, comprehensible, disquieting. On the other hand, the state of mind of the army ranks must be remarkable. In the end, the radicals and the socialists blow on all the fires. To power, then—that is to say in the Chambers and the Cabinet, men obliged to count with all these elements, and who *want* them all. By climbing a bit higher, we see the nothingness and the weakness of the republican principle in all its generality. The shapeless debris of the reasons of State disputed by the *free* press, the whole of social space open to the expansion of every idea, as a result of the following curious fallacy: "Every idea is necessarily good for all. Absolute freedom to every idea." Now, there is no direct or simple relation among these things. Nothing is so curious as seeing the socialists, for example, leaning on the theory of evolution. That is to say that a hypothesis as hypothetical as possible, and in any case billeted by force in the domain for which it was made, may lead and will lead to cracking the head of a number of people, etc. . . .

In the end, I am teasing you, and you are right in making fun of me. But the questions leave you cold and you walk out, where on the other hand, I simply discover them again. . . .

I am looking for someone to be bored with, without finding a shoe to fit my foot. I really need one. At this point, when by chance I am again thinking of my tricks and systems, I would need to expose them in conversation so as to clear up various things coiled and twisted inside me, to clarify and be done with them. Writing cannot help me in that because I stop at once, seeing the difficulties, the least ones, whereas speaking would oblige me to go ahead—a great point. In the end, I would thus be obliged to *see* as a group. But the shaved man needed is not yet born.

One evening in the last few days, I put myself under the lamp light to write the beginning of the following story, which I shall never finish because it is too difficult. Given one of those women who sleep two, three, or ten years at one interval, it may be supposed (quite gratuitously) that she dreamed the whole time, and that she can recall this dream on waking. Now, for two, three . . . or ten years, there has been no sensation for her: then study the deterioration (or something else) of the given data on which she fell

asleep. This is a problem in transcendent imaginary psychology, which is very hard even to envisage. The successive
zones of alteration of the images, etc., the variation of the
thought becoming little by little empty, would be curious
to realize. The theme excited me for ten minutes. Then,
v ‾ ‾ ..o enthusiasm, I wrote a few lines of the beginning,
foreign moreover to the problem, then I stopped. But, a
very typical thing, I set aside this statement of the facts to
study at leisure, geometrically, and outside all literature. . . .*

Your slightly ripe VALÉRY

[Valéry to Gide]

[Paris, February 14, 1898]

My dear André,

I am ending eight diabolical days during which I have
fabricated in all haste the treacle on *Durtal*, a thing without
a name, due and hurried by the *Mercure* where I finally
carried it yesterday—even finished it on the spot. The most
annoying part is to have caught a total insomnia, which has
already lasted for five or six nights and is exhausting me.
I am sorry to have been so harassed, to have had to work
evenings at a gallop, which I detest, especially for a thing that
I couldn't, in short. , ᵕ at all and that appeared only on
paper, and hardly ᵢere I regret it because, at the end of this
record, I was be· ᵢniᵣ ᵤ to be interested a bit, that is to say,
to rediscover ꜱome thiᵢgs: subjects thought about in the
past, plus theᵢr linkiᵣg- ᵤp to the present current.

All this expiᵤᵢ ᵥs vᵢhy I have not answered you sooner.

This morning I received a *Holy Grail* where we still have
some genius, but with Goldberg and others—then *dame*!—

* Valéry gave the title *Agathe* to this work, but never finished it.
[It was first published in 1956. See *Collected Works*, Vol. 2, p. 205.]

one prefers, perhaps, to be simply not stupid but apart.
I finish by swallowing this luminous loony who seems,
moreover, ignorant as a carp, wily as a fox and mystifiable
ad nutum. His c——*rie* is truly phosphorescent.

What transports me in regard to this case is that: it is like
a diagram, or a marionnette of the "Great Poet" type.
Emmanuel★ sums them all up. And he speaks an undeniable
truth when he proclaims it.

If one abstracts himself from the question of results, the
restatement of a question, etc., one can see in it the concentrated juice (ideas or lack of them, ways of associating,
etc.) of the more or less gigantic lyrics—*that is: vague*. He has
all that constitutes them. It is like them, an image mill, that
turns without knowing what it grinds. It is all very pure,
very agreeable and easily dismantled by the above-men-
tioned.

Do you know the grand style? Little live tortoises, the
size of a forty cent piece, and carrying precious stones and
gold settings on their backs. A very fine gold chain yokes
them to the women's necks, on whose breasts they crawl,
and, so it is said, drop their excrement or die, at their little
pleasure.

This is Des Esseintes. It seems that the beetle is also used;
I have seen only tortoises.

I bought at Durand-Ruel's a few photographs by Degas,
which brought me to violate my anti-iconic principles, but
since I came here I can hardly, any longer, maintain good
order in myself.

I am still very much annoyed everywhere by the Dreyfus
affair. God knows when that will end. I spread the good
word as much as I can, that is to say: what does this devouring

★ Emmanuel Signoret.

of insects matter? Let us seek true freedom, the kind to be furnished to a man with the burden of State.

In a short time, anybody can rise up and will have a following. Let us hope for the brutal and disinterested man who will feel keenly what ever is interesting to do. But at bottom I have little hope. Perhaps with a sufficiently keen eye, someone might see that the machine is done for and everything is broken, thrown away, except the individuals who remain naked and worthless.

Your P.V.

[Valéry to Gide]

[March 28, 1898]

My dear André,

I don't know whether it is my turn or yours to write; I have been a bit sickly these days. This filthy weather gives us nerves everywhere it shouldn't. When I am well, I can already hardly work, but when the atom suffers!... *zut*!

However, let's do like Pierre Louÿs—or like you.

I shall write (about Degas not designated any more clearly):

Monsieur D. or Painting

and then also:

Notes on "Agathe" or: *Agathe or Sleep.*

Finally, in the eternal fog where works that never appear and never will may be found, read this little piece:

The Dinner in London (formerly *Supper in Singapore*).

But this is something nice.

Besides, I may perhaps do as I did for *Agathe*: I shall

publish it as notes. This is a charming trick, no more embarrassment, but blanks and suspension points.

The *Mercure* is somewhat in revolution and our little Fanny, not without Chanvin, on the verge of an expulsion, half undeserved but which I can face without disturbance.

Yesterday I reread my *Durtal* with a kind of contrition, and this disappointed me. I would have thought I could yell against him louder. But he was either less loud or I was more so. You must have made a pretty face when you read that. Foreign policy would stir me at this time if I were free—I believe I would explode with articles. Everything is going as hoped for. All is moving easily, clearly, with the help of three or four ideas, and this is coming to be really a game in which one can reason, or look. This will soon be better.

But all my animal spirits are in disorder. Hatred transports them from one end to the other of my self. I would like to hold and punish—and one must remain in his chair, to await five o'clock then await seven o'clock when one dines, then the hour when one goes to bed and then, etc. From here to there, my mind will be occupied *uselessly* with twenty subjects, mixed with causes for boredom, if my body allows it to do so.

Impregnate yourself, bring back to me some of the Roman air, of the compact fever and of the demon of organization. I know very well that one is caught between two things: either to think only of viable things, or not; and in the first case, perhaps a great part of the possible is lost. . . . I am talking nonsense.

Your VALÉRY

[Valéry to Gide]

[Paris, July 8, 1898]

Dear You also,

I am still on vacation in my room, with good moments and bad. A sot, in short. I profited by it yesterday, getting up, to scamp a bad *Teste* which left at once for the waste-basket.

It is a matter of getting well, to go to Cuverville. I shall confer today with Julia on this point. In case I can go, it will be by way of the train you indicate, at 6:52. There is a restaurant car where I will dine. Here is a semantic fact of the new savage language. The root *W* is declined and signifies thus all the needs of the body: W.L., W.C., W.R. (for love, W.A., the synonym for bed-toilet, etc.).

For remedies, Julia gave me an agreeable one to compensate for the frightful mustard-plasters. This is a fumigation: menthol, 2 grains; alcohol at 70 percent, 60 grains. A spoonful of this juice in boiling water, and nose and mouth above it. It is rather extraordinary. At the first sneeze, try that.

My dear (Monsieur Teste would say), as for *Saül*, since the question of confidence has been posed, I am going to "bring the light" immediately:

(1) *Saül* is not, for me, indifferent.

(2) First, *someone* tells me that you are doing a *Saül*. Good. I am talking to you about him. You talk to me about him; but, agree about him without words. I don't insist. Why? Well, I know that it is not good to talk about things before they are completed. Then, it is understood that I am a bit noxious for literary work, and I believe it in fact, all reflections considered. So, I am closing my box. I am waiting

for you to exhibit. What will interest me will be *Saül*. What doesn't interest, then, is what doesn't exist—for me at least—yet. I see no inconvenience in waiting and I find that you are right to put me off for the result.

(3) But *someone* is again talking to me about him. *La Revue Blanche* is publishing an extract, which I haven't seen: in the end, several persons know the entire work. Someone is making me the greatest eulogies. I don't know what to respond to them. First I have seen nothing, and then those who talk to me about them have no doubt that they are offending me somewhat. Nevertheless, I reflect. I appreciate the reasons which have probably led you to begin your experiments, rather by certain reactives than certain others.

You have seen quite clearly that this did not keep me from asking you for news of the King Youpin in question. Yet, observe how much, when I shall know this drama, it will render my judgment difficult to make and difficult to speak. Devil!—Note, as I have already said, that I learned of the very existence of *Saül* from X or Z.

I see no harm in your directing to your taste the relations of your literature with me. But the question changes when it is a matter of the relations of you to me. I confess to you that they seem to me infinitely above anything that we can, each of us, splash onto paper. That is to say that I am naturally led by you to neglect that about which you prefer to address yourself to others. (Ouf!) It is obvious. I repeat to you that in literary matters, for you, and in loufochistic matters, for me, I consider ourselves as independent variables, making our salad as it is convenient for us.

When I give you an opinion about your writings, first of all it is only an opinion, and then you must by now know me sufficiently by heart to know that I have a very special and impractical way of seeing these matters.

That will not keep me from making a clear remark to you: to my mind, you should beware of those who—on a small scale—think as you do. The search for an opposite temperament is the beginning of wisdom. One must use those who are antipathetic (as Monsieur Teste would say). This theorem has its corollary or rather its reciprocal: one must not try to excite those who are inclined to excitement. We give imprudent habits to everyone.

This must be clarified by the use of words.

Another response to a sentence in your letter: when you have something on your mind, you have only to speak. It would be fine no longer to fear ridicule between us, and that you should have told me squarely: "You don't talk to me about *Saül*? Why? Is it that you don't care a f——?"

But that is not easy and, in your place, I agree that I would not have done it.

All the same, *without your letter*, I would still not know:

(1) that *Saül* is indifferent to me,
(2) that this distressed you!

In short, as Tinan would say, that is better than if *Saül* distressed *me* and that this should be indifferent to you.

Then good-bye, no doubt.

I shall write to you as soon as I am sure of coming, about Monday probably.

You shall have your goose feathers. I think that they are, in fact, feathers and not beaks that you want.

Your PAUL VALÉRY

[Valéry to Gide]

[Paris, September 10, 1898]

Dear one, I am overwhelmed. Mallarmé died yesterday morning. Last evening I received a telegram from his daughter and I am busy writing to right and left.

I felt last night, when I could not go to bed, all the affection that I had for that mind—and the more I tried to penetrate it, the more I feel this death in me.

The burial will take place tomorrow, Sunday, at 4 o'clock.

Your P. VALÉRY

[Valéry to Gide]

[Paris, October 7, 1898]

My dear André,

I have been ill during the entire week: yesterday, however, I had to go to Valvins, at the call of these ladies who remain. This was a tepid impression, immense, smooth, a mixture of the great calm of such a beautiful land, of my physical suffering, and memories. A long talk, watered at moments slowly with funereal things, turning at times even into laughter—as it were posthumous—with moments completely moving.

I tell you between us, first, since this must *not be spread at all*—that I was led into the mortuary chamber and there on the table, intact, someone gave me a paper all scribbled over to decipher, written on the evening of his death. In it I read the order to show none of the papers, to publish nothing unpublished, and to burn "this half-century pile of notes... which I alone understand." That scrap was frightening in its convulsed handwriting—and beside it, two fragments of *Hérodiade* almost finished, the last work. I was permitted to read them despite the interdiction. One is in strophes in the manner of Banville (8, 8, 8, 4), this is the *Canticle of John*, the other about fifty alexandrines; not one line remained in my head, but I have the impression that *The Canticle* is very beautiful. You understand that I was lacking in composure.

Strange and painful impression—going back in the train —to see that not one line of these fragments had remained with me.

Now, I come back to business. I shall be brief and clear.

In talking, I persuaded these ladies to reveal to me their pecuniary situation. In brief, they have about 3,400 francs to spend. They remain at Valvins—at 400 francs a year. It is then that their regrets shone through—they confessed that the house in Paris would have to be done away with—and they showed me so much chagrin that—*dame*!—I put myself forward. I thought of you and of me in a rapid little mental calculation and I said, very vaguely at first, not daring too much, that . . . some friends *had* thought of those things. I saw the pleasure that this gave them; I added a bit of boldness, and promised to clear up the matter.

Here is my idea: the Paris rent is 900 francs a year, that is to say, 75 francs a month. This is not the devil. But alone I can't go beyond 25 francs a month. On the other hand, I don't wish, naturally, to send out the call *en masse*, which would be without discretion and consequently would go against the objective. Then I thought of you. Tell me what you can do in this direction—if you wish. I won't hide from you that the merit and the difficulty of the question is entirely in the result, and the REGULAR CONTINUATION of that rent, no less than in the absolute secrecy required.

Answer AS SOON AS POSSIBLE and give your advice on that other point: after you, and only after your response, I shall address myself to the following friends: Dujardin,

Griffin, and perhaps Fontainas. I need people, primarily of heart, secondly of honor, and thirdly with a regular purse and of special discretion.

Once the combination is regular, I shall inform those interested with the names of participating friends. Whatever may be your response, radical silence! I am charged on the other hand to thank you for your letter. I must write to various persons for the same reason.

Were you informed of the birth of my nephew, last week?*

Your VALÉRY

[Valéry to Gide]

[Paris, July 12, 1899]

My dear André,

This morning I received your "supplies" and thanks for the punctuality. Mardrus, who had appeared two days before, left yesterday evening for the sea. The second volume will appear in September. The Natansons† predict 100,000 to 150,000 profit! The fact is that the fourth edition of the first volume is already in the press. Your phrase *copulomimetic* is excellent; it makes us want to give the sign and the gesture.

Work. It is time, France makes nothing now but translations: Nietzsche, Haroun, and that stupid Wells with which Davray is flooding us, and that amusing Kipling. But it seems to me that our best literary periods have been these in which excellent translations have appeared. Nietzsche pretends that France has a female genius: she gives birth to

---

* Jean Valéry, the son of Jules Valéry.

† The Natansons, directors of *La Revue Blanche*, who published *Les Mille et une nuits* [*The Thousand and One Nights*].

ideas but doesn't engender them, a role that he gives to the Jews, to the Romans, to the Germans. But we have had, nevertheless, a few males. But what is it better to be? Who enjoys most? Here the female. For me, it seems that I prefer the masculine. Besides, all this goes back into vague ideas. Concerning the vague, I notice in passing that it is the vague idea that is most generally understood—and that a man is taken to be obscure as soon as he is precise. That comes from the fact that there are degrees of comprehension and that most people imagine that they understand more than they do. In other words, if they are urged towards an idea which they *feel* that they know deeply, they splutter.

I go bad like an old roquefort over a fragment of *Monsieur Teste** promised long since and as invertebrate as possible. You know my destiny. Everything that amuses me bores the public, without exception, and no one does as badly as I the things that don't amuse them.

I am still uncertain about the use of my short leave and my infinitesimal resources. To do it well, I would have to divide myself into segments, go to Genoa, to Montpellier, and the Aveyron. That is absurd.

Your P. VALÉRY

[Valéry to Gide]

[Paris, October 16, 1899]

My dear André,

I received your dispatch of no words and concluded from this silence that your cure was well under way.

After leaving you a moment ago I smoked a cigar, with various reflections on certain subjects, which our meeting had

---

* *Teste in China*, which was never finished but which appeared in another form thirty years later as *Le Yalou* (published privately in 1928, then incorporated into *Regards sur le monde actuel*, 1931).

interrupted; at home and in bed I left all that, to come back to the very place where we talked. A place in the mind, of course.

You had thrust your nose into my anxiety, and at once I reexamined this disgusting faculty of mine. There I was in agreement with certain previous conclusions concerning this subject. The true name of this anxiety, which continually stops me, is the irregularity of my strength and my mood. My means are fantastically different, according to the moment, and I discover this discontinuity in my physique. I have used it as often as I could, and I consider as certain that some of the results I was able to attain are precisely due to this way of being. But no one is strong and effective unless he is regular. ... My present existence has, in some way, consecrated this condition by its absurd distribution, which introduces into my current certain artificial flaws (in addition!) and, on the other hand, the annoyance accumulated by the hours spent in the office. In short, there is nothing to be done on this point: I am a man who pitches like a ship.

As to what concerns my practice of criticism (in the worst sense of the word), I must agree with you that I ought, perhaps, to have made nothing but my own delights. I drew attention to my emptiness by using, for very simple observations of my contemporaries, the leisure that it left to me. But my defense seems, necessarily for them, harder than my objections. It is enough for me to reply with the simple truth: "You haven't seen that I was only asking for contradiction. *You cannot refuse me this: that I have always given reasons and that they were not always bad.*"

This aggressive kind of sincerity—of which I tend to rid myself because it has not given me what I was seeking in

adopting it, that is to say... terrible extreme intimacies—
made me realize in myself that I was not a social being bu
indeed—solely and enormously—sociable. By *extreme*
intimacy, I mean a condition among several persons where
one would be able truly to say everything and where one
would find the comfort of a conversation between active
thoughts, without monologues of memory, echoes, etc. All
would look at each other mutually, finding all *à mesure*...

As for *this* disdain, it is entirely justified by the enormities
that I have heard spoken, that I have seen written for the past
ten years and above all by *the will not to see what is, as conser-*
vation of the literary talent that we suppose we have. That has
always seemed to me admirable, and deserving the most
vigorous of smiles, infinitely thin and infinitely clear. This
adds moreover to that ignorance and that disdain, so dis-
dainable, which our world observes with regard to other
efforts than theirs. He cannot conceive that one may see
terrible difficulties in the very ease of its train-train. He no
longer conceives himself, if the hope of having genius is
taken from him!—just as a Christian needs his heaven to live.

I find then that I have not had good judges. I find them
either biased or incompetent, and I feel that I cause them—
rarely—a boring problem in their heads.

You will tell me that *I also* keep my *secret* documents.
But I have never said that my ideas were completed and that
I might stop and give the results. The little that I have
published shows in itself distances sufficiently great; it
appears at sufficiently distant points; I believe, however, that
it shows a quite singular homogeneity of work and research.
It is impossible that it should not be felt that I am founded
on something that, at one and the same time, is very confused, very solid, and that *to me* seems of the first importance.

Finally, I talk—and I talk about myself willingly. I even talk about myself with the naïveté that makes me say, "At that moment, I had an excellent idea."

As for the very root of "miscomprehension," it is the principal tendency of my mind, which is extension, endless generalization. For me it is completely impossible to attach myself to anything at all peculiar. I can moreover, today, give you a precise notion of that. Every definite subject may, for me, be reduced to a series of physical and mental operations among terms. These terms are invariable, they are as fully thought out as possible. Now these operations, especially the mental ones, can be acquired. The only difficulty is in nicely analyzing the given subject to reduce it, in all possible cases, to a group of elements positively dead and to the diagram of a series of spiritual acts more or less arranged. Finally, mental operations are certainly of a number finite and small. The system that I point out to you very roughly exhausts—already—many things, and even without my detailing for you its procedures and its needs, you must see its bearing. One of its greatest advantages is to restrict to the minimum the chances of nonsense due to language, since it keeps no account of words in replacing them always close to their *signified* correspondent.

Besides, my tendency would exist, even beyond all method. Typical example, in a domain unknown to me, in music. If I were a musician, you see from afar that I would think constantly, for example, about the group of all possible melodies, I suppose. This would dominate me. I would search to draw them one from the other, to classify them, etc.

In brief, I don't generally want to see things as everybody else does. First I take an impression, as instantaneous as possible, then I come back to that, trying to rediscover those things by a sequence of conditions independent among themselves and consequently more general than my object.

What becomes of literature of that kind? A problem, an application, but not an aim, nor a fundamental point. This opinion will certainly be vulgar after a certain time. The medicine that was an art, with all its marks, with the genius of diagnostics, with the tricks and the charlatanry of the practitioners, with the superstititions and the infatuations of the public, has really become a special problem in chemistry, on the whole.

To summarize this colossal letter, I put a question to you. What to do when: (1) one has an irregular temperament, (2) one believes in certain things that shock public feelings, that annoy people when one states them or that offend them in their intimate household gods (hope, enthusiasm...), (3) one does not have the MATERIAL time, (4) one does not believe in what animates the people around you?

So, one does as I do:

One works when he can—and so oddly that no one would recognize anything of my true ideas in my papers, when I am no more.

One displays the best humor in the world—as far as possible.

One thinks what he thinks and lets others talk. One praises and blames as chance and humor decide, since *here* what is published counts no longer. What is said counts not at all.

One seeks the small so-called pleasures—vulgar, since in the end one has known, very widely, pains not vulgar at all.

One allows his ethics, exterior conduct, etc., to follow chance because one knows too well that this is indifferent, since it cannot penetrate the ultraprofound dogmas.

One talks with anyone, since that comes to the same
thing—all ears will be alike.

And sometimes one has the right to despise vast groups
and well-determined morals, since one in due time took
account, and weighed them.

Your VALÉRY

[Valéry to Gide]

October 25, 1899

Dear one, I see that my letter stung you, and this brings me
the good fortune to feel that you are taking the offensive.
I was afraid long since that you might have become indifferent toward the group that we would form together; it
seemed to me that we haven't the leisure to be useless
ourselves, and I took from that idea the permission to write
you several vague and annoying pages.

You considered as a judgment on yourself the statement
of needs which are personal to me; and I find this result
excellent. I love you, my dear man, because—and among
other things—the problem of the *difference* is posed between
us marvellously. This is one of the questions of existence that
I have passionately watched developing in the course of
many an intimate relation. One is in a tray. One puts in the
other tray a woman, a stranger, an imbecile, an intellectual,
an imaginary genius; and oneself furnishes, also, the support
and the scourge of the machine. The sensitivity of this balance
is peculiar. It depends on the quality of what is put into the
other balance. When it is you who find yourself there, mine
becomes much more sensitive than before.

I think that our differences are not at all great. What
makes their value is that they seem to me extremely supple
(like capillary blood vessels) so that to encounter them, we

can approach each other much closer than the greatest number of couples of mind. And that is, at bottom, what we have done. We have glimpsed—perhaps without saying so— that, in general, everything that one of us does is precisely what the other must not do. Each impulse of each one of us is, for the other, a priori, an indication about himself and to the contrary. Until I had thoroughly understood this mechanism, your successive new relations (for example) positively intrigued me; I shall not tell you exactly why. In short, I could enumerate a crowd of points on which the said mechanism has functioned remarkably, half without our knowledge.

You notice in passing that this suggests the conception of "ethics" as multiple correspondents among themselves. One imagines groups of people and one supposes for any one of them a kind of "ethic." One takes on, then, all the others by supposing that one will act by inverting, or exaggerating, or omitting the fashions displayed by the man chosen as a base, etc.

I believe there has been a misunderstanding between us, the error of people who wish to suppress a precious thing and a fundamental difference, instead of taking it as the key to their music. This error has certainly been more my fault than yours; it goes back to the time when I was floundering conscientiously among your tendencies, with the confidence that only the beginning is given by the use of a general analysis. I would have been entirely right, if these tendencies had been mine, and I was right in certain ones of mine. One may say: "I think A and I find A false," but one may not say: you think A and I find A false," because you think: A is inaccessible to Je. But all these *tu*s and all these *je*s are stolen by language and abominably half suppressed. The result of this is that your *toi* was protesting against the purely verbal massacre that I managed to make of certain ideas of yours, in so far as they are expressed. Here begins your part of the fault; at least, it seems to me that it would have sufficed you—then—to oppose me, as a simple fact, the irrepressible part of the incriminated tendencies.

You are mistaken, as I am, when you reproach me for believing that I am alone in thinking *sicut meipsum.** I think as I do because nothing, in short, in the acts or writings of another shows me the contrary. This is precisely a point where I wanted to sound out my contemporary. You know him, that millionaire! Moreover, I was one, and like him I knew that fear of being bored, of which your letter speaks.

Well, I found him, at the age of twenty, full of extended ambitions and of a certain charm of boldness and fear; at twenty-five, with all the talent you would wish, but already smelling rancid. He is founded on ideas as rare as they are commonplace, that is to say, not exactly his. He is so afraid of being bored that he bores me. He is horrified really of any change in vision, since he knows that his professional value is attached to that. Certainly, he does the same thing better and better. (And you are, in parenthesis, almost the only one for whom this is not the case.) I know perfectly well that if I had continued to write fourteeners, I would do them beautifully now; this is unavoidable. That is why stupidity and talent coexist so frequently. It is that fellow, moreover, who invented both genius and talent, like an officer and a petty officer. He invented Art just as he invented Life, Society, etc., and he would be a prodigious inventor if his discoveries did not all tend to exempt him from discovering. Me, I put the question to him whether he wants to be bored

* Like myself.

or wants to *rise*; whether he wants, in the end, to consider all that is made, all that *he* has made, always as *nothing*. And he, who makes what he makes only so that it may be *already* made, who wants to give himself a comfortable past, laughs in my face. I talk to him about power—and he answers me by success.

We talk about literature. I look for an author and I find nothing but a man—not even a man—a seamstress. I have all the more a taste for being severe because I have known, here and there, few individuals more hardy and vigorous, minds who did not see everything as substance for the printer, who required difficulty and who trusted their non-satisfaction. Those men have spoiled my contemporary for me. I would like him more enraged.

You speak evil of "false flowers" and of Wagner. But notice—and this is my whole system—that if they are less than veritable beauties, they carry it off from the point of view of making. The mind of the worst sculptor is agitated, and the mind of two men who are drinking a bottle is porridge. I know very well that the happiness of a day and twenty years of research may come to the same thing on paper and in the *visible* result. But in the long run—or in the mind itself—calculation prevails, for its essence is to fortify every moment.

In the end, there is for me something real, something endowed with a future and viable in that instinct that came to me to try to move between kinds of thought, more than between thoughts.

In the system of real flowers, life becomes line-fishing. One manages quickly to compare the value of the pike caught to that of the time consumed in waiting for him. In the system of false flowers, I believe that one can scarcely

ose an atom of time. I know of course that there is
)oredom. ...

Finally, since we must count everything, I must confess
also a certain bad humor, latent as always. Recently it was
the care of tomorrow. Now it is the care of today. Often I
despair a bit in the morning on leaving the place and the
moment where I would have worked well; and every evening
I look at the day from which I have just fallen, for nothing.
At times a madness takes me to conquer time and to want to
find in one second something far more important than all
that I might have looked for during the whole day, if it had
been mine. This madness has served me, but rarely. I fall
asleep with something painful in my mind, even if I mock
myself in saying: "All is the same." Or again: "But you
would have done nothing." You see that I am still happy
to have the head that I have, to have no need of "literary
production." Where would I be in that case? It is true ...

I am interrupted, that is better. I send you this as it stands
—and it is certainly enough.

Your P. VALÉRY

[Valéry to Gide]

[Paris, November 7, 1899]

I want to answer you today, but I don't think I can do it
as it should be because I am quite exhausted by crises and
considerable nights, things which moreover have nothing
to do with this.

To tire myself less, I shall only reread your letter and
annotate it.

So this sentence:

"Precisely because I collect the hostility of others, I *ought*
to collect your praise also, or perhaps my way of acting, of

writing, of living *must* seem to you like a tissue of practical blunders."

No doubt! I quickly reply to the first horn of the dilemma but the quibble lies in this word: "the others." In the whole group of others, some praise you, the *others* tire you out. First point, if you accuse the lack of comprehension of certain ones among the latter, be just and see it also in several of the first. As a rule, is it not probable that those who criticize us understand us (on the whole) more than those who praise us? If, moreover, you put each *against* the preceding one, how do you judge those who like them all?

At bottom, I can scarcely distinguish, therefore, between the hostile and the favorable. As for refining the admirers— alas! Wait—who more than Mallarmé could pretend to that? Well, I know by heart the detail of their admiration. I am myself seen among them, and, on this special point, I prefer me. Now, they, this small assorted number, do not seem to me in general to have grasped the most obvious and the simplest principle of the poet's general intention, and, for me, I know quite well that what interests me is the difference from that intention.

I come back always to saying: literature can have only three aims—that is to say, whatever one may do, it ends with the following three things (of which one must imagine the maximum number): (1) money, (2) number of persons who know your name (and the consequences), (3) personal instruction, by problems of a general kind to which technique and the exercise of art lead.

1 and 3 are my favorites. Anything is preferable to 2, except that 2 gives 1.

If you choose 3, either you give up literature, or you keep it, but for a particular, episodic reason. Moreover, one is rigorously led to theories analogous to mine, that is: the greatest possible consciousness, and the approximation of a more and more urgent calculation. In fact, to do otherwise (in hypothesis 3) teaches us nothing, and the puddle of *genius* once vomited, we are like anyone else. In other terms, our manner of thinking is in no way damaged. Understand me— I don't mean to say, by way of thinking, opinions, taste for a particular thing, sensual pleasure applied here or there— I mean to say the manner of seeing everything and dependence upon that manner. A change of syntax, and not a change of words. A change of countries rather than a change of regime.

Never forget that in literature the most beautiful book of the most beautiful writer is immediately balanced by the narrative of a Cook* or a Bourgogne† and that the public or reader does not have to take account of all the singing and buzzing necessary to the man who has nothing but his head to give you the Russian campaigns. But that head must pay for itself and with its own money. ...

It is true then that I don't understand your sport. I find that you think about your public too much or not enough. I am even sure that you are aware of this. You feel certainly by minutes—how can I say?—the sudden need to recapture a sort of average that you were forgetting happily. On the other hand, it seems to me that this can be seen in the history of your relations?

It is impossible for me to mistake you for the literary *littérateurs* of whom, were he a Hugo, the true portrait was

---

* James Cook, *Relations des Voyages du capitaine Cook aux deux Pôles et autour du monde* (Paris: Éd. Lerouge, 1811).

† *Les Mémoires du sergent Bourgogne* (1812–1813), published according to the original manuscript of Paul Cottin, in 1898.

seen in numerous copies in the receptions of the Sabbath a
Heredia's house. In other words, I hope and am sure tha
you don't do *that* as one makes sugar or medicine or teaches
(even with enthusiasm). The proof of it is that you ge
excited in order not to *imitate* (let us understand each other !
—this would require an explanation, here I give to this word
great extension) and so as not to *imitate you*—and that you
always prefer, no doubt, to interest others less and yourself
more.

Look, if I tell the truth, how gentle is the slope from this
way of *believing* to that number 3 of page 3 above. This
posed, you understand how much I must misunderstand
your game.

It is true that I am not made for this comprehension. All
that I have done or thought is tied to my existence—
IMMEDIATELY. This is strength and weakness. Now, precisely, this existence, this sense of being or not being, and—
especially—this sense of being in a certain manner (it is *that*
that is prodigious!) finds no interest or pleasure in constructing thwarted works to deceive or astonish the people
round about. On the contrary, everything carries him
(carries me) to give himself additive properties, to bind his
moments (under the condition of allowing them the greatest
diversity, and, in that class, you have noticed that I don't do
badly!) so that I could describe in this way the perfect or
theoretical state of my being: moments; and—in each of
them—*rigorously no matter what*; but, *around them*, a tendency
or an art that comes out of them, without altering their
particularism, and which consists of trying to guess the laws
of their transformations or of their mutual substitutions—
and to do as if these laws were known. This allows me to
pass everywhere. We are not responsible for the ideas that

come to us but, *at the very most*, the destiny that we make for them. Here, there is perhaps something of ourselves. Our hand here feels itself more distinctly. This hand, that is what interests me. The going-and-coming also, but whatever goes and comes leaves me cold, were it what the mind of others calls a genius's idea or filth or, *etcetera*, this is Job's fortune.

Of all the possible feelings, the strongest in me is that of *security*—or, if you like, of infinite distrust. I can have no confidence in what goes and comes. I don't trust myself in this, that is why I have sought the more constant things. I do not distrust them (consequently), that is why I deprive myself of nothing (in the mind).

Here and now, I can imitate the amusing collection of opinions which your letter contained, according to you.

Kolbassine used to call me "the freest mind that..." (Happily there was no Dreyfus at the time! Passion would have—as they say—blinded him.)

For Heredia, I am a lazy man. (You are right!) For a thousand others, very clairvoyant but only to the belt, I am the gentleman who will never do anything, or the abstracter of quintessences, or a poet who died young, or a practical joker, or a bore (those are exact). For various ones, a very original mind, complicated, etc. In other respects, I have been called good and wicked. I have the esteem of Mr. Ubu. There are also feminine opinions, no less diverse. Finally, I am the geometrical point of all contradictions.

And me, Valéry, my true opinion of myself? Valéry is an irregular being, extremely sensitive, who will never adapt himself to the idea of being what he is, at a certain moment; and who continually makes off in the midst of the incessant

sensation of not having said his "last word." This last sensation proves nothing, but I still have it.

All these opinions are just. Above all mine.

. . . .

Let us stop here for today, duty requires me. This letter
will have neither tail nor head, which is a great advantage.
I find it however less stupid than in the beginning I had
foreseen it. If you knew by what basso continuo it was
accompanied, you would find it perhaps more interesting.
I am at present facing a good number of things. I am not too
bored. I am out of patience; I aspire, after so many domestic
wars, to peace, but the means of honorable peace disgust me,
and the enemy who kills me pleases me.

P.V.

[Valéry to Gide]

[Antwerp, June 8, 1900]

My dear André,

I am very happy. I breathe in the vague with as much
delight as I have in fleeing from it. There is also the happiness
or vanity in finding that one can suspend a very old discipline.
Across all these beginning moments, I believe, a sort of
insipid Belgium is passing. Bruges, seen from rather close on,
left me quiet. Only its picturesque quality disgusted me a bit.
Antwerp disappoints me, so far. My new state deprives me,
it is true, of such explorations or *riddeks*, which would be
well to see not to be robbed.

But I am particularly pleased to notice nothing—yet!
I look only and scarcely, into myself, a sort of elementary
ebbing of rather ancient states. This return amuses me
because I shall not tolerate it for very long. Otherwise it
would be necessary to begin again being stupid, a poet, etc.

At the bottom of my suspense between an unknown and Monsieur Teste, there are also several anxieties, certain and serious. My mother wanted very much to remain in Paris, and there she is, unreasonably alone in a boarding house! Then the eternal spectre of the Artillery torments me. Finally, the uncertainties or perspectives of moving out, moving in, worrying, all these confused and arithmetical things called the serious side of life. . . .

Someone writes to me that your library is very very good. If, as I believe, it is a turning thing, and supposed to be at the fingertips, I see it filled with my reference books—that is, numerous mathematicians—one *Henri Brulard*, one *Divagations*,* in short, my fixed points. Perhaps you are going to deliver me of my eternal congestion of the table. Believe that this is a remarkable thanks.

Good-bye, my friend. Imagine that I can now write: my wife, etc.†

But, for this time again, I shall not fill the blanks. I shall not trace what *she* asked me to put for "you" at the end of this sort of letter. That would already be too much domesticity, I felt. And then, there you are, all the same.

Your old and recent

P. VALÉRY

[Valéry to Gide]

[Paris, August 29, 1900]

My dear André,

I didn't write sooner because I imagined I did not know where Cuverville is. I soon thought of Criquetot–l'Esneval. . . .

---

* By Mallarmé (Paris: Ed. Fasquelle, 1897).

† Valéry was married to Jeannie Gobillard, the niece of Berthe Morisot, on May 31, 1900. This letter was written during their honeymoon in Belgium.

I am continuing my function at Monsieur Lebey's house.*
It is agreeable, in short, and restrained. In fact, he is full of
respect for me and at times recounts corners of contemporary
history or business episodes that have their flavor.

I still have the anxiety to know what will happen at the
expiration of the six months of leave. There is the shadow.
I sense that I will be prodigiously annoyed to go back to jail.

Another annoyance is the health of my wife who is very
anaemic these days—with weaknesses, headaches and other
forms of discomfort. This reacts somewhat on me, and we
take care of ourselves between us.

But it was necessary to interrupt the useful work of a clear
dictation of my notes, which already were taking shape.

I feel, in looking at this little package, how much, if I
were publishing the reasoned collection of my *Questions*,
the eventual reader would be annoyed. My aim being purely
linguistic, representative, and consistent in seeking a convenient figure of knowledge among an infinite number of
others equally possible, I deprive myself of the metaphorical
lure completely. I see no good reason why a philosophy or a
psychology should furnish more ideas about the great Boats
(Life, Destiny, Me, etc.) than geometry.

It is curious that no one finds in any professional philosopher the preoccupation to establish as rigorously as possible
the correspondence of words and phrases to interior facts.
For me, it is a study full of amusement, which was suggested
to me in principal by reflections on time and by the theory
of the construction of geographic maps, that is to say, transformations of figures.

* Édouard Lebey, director of the Agence Havas, whose nephew,
André Lebey, a poet who belonged to the *Centaure* group, was a
friend of Valéry. Édouard Lebey took Valéry as his private secretary,
a post which Valéry filled until Lebey's death in 1922.

The theory of the verb occupies me then these days, and it seems to me to grasp the principle of it. We should see in grammars the definitions we give of the verb! That reminds me of the definition of the straight line, on the subject of which the geometricians, from fear of calling on what exists (that is to say, on image and a rather simple property of that image), have invented propositions that are the most vicious circles in the world.

On the other hand, I rarely rewrite a sentence from the debut of *Agathe*. It is very hard. But where there is no discomfort, there is no pleasure in writing.

Not seeing a soul of the *milieu* alive, I shall teach you nothing on this head.

I suppose that your wife is at present free with her gestures, and is recovering her strength. If it is permitted to give handshakes, I would be happy that she should reserve for me one or rather two and even three since I am several.

But you must not fatigue her.

Your P. VALÉRY

[Valéry to Gide]

[October 17, 1900]

My dear André,

I am responding as soon as possible to your letter where a certain discouragement perspires. Why this cure at Lamalou?

I had written to you at Cuverville, but I had not put in the important thing, since you imagine that I am going to award just anybody with the armchair that belongs to you in my intimate storeroom. Nor will the *marriage* deprive you of it. Our bond is too . . . abstract for the diversity of life to bother it, and we interest ourselves enough to interest us forever. All adventures, even that kind of enemy friendship which existed for a moment, at your preceding Lamalou, our own and extremely narrow, turned only to mix something enormously and to unravel very happily all the rest. I hope that we very often serve mutually as definite types of another mind than ours, and as sympathetic and as different as possible! The ideal would be: as possible as possible!

What is stupid in this matter, as in all others, is that there is only one word (friends) to correspond to very diverse reciprocities.

If you wish and if you believe, I would say that we are in a certain sense harnessed to one and the same shaft, and that we know ourselves as such, or subjects of one and the same power, that power placed as constantly apart from all others as you will.

But you can find a thousand better approximations.

In short, what I have written above is no doubt not clear —it is tossed—but it is very determined.

I have not yet perceived in myself any change other than existence, that is to say, in a way to lose that time, which one always loses in any existence. It seems to me that the rest holds.

Except that I am considerably bored in writing *Agathe* as a *pensum*, seeing the chill of that subject. I am condemned to write retroactively, with no warmth, no aim, no desire, and no pleasure—like a perfect imbecile, the imbecile being the one whose duty is tedious, and who fulfills it....

I am struck by the coincidence of your depression with that of Pierre Louÿs. They are quite different, I know, but less than the two of you. Until now, I had almost the monopoly of these filthy states. The more I go, the more I feel myself a slave of the physical, that is to say, of I don't know what, and I thought that you were less bound than

I am to your flesh and nerves. Here is a good title to meditate on always (so that it may be good for something): theory of the disobedience of the body.

I went to the *Mercure* a few days ago. Centuries ago. Talked rather gaily without any interest. Decidedly, it has *become* impossible to give oneself up to this charming sport. At moments, I want to ask for interlocutors by "way of advertisements"—this is annoying. I like people who jump up as quickly as I do and who can forget while talking as one forgets in a quick movement. The true *verbal* analogue of music (if there is any) is conversation that allows all the passages and all the discords. But no performers or no music and none of us yet has the *grandiose* to execute the solos of Mallarmé.

There is a pleasure *foutu*.

Bloy has just written a book against Zola. It is filled with excrement but there is so much of it that it is almost imposing. Finally I writhe in the reading. So, thanks and glory to the author. I am letting go this letter infinitely an-harmonic and moving out, to give *Agathe* one hour before dinner. You will consider it as a *bavardage* that I have almost prolonged to avoid my above-designated labor.

This is not a dialogue from you to me, I still have too little place (and places) to chat comfortably. Then, I am not yet a regular customer to my wall and table. . . .

Your P.V.

[Gide to Valéry]

Lamalou, October 21 [1900]

My dear Paul,

Why this cure? Oh! That is what I am asking myself at present since I am at Lamalou and I am well enough there to be bored to perishing. But I didn't ask it of myself this summer, when I promised myself to go there.

The tone of my last letter will have deceived you: I am not in a slump, and the depression that you could have glimpsed was completely sentimental, and just at the right point for you. I was sad not to have been able to see you again in passing and *to assure myself* again of you; I was wrong to be sad, as your letter excellently shows me. And now, if this letter still seems dull and ill-advised, see in it only the effects of the cure of which the first benefit is to make one stupid.

Impossible *all the more* to work; one can scarcely read; I discovered a piano in an abandoned neighboring villa; in front of it I spend the greater part of the hours that, last year, I dedicated to boredom.

I am rereading *La Cousine Bette*, who cannot decide to stop being detestable until the fifteenth chapter, but who then, suddenly, turns to the masterpiece. I would like to see *Agathe*. What will you make of it, now that there is no more *Centaure*? Useless to tell you how much, if you don't think of letting go either with money or honors, *L'Ermitage* would be happy that she should sleep there. But I don't conceal that this is not a famous springboard: to live there, one must renounce many things, and above all, jumping.

I was very stirred by what you told me about Pierre Louÿs already in your last letter. It is impossible for me to get *indifference* from myself in his regard, and without more hate than love. I will always be interested, with a certain passion, in all the narrow passages along his road. It is certain that what you tell me about him, this letter that he wrote to you, etc., awaken in me a very lively sentiment that terribly resembles affection ... but what good is there in talking about that?... None the less I would have wanted to see that letter.

And Régnier? I haven't seen him since Blanche told me about a curious dinner at the Mettmans and a few topical anecdotes. From various sides, news of him comes to me (oh!—very external news, I am simply told that he is better now, but that he had a narrow escape, etc.). The sentences you speak of, which he may have spoken—and which you know how!—can't be confided to a letter? I mean, when shall we see each other henceforth? I don't know whether I shall come back to Paris this winter, and I greatly fear the *lacuna*.

Explain to me now why you still write to me on paper from the Ministry. Good-bye. A good moving out. May your wife not be too much fatigued. Please give her my best memories and bow respectfully to your mother for me.

Good-bye. It will soon be 10 o'clock, and after nine sleep begins to gnaw me.

Since various reasons will make me shorten the time of my treatment as much as possible, I don't know whether I shall be able to go to Plaisance. Question to be studied.

Your ANDRÉ GIDE

[Valéry to Gide]

57, Avenue Victor-Hugo
Sunday [June 24, 1901]

My dear André,

It is finally decided that I am going to leave the Ministry, with a formal and precise promise of a place at the Agency. Truly, I did not make them beg me too much to give up the idea of going back, and I made my decision. So, I built on the unknown, but the known was so boring! My mother left yesterday for Montpellier, changing the direction of her boredom by going away. My sister-in-law is ill again. This malaria is endless (although *Paludes* gave it up).

And I am dying of the heat, here. Sweating room and notebooks.

From time to time, a resolution is settled. And according to my custom I see it at once as a sort of forgetting. I begin none the less to put it in force, sure that I or something else is going to interrupt it.

In this way, I wrote a while ago at the top of a page: *Definitions*. This title raised some difficulties for me. Whence six or eight lines in the eternal book of notes always gaping. I come back to my white page, and I write a half-dozen definitions of my kind. There, I was interrupted. I stood up with the certainty that it was radically finished with a very useful work, when needed, to recognize me in my digging.

The fact is that I never retouch it. I have happily come no longer to count any but the present moment, so that I leave behind me each day a page that, in general, I never turn again. Whatever survives this calendar, I esteem, for it stayed in my head. To have been struck by what one has made, to the point of keeping it, this is a sort of sign, in short. No worse than any other.

At the Mallarmé wedding, few people.* I had the glory of giving my arm to the beautiful Thadée Natanson.† Madame Mallarmé began the march with an old general, red and gold, etc.

I read *Eureka* to my patron. I felt that I was perhaps wrong ten years ago not to have written an article of some sort on Poe. Now, I have no wish to do so. All the same, that man

---

* Geneviève Mallarmé married Dr. Edmond Bonniot, who had attended Mallarmé's "Tuesdays" and was his great admirer.

† The wife of the director of *La Revue Blanche*.

has a unique title. He is absolutely the only writer who had the intuition to connect literature with the mind. I deduce it entirely from these propositions.

Literature is a property of the mind. Now, the mind is a *certain thing*, so, etc.

This idea is so simple, one lone man found and applied it (in part only, for lack of great details, in the minor of the syllogism above). If the writing has the least importance, this idea is as important as the great *lancé* of Descartes. And it is a matter of nothing less in the two cases than to substitute a general type of research and hypotheses for empiricism.

Mallarmé, at bottom, has done in detail, I mean to say expression, etc., what the other has done in principle. . . . But the field of application is a great deal more extensive than the notion of *method* suggests at first, and even any particular possible work.

Today I can measure all the influence that this former obstinate reading has had on me.

What I hold against most literature, then, is to juggle with things of which the author cannot measure the full bearing. This reproach is only personal, naturally; I mean to say it is *that* in which most literature fails to grip me. And then what comes of that sport, if it encounters a reader of my kind. I would be terrified by a reader like me. And if I don't write for someone like you, I write in the vague; I shoot at an empty hat; I don't encounter the milieu where I can *reproduce* myself.

Literature cannot bear objections. That is why the beginning is delicate, the continuation narrows, and the end is always false. The whole affair is to decide whether there is room to transpire on one's paper in sight of the one who is not fit to make objections. And every author implies a sort of bizarre faith. That one—the eternal Client.

But it is understood that I speculated purely. The *Mercure* is not going to close its doors after my advice. And yet, I am right. What antics, after all, to read a book in which one is sure that the author could not justify three lines. Stendhal himself could almost be reduced to puppets. And yet I like Stendhal, and I shall almost never say to him: "What matters to me if it doesn't resist me?"

Relative obscurity gives resistance to Mallarmé.

Let us leave these noble and gloomy subjects. The Avenue Victor-Hugo is deafening this Sunday, where the heat brings out the imbeciles, who ought all to be naked on their innumerable beds. ...

Your P.V.

[Valéry to Gide]

Paris, July 14, 1901
Saturday, I think.

My dear André,

I am dying of heat. I insisted to my wife that she go at least to breathe among the trees, but you learned that my sister-in-law is still ill—so it is a sunken project. I would have loved to go to your house with them. There is so long a time that I have not known rustic phlegm. ... Finally!

An anecdote, but keep it strictly for yourself, if you please. Yesterday I went after dinner (as every evening) to the house of my "boss" whom I found in his little garden, facing the jet from a waterpipe, and I took the seat beside his. The night was coming on. Suddenly he said, "Do you know that you have had an enormous influence on me?" (Exclamation ...) "...Yes, on my mind—you have made me come back to religion. —??!!— I have found calm in it and I am grateful to you, etc."

It appears that it is the result of my critique. I was quite touched by that act. But who would have believed it?

A curious thing, this is not the first time that this adventure has happened to me. What an odd apostle I make then? I must say that I have a passion for the Church. I have not found in it one screw which is not marvelously placed, nor one absence. All the qualities of the ideal mechanism and in the first rank of independence of the game as with the value of the agents, etc. But these appreciations are rather suspect, at bottom more terrible than heterodoxy or free thought. However, there is the effect. Then?

The storm is at the full, finally it bursts. Nothing is more curious than the noise of thunder. *Agathe* sweats and steps back. I sense that I am going to remove the half of my second notebook. In a subject where there is no possible order since precisely that happens *before* all order, I can't manage to juxtapose my ideas. They are so very rarefied, made so irreducible that I cannot close the vault and go away from a deadening parallelism.

I knew in advance the *Naturally*.* But I don't understand very well or then it is very far from the state of mind that I had told you about.

I am very much more satisfied with my eternal little notes than with *Agathe*. It seems to me that I have advanced rather well these days. But the more I go, the less I see a whole. I have, moreover, on this point the absolute conviction that it would be (the case fallen due) a book for nobody. Some are infected by their studies and their crazy vocabulary. The

---

* An allusion to the dedication by Pierre Louÿs on a copy of *Les Aventures du roi Pausole*.

others would not get the point. My novelty is to serve myself with conceptions as with procedures and not as realities, while considering, moreover, the various conceptions as transformables, the ones by the others. On the other hand, a crowd of observations together furnish me piles of problems, all of which come back to questions either of duration or of language (in the most general sense of this term, that is to say all notations). So I have made in its overall lines a sort of general theory of notations, which was lacking, I believe. I had observed for a long time that the philosophers have scarcely stirred in reality any but the meaning of words. So that they teach us nothing clear about the mind but only the interior relations of language, this language resting on nothing. It is easy to demonstrate. Thus you would seek in vain from them the solution of this general problem which I find to be capital: "What does language conserve?" Let me explain. A geographic map, following the system of projections adopted, conserves, for example, the proportionality of the lines of the terrain among them, or the angles of two lines of the terrain, etc. You see that there are no such rules for ordinary language. The language of algebra conserves *ad libitum* the personality of quantities and operations, etc.

But being interrupted, I leave you. . . .

Your P. Valéry

[Valéry to Gide]

[Paris, September 17, 1901]

My dear André,

I came back to Paris yesterday morning, recalled by Lebey, who was alone, and leaving my suffering wife there with my sister-in-law. She is in one bed, the other in the other, and since they are one above the other, they talk to each other through the thin ceiling of pine boards.

These shaken-up vacations were almost amusing for two or three days. Several conversations with Fontaine or Redon, a pretty walk and no work at all, even negative. But, to end them for me, this rather sudden departure, at the moment when my wife's health was troubling me, had to take place.

I am making a gigantic effort to write to you, but in the end I can almost manage it here, whereas over there I would have already let go of the paper.

The country is gentle with its attenuated ocean and the handles that are called "conches" all the time. In the direction of Royan, that is towards the northwest of Saint-Georges, in each "conche" there is a bathing establishment, a clique of a sort, and since they are quite separate, each one has its own horizon to itself. We have rented a villa quite near the shore, very agreeable and large. In the end, by good luck, I happened onto a doctor, a gentleman, conscientious, whose only pleasure in this country is to wait for October to enjoy the sunsets.

However that may be, I held him close, and I almost summoned him to act energetically. It seems that his treatment gives results and I noted a relatively great improvement.

How I have regretted at times not being a doctor myself and being unable to be one! In the case of Paule, I have watched over her minutely for hours; it is a very curious case and it seemed to me that, as a doctor, I should have read her.

One scarcely begins in medicine to notice the functioning of the whole organism. Now, all the strange ailments are strange because their symptoms have no visible and anatomic connection, and there is no science of *will-o'-the-wisps*.

But since one follows, all the same, the vacillation of general energy! Life in units of time has theorems still unknown but almost predictable. The doctor sees the rods, the pistons, and a bit of the machine's metal, but as for the work and the power, he still sees nothing. Example: as for the nervous system, where in reality no physiology is visible, the therapeutist caves in at the sixth floor below where the occultists, the estheticians and the philosophers eat their own feet. The best to you,

P.V.

[Valéry to Gide]

[Paris, April 9, 1902]

Dear Horticole,

... As for me, my weakness would be the spider. Every spider draws me. ... Don't be frightened; I am not going to unwind my thread here. My notebooks will suffice for that. Days when I treat myself well, I see myself running across a difficult web, sensitive as water, a linen where there would be enormous stupidities caught, but they escape.

I don't know if you know that I have added to my twaddle a part (obviously shameful) independent of my ordinary point of view. If I have admitted it, that is because it came of itself and was not a deliberate invention.

I have tried (after long and ancient encounters with various difficulties) to serve myself, in the rough sketch of man, by a conception analogous to the energy of physicists. You sense, perhaps, the advantage there would be in representing and in unifying all that in the "mind" appears to us in the form of waste, conservation, successive transformations, instantaneous states, reversibility, etc. All that, as realization, is only a question of good definitions—to begin with. That done, the benefit would be to be able to represent with great precision the state of knowledge between two given instants.

I have spent my bit of useful time these last days in carrying this effort quite far. I shall not recount the detail to you. It is boring to write.

Up to now, no one has ever dared to involve the head in the total energy of the universe. And, for lack of the ability, some have gone so far as to call the phenomenon: a mental epiphenomenon. Which is rather comical.

I took another turn. I fabricated a special notion for these phenomena by observing that the difficulty is the opposite. In the physical world it consists of finding the unity beneath the forms, and here it consists of rediscovering diversity. The unity is given.

The whole question will be to see if I shall manage to find my energy parallel in its laws to physical energy. These kinds of analogy constitute the method of physics and have led to this great edifice of general physics—which is no longer more than a limited pile of purified and perfected concepts.

Scorn these lines and lock them up. At this price I promise you the energetic theory of syntax.

Your P.V.

[Valéry to Gide]

[Paris, September 18, 1902]

My dear André,

My wife is at the top of the stairs reproaching me for having refused—disagreeably—to give you any explanations concerning my works. That denied, I am writing to you.

It is true that I was not disposed to talk about them. Their condition is now ineffable. So many very different considerations occupy me, so many beginnings or roads sketch themselves that I could not display them clearly. You know that there is no one more than you to whom I would prefer to talk about my endeavors. To leaf through together, in a safe corner, one of those notebooks that I keep from day to day—and in which I form the only tie—would please me profoundly. You can well imagine that, despite my constancy, I find at times an immense doubt concerning all these closed adventures. I would need to recount them, were it only to remind myself of them and to test them better in the rapidity of discourse. It has come to the point that often I speak of them to Mr. Lebey. A monologue in which he has the kindness to pretend that he is interested.

He asks anxiously: "Did you write all that?"

"Yes, sir, I noted it."

But, God knows whether I would want to be able to measure all these ideas at a glance. You know what it is: minute observation of the *truly* mental, the systematic reduction of *all* language to certain properties, endless research on the units (as it were) to which every human step must return. In short, for the past several months I have added new chapters, which are closely related to physiology, which are in a way the reduction to axioms and formulas of the physiological facts indispensable to knowledge. There I still have a great deal to do, etc. But that says nothing without explanations, without accuracy, and I repeat that this is not the moment.

There we are. I am slipping away to number 38.*

Your P.V.

* The home of Édouard Lebey, then 38 Avenue du Bois; now Avenue Foch.

[Valéry to Gide]

[Paris, December 3, 1902]

My dear André,

Coming back from your house, I realized that a remark or a parenthesis was lacking in my whimsical exposé of "classic" art. Here it is, for it supports this thesis somewhat without diminishing, moreover, its purely conversational bearing. . . .

You remember that I talked about laws—arbitrary, perceptible, external to the subject?. . .

Well, here is the remark. In the so-called classical periods (antiquity, the seventeenth century, etc.) there was general belief in the possibility of the arbitrary. It was not generally thought that everything was determined, partial, and precious in itself as a document or a fragment of laws.

Then, *laws were laid down*. One constructed a priori a similarity between the work of art and the natural fact considered as the product of Fate, of perhaps foreknowledge and divine powers.

The situation is reversed. No arbitrary will, an infinite subordination of impersonal laws. Such is the present sentiment (I do not discuss it, of course). So, the most ordinary fragment of the most ordinary work belongs necessarily to the great mechanism . . . modern importance of notes, pieces of paper, which often cost us more than books well made. Realism, Vitalism, Naturisme, in short, all the heresies. Then also, why compose? It is merely to make *false books*. There is no longer any feeling for composition because one wishes or one believes that he feels the relation of *no-matter-what* with All.

And in fact—by adding an individual to anything whatever—the sum is always COMPOSED.

On the other hand, I find it right to consider the work o art as false logic and psychology. But this view constrains ar enormously. Then?

Truly, I believe that what is called *art* is destined either to disappear or to become unrecognizable. Art is on the way *no* to escape experience and exact analysis. I feel it and I see signs of it. The day is not far when certain kinds of research, still young, will come to it. If nevertheless something awakened can materially survive the present popular mud and slush.

In short, you see what I mean to say: we know almost too much about it to be true classics. Euclid, who *was* classical science, has been himself penetrated after twenty centuries of *beau fixe*! One sees in that work what makes the absolute classic *chic*, the rigor of the arbitrary.

Today, one must be resolved to the *sacred* personality! Who would wish to bow—and why?—before a regulation? See the verse, see the music. Talent, on the contrary, is marked almost by the power of dissolution. Equality— which is a sentiment—ends by suppressing what was common to all men. Death of criticism, because of talent and lack of discipline.

Etc.

Your P.V.

[Valéry to Gide]

[Paris, July 3, 1903]

Dear André,

I should have written to you. Everything is so heavy for me that I did nothing about it. My wife, ever and ever tired, overworked, almost without respite, is again at *Le Mesnil*. I was hoping for a zone of relative peace and calm. The fact is quite otherwise.

At bottom, and soon, the difficulty of the return—and, finally, the crisis.

And me, physically ordinary, I remain a pig here at the mercy of every idea and every discouragement.

I hope that Drouin and his wife are more courageous. Besides, they have already passed through these ups and downs. But there is, no doubt, always an accelerating oppression, which cannot be avoided. Give them my very particular affections, which means that at this time we can very easily imagine each other.

I have received *Prétextes* and *Sanguines* and even *Les Trente-six mille Nuits*. The plurals dominate. I saw Pierre two weeks ago. On arriving at his place, I caught sight of him in his garden, small, but near, very near, gigantic trees (for Paris); he was happily watering a lawn with a lance, in a frock coat.

He seemed to me in very good health, very old—friendly. I spent an hour, rejuvenating and almost Wagnerian. We discovered in talking that we had both passed half of the night, from April 11 to 12, watching the eclipse of the moon with binoculars. He concluded from it at once that alone among all of our friends, etc. This idea delighted him. And when an idea of this kind delights him, one is ravished and delighted with him. Not true?

The sure thing is that both, by very different roads—I think—came to the point of killing the hours by watching them *in person*, with a lorgnette, on their parallels. I constructed for myself a sort of astrolabe in cardboard and I tried to fabricate an astronomic telescope with borrowed lenses.

I ought to talk to you about *Prétextes* in my manner, instead of telling you this stuff and nonsense.

If I were lucid, I would do it willingly, but I cannot lif
my spiritual members. Besides, it is a book of criticism, and
there we must begin at the beginning. How much chicanery
my friend; I am annoyed simply by thinking about it! It i:
only in conversation that I can cover quickly enough the
road *necessary* before broaching the question. This is one of
the things that turn me away from writing, this immense
road, unending and bare, before drinking in safety. It is
better not to be doubtful of it. But when one has doubts
about it, it is finished: he is unique.

Look, the article on Villiers is capitally interesting. I don't
understand, however, the word *imposture* that terminates it.*
In your lectures there are notions, "great man," "nature,"
"art," that mislead me, and it seems to me that you mix in
your judgments several modes, for example, the intentions
and the execution, etc. I mean to say that these pages are in
the full atmosphere of literature. Then arises my conflict
as a reader between pleasure and profit (two ignoble words).

I am stammering in half-words. All that is above is
unintelligible, but I am elsewhere and I am very concerned.
Many friendly greetings to your wife, who is of a kindness
truly rare, and to you.

Your P.V.

[Valéry to Gide]

Sunday [July 13, 1906]

My dear André,

I have just returned from Mesnil, where I spent 36 hours
seeing my women and children. When I come back to Paris
after this endless voyage, I am half dead. I get up at six, I

---

* The final sentence reads: "Son art n'apparaît plus alors qu'une
admirable et éblouissante imposture."

rrive at ten, and I read aloud until noon. It is 2 o'clock and
am bursting with a revolting torpor.

Towards 5 o'clock, it will again be necessary to preoccupy
oneself with the Russian National Assembly (instituted in
1905) and the falling away of the coast.

But the bottom of my thought will again be fatigue, the
desire to sleep at last one veritable night and not in detached
pieces, an anthology of dreams (where you figure) as co-
herent as if it were due to v.b.* This will be also—on the
garden side—all the caresses of my little noodle of a son who
never stopped kissing me (is this French?) yesterday.

And so much for M. Teste.

. . . With my wife, that same yesterday, I made a visit to
Raoul Pugno, a country neighbor and mayor of the place.
I talk to you about him since you are a pianist. . . . And then
there is a problem.

A droll and profound problem, these virtuosos who,
according to all the musicians, all the ears not yet asinine,
are, in short, artists, producers of silent music, exegetes
capable of radically transforming a page and who, however,
and nevertheless, have prodigiously, almost all, something of
the *mulatto*. I don't see them white. They are never very subtle.

And all the same, someone would ask me, a priori, what
he must think of one who derives a really living being from
a certain sonata, concerto, or prelude—or who reconstitutes
the best of these deliberate stops—I would call for a singular
intelligence—a reader of bad faith and of excellent will—and
a man, therefore, several times stronger than the work itself
requires.

* Adolphe Van Beyer, who in 1900 publsihed in collaboration
with Paul Léautaud, *Les Poètes d'aujourd'hui* (Éditions du Mercure de
France). Valéry was included but not Gide.

Moreover, *he* is charming in his great belly, and his furnishings, brought back from his concert travels, are indeed worth all the admiration he desires with good fortune that one has for them.

You must agree, I put my thumbs into it. True artists are like drunkards; inspiration is all; lucidity is its negation. Art in full light is a pure fiction. The little one has seen of it is only a laboratory test, not to be thought of to invest his capital.

I received a small volume from Ghéon. And since this peculiar poetry did not leave me indifferent, I am very much embarrassed for my response. One feels at once that his "temperament" is too much that of a poet to *execute* verses; it is the libretto of a nervous system. It is difficult to say, but I would like to make him understand that *this* interests me.

And myself, here I am again at the end of a heavy note-book. I am going to buy another, just as one renews the canary's cage. I would like very much to know what you do and in what sense you do it, but I shall not ask you to write it for me until you have made me guess it.

Your P.V.

[Valéry to Gide]

Wednesday [Paris, March 19, 1908]

Dear André,

I am sending this to Santa Margherita. Between this card and the other, I underwent a crisis of the hardest kind—twenty-four hours—entirely *intellectual*. I am destroyed by it. This time I had the punishment of all the devils to get rid of myself. I am done in. Imagine what it is to find, in the midst of work, two or three ideas, the most cherished, the most *original*, the most central—almost discovered by someone lse—largely utilized. And it is not a matter here of a *theme*, or a literary detail, but of capital. When one has reduced everything towards that, trimmed his being and his possibilities as I have done—to feel oneself outdistanced as in oneself and in its deepest depth—nothing is harder. So beaten that I talked about it to my wife.

And now, I am getting along nicely with the ideal adversary and my illness. . . . I won't tell you a word more about it.

Genoa and its people are marvelous. And those narrow streets between eight floors, whence through the grilled windows filthy brats shower the stranger with their lice, packed in very small papers. What peculiar churches! I thank you for the pineapple, which is not yet here. Instead of the cinema, *in my time* there were: marionnettes, and a prodigious theater for drama, like that of the Gobelins, but at Genoa. Have you gone up to the highest fort and to the lighthouse admirable for its proportions? That was something to do.

Your P.V.

[Valéry to Gide]

Wednesday [Paris, July] 15 [1908]

My dear André,

Degas returned the photographs to me, in these terms: "Many thanks to Gide and Piot for having sent me these photographs. Tell Piot that I envy him. If I were younger I would hasten to put myself under his cutting, I would make myself his student. Ah! what an admirable craft is fresco! It is that, which made the ancients such strong men since it prohibited the *messing about*, which ruins us, necessarily (seeing that it is obligatory for oil)."

And he congratulates you for having ordered this work

Such are, approximately, his words. Approximatel
because I retain poorly and because for him the tone i
three quarters of the song.

I dined several times at his house in recent days, whicl
didn't fail to be painful at times; he has become much olde
(less than this winter, however) and conversation is at time:
difficult.

At one of these meals we were talking literature. He
didn't know Rimbaud. I was amused to repeat to him a few
lines of the *Bateau ivre*. His expression was a mixture, both
comic and willed, of despair and *blague*.

But me! Just imagine, my friend, that at the same time
that I was reeling off my *Bateau*, I found all that more and
more stupid. And not me—the boat! I had not again seen
nor chewed over these verses for many years. Here it all is
reappearing at the entrance to the port of the mind and I find
it...useless.

Would Mallarmé have been right? But the *Illuminations*
remain, I think. Would it be a child's *bateau*? Is it he, is it I.
Say *me* if it is you.

I have been very ill this summer. Sick as a dog, from
the stomach. Horribly *foutu*. A bit better now but by a
killing discipline and, no doubt, for only a moment of
respite.

Read by chance some Michelet, *The Revolution*. The
literary indignation is to be declaimed in some popular
university and not a word that is worthy of being *reflected* on,
not a sentence that might lose its shirt and sleep in the mental
bed of an honest man. Those machines have never been
shaken up in the intellect (which might have dissolved and
unglued them), but stammered for the public surface.

What are you doing? I am sending this to Cuverville. received from my friend Féline a curious little letter from Azemmour. I deduce from it that the government lied very naïvely in this affair, which was *a war operation*.

Your American pens are *des cochoncetés*.

Yours, without further words, P.V.

Gide to Valéry]

[May 31, 1912]

Dear friend,

You are taking it on yourself, aren't you, to send to Gaston Gallimard, 79, rue Saint-Lazare, your poetry— *La Soirée avec Teste, La Méthode de Léonard*, the divers fragments from that period—in short, everything that should go into this first volume of your work.

You will decide if it is advisable to include the article (December '96) on *Une Victoire méthodique* (*La Conquête allemande*) (and my advice is: YES) of which I found the manuscript along with the first proofs and sketches for *Monsieur Teste*. As for the manuscript of your poems, I guarded it so jealously that in the hurly-burly of leaving for Cuverville, I can no longer lay my hands on it. But you have a carbon copy, haven't you?

Your A.G.

[Valéry to Gide]

[July 1912]

Dear André,

I am late. But what can I do? I have ten letters in suspense, and things from Havas; I don't speak of works in hand, essentially interruptible. My overloaded brain is breaking down.

And the worst, as an obvious sequence of emotions, m
chest hurts, and an annoying shortness of breath, rathe
anguishing, continual.

. . . .

The military article: Féline is now publishing his book i
hot haste, in view of utilitarian ends; career, return t
Morocco. I believe that meanwhile he has spoiled the chapte
that I saw published in a review. And there is no way t
understand one another by correspondence.

As for me, that is to say, in the collection or herbarium o
dried-up things, I dream of it, scratch in the drawers, an
disgusted—and all to the good—for if I regretted, what an
increase, O Lord! Up to now I don't see this volume: not
its form, nor its substance, nor its necessity.

Then, to appear two minutes after Mallarmé, this is in
three or four diverse ways frightening. Is it necessary to
mount the stage which, after all and in truth, is not mine?
To see the articles from the *Mercure* or the *Phalanges*, relive
without desire, endorse the sonnets of a former self? Is not
my domain, since that time, this table, the kitchen table
where I have suffered so much and not generally "for Art?"

To publish what I have done, is it not to consecrate the
abandon and the catastrophe of that for which I had abandoned what I have made?

Often, in my mind, as if issuing instantaneously from
pain, I have left you a bundle of all my papers, and I have
foutu le camp au diable, having again become alone and
unfettered.

You see (in parenthesis) the people who talk about
utilizing their suffering; they are simply people who haven't
suffered enough. And the martyrs who did not give in, the

onstancy of martyrs proves above all that the hangmen
lacked imagination.

One is endowed for suffering as one is endowed for
music. Everybody hears, but there is only a small nucleus
who have a stomach-ache from it.

"However that may be," I number these *sacrés* poems
that make very few verses. I have another idea: to make a
volume very uneven—prose, verses quite mixed—like a
notebook of very artificial works, without deciding to be
more specially a poet than something else.

Then, if time were willing, I could tinker with *Monsieur
Teste*: (1) *La Soirée*, (2) the ex-beginning of *Agathe*, which
would make *the interior* of Monsieur Teste's night, (3) a little
tour with Monsieur Teste, of which I have the beginning,
and someone would make his belly with snippets from my
notes.

After all, a book entirely of verse is boring. It seems to me
that Nerval made this mixture, and for the very "little"
poets, it is an advantageous mixture.

Your gaunt old P.V.

[Valéry to Gide]

Sunday [Paris, July 21, 1912]

My dear André,

I was expecting to see you these days and precisely
yesterday. I was having the nostal-gide, and by way of a
letter from your wife, communicated by Dr. Mesnil, I knew
that you were in the air.

Since you always do me good I was awaiting you. In the
end, so much the worse.

Now, tell me: I really regret not to be able to go to
Orsay. I should have done it quite willingly if the business

had permitted, but on Monday we have the general assembl
of the Agence Havas, and morning and evening there
nothing but debates, telephoning, etc. Moreover, I have th
impression of having written a very brief note to Ghéon
besides, I was unaware at the moment of the accident t
which your wife made an allusion.

So, do you think he would accept coming to breakfas
with me, here, alone, in a few days? I don't dare propose it t
him without your advice. . . .

As for me, I sleep off my anxieties and ambitions. Slee
and the stomach or insides, always difficult. Fatigue tha
I cannot manage to liquidate after so many months. Brair
confused, vapors always stinking, never wide-awake, neve
quite asleep. I drove my wife to Mesnil by auto. She held u
well under this rather bumpy ride. I have no bad news or
rather no news, since she doesn't speak of her health to me.

As for the Book . . . my hesitation exists. A very simple
mixture of disinterest, pride, fatigue, even to dream of
proofs, of this inborn contempt in me for my fundamental
incompleteness, and in the end, of molecular demolition.

At a certain period, I began to live on the footing of a
hundred thousand days per year. That could not succeed.
Then came the Harpies and the Chinese torture. Between
waking, which destroyed my health, and the morning after
which, in three or four ways preoccupies me terribly, *I am*.

If I have not absolutely, and beginning with your first
words, refused to go into print, is it *not* in consideration of
precisely *that* tomorrow? I may find myself, at that moment,
in a very embarrassing situation, and I say to myself, despite
all, that perhaps a published book, then, would serve me
somewhat. But then what? And here is another question.
It seems to me that I would prefer to publish my verse in a

pretty edition and I see how it could be realized, in what printer's house, and in a certain form. I am disposed to pay the cost, the *Nouvelle Revue française* having given me its mark as publisher, in case I did not wish to publish elsewhere than at home.

Then it would be the debutant's *plaquette*.

There would remain enough to make a book of prose, *format et gueule ordinaires* in your series.

I am going to write to Gallimard and talk about all this with him. I have talked to Pierre Louÿs about this project, since the verses have been dedicated to him for twenty years. He has approved, and suggested to me a good title for the prose and verse volume: *Mélanges*. What do you say? But any other plan suppresses this title.

Speaking of Pierre Louÿs, you know that there is a subscription for the Heredia monument. I feel obliged to go with my *petit louis*. If your heart yells in you, in passing by Leclerc's* house for me, I shall contribute for you, but you are free (more than I).

I am writing to you on what I find at hand: in the midst of inextricable bits of paper where I never manage to find myself. It is an analysis of surprise and waiting, which I should like to liquidate, and I am bursting and yawning.

A thousand things to the Drouins, if you have them. I am absurd with Drouin. Ten times on the point of going to see him, ten times stopped.

Tell your wife all the affection of the poor monsieur who came, on a certain evening to her house, as others rush into a church.

Your P.V.

* No doubt the architect Charles-Alfred Leclerc (Prix de Rome, 1863), who erected numerous monuments.

[Valéry to Gide]

Sunday [July 1914]

My dear André,

I have no time, and yet I must write to you again. Firs
to tell you to read the Bourget, which is about to appear
Le Démon de Midi.

I have read, by chance, as I read things like this *book*. An
despite all the possible contempt for the miserable author
the impurity, the intellectual bric-a-brac, where the medica
the theological, the Balzacian compose a salad, despite th
ever-present shame, nevertheless, this is his best book. Th
one, then, where he appears in all his naïveté.

There are several phrases that have *tone*, believe me. I sti
admire in Bourget the comic procedure that consists in
making a sententious maxim with the first incoherence a
hand. As many arbitrary events as judgments.

But in the end, read him. I tell you this. I am sure that
you will be amused in three or four ways.

This has no connection with the *Caves*. But it appears
at the same time.

The hero is of the Baraglioul family, etc.* I await you
after the reading.

Ma, Signore, come si può far romanzi? [But, Monsieur
how can novels be made?]

Let us go on to *drama*.

Another thing about which I am embarrassed to have an
opinion.

That is to say that I am astonished that such things are
done? Sit down at the table to draw tears? To milk? Whom?
Some...? That is to say the c—— part of each one.

* The principal character of *Le Démon de Midi* has traits in common
with Julius de Baraglioul of [Gide's] *Les Caves du Vatican*.

Poe wanted to bring women to child-bed by the terror of plays that he imagined.

This is the Grand-Guignol. But there is no midwife. And then, since it is *foreseen*. . . .

. . . .

I have read Rivière's first piece on Rimbaud. I am very sorry for Rivière, whom I esteem highly. This is worth nothing. It is made of insignificant exaggerations.

Precisely, I have just this week clarified a little problem which intrigued me.

I managed to convince myself that the Mallarmé of 186– and the Rimbaud of '69–'70 differed very little. There was a moment of crossing. And some others more obscure were there.

This may be explained by the *epoch*. If one is willing to forget that these encounters *on the contrary* define the epoch!

I saw at Bonniot's some ancient poems, very young, of which the reflections, the pieces, are found in *Le Guignon*, *Le Mendiant*, etc., under a thousand retouchings.

Now, the enraged verse line of Rimbaud was sometimes written by Mallarmé. There is a sonnet that is perhaps the prototype of the famous sonnet *Blasphèmes* (the spermatozoid, etc.), which (if Mallarmé had confessed it) would have placed him between Rimbaud and . . . Richepin.

And also the ways of feeling: a complete *revolté* quite surprising in relation to Mallarmé whom we know, but mixed with the admirer of Banville. A revolter who finally gave to his revolt so much disproportion and depth, a revolt so penetrating, so molecular that it ended in the universal smile that we knew.

Or again: unable to destroy it, he created a kind of "world."

Detail: in a rather mediocre piece, this hemistich: *feet that would calm the sea* (beautifully repeated in *Hérodiade*).*

Your too long P.V.

[Valéry to Gide]

La Preste, Wednesday [July 22, 1914]

My dear André,

Where to begin? You see where we are. It is a blind alley of rocks, the bottom of the Tech, this bottom at 1,100 meters, the high points at 1,500 and 1,600, green or greenish. Spain begins on the crests. The establishment is forced between the rocks and makes beneath itself its sulfurous waters.

A great terrace where the urinary wander, almost all the old men of the regions of the Aude and the Pyrénées-Orientales.

Every evening a storm.

My wife made a journey extraordinarily borne. Imagine that we left on the fourteenth, in the evening, in a railway car where the thermometer marked 38 degrees. At Montpellier, Paule and Agathe were lodged in the old ruin on Urbain-V. I have again seen this apartment. The others were in my brother's house. Montpellier gave me pleasure. I would willingly have remained.

There I talked for a long time with Jeanbrau.† He is a curious mind, very political, a calculator, I believe. Finally,

---

* Les lions, de ma robe écartent l'indolence
  Et regardent mes pieds qui calmeraient la mer.

  [The lions lift aside the indolence of my robe
  And look upon my feet that would calm the sea.]

† Mme Valéry's physician, a professor at the University of Montpellier.

smell someone. Among other things we have envisaged his real death of Montpellier under the appearances of a university. For him (and it is true), there is nothing to be done south of Bordeaux. The winter being too beautiful, the summer too hot, consequently: he finds no students to help him, even in the easy works of bibliography.

Palavas.—I took two old baths, as of long ago, but with the children.

Cette—lamentable. Three boats, no crowds with absinthe at the cafés along the canal. Always beautiful and always more beautiful, the cemetery with pink laurels and cypress.

From Montpellier here, a killing journey, changing three or four times with women, children, and packages; heat and dust.

The valley after Arles-sur-Tech has no interest. But Prats-de-Mollo was charming—the festival, the dances, the evening—immense trees and small places filled. The auto from La Preste carried away my people and others. After various scenes, I stayed there, awaiting the return of this carriage. Night fell. I spent an hour sitting on a bench.

Here I am not very well. I feel even quite tired. I give myself up. Nothing speaks to me. I am of a punctured indifference. The increasing impression of surviving is unbearable. It seems to me that I *am* only at the surface. And it would be idle for me to think, to say the most profound things (which doesn't happen), that I would have the sensation of dead members, of words asleep, of things that someone agitates without being there.

I have always been too present or too absent. But the balance leans and the statistic is altered.

As for my wife, she is scrupulously attached to prescriptions. The Jeanbrau suggestion has made her do unheard-of things for herself. At Montpellier, she descended and mounted the stairs. Here, she descends and goes up again between bedroom, baths, and the refreshment buffet. This morning, she was rather tired of these gymnastics. The doctor here pretends naturally that these waters will do her immense good.

The fact is that they have already singularly mobilized her. To go to Mesnil, come back, go to mass—this was a story—and here it is on the frontier of Spain!

Your P.V.

[Valéry to Gide]

La Preste, July 29, 1914

Dear André,

We live here in anguish, without recent news. The fifty-odd bathers hurl themselves on the postman at 2 o'clock to have *La Dépêche*. And that is that for twenty-four hours.

I am very uneasy, otherwise I would observe with curiosity this microcosm, this colony lost as if in the sea, caught in the rocks. I am very worried—I don't know what to do—and moreover I am not very well here: fog, cold fog every day. I haven't seen the sun.

I left Paris without my military papers. In case of mobilization, I don't know how to manage in order to join up. I will give myself over to the police, who might perhaps know where to send me. But the point that distresses me if everything cracks is my family. I cannot see them returning to Paris in the confusion of troop trains. Moreover, I prefer that they do not go to Paris, where anything might happen. But how are they to manage? I will leave with them the little money I have. And then?

These are my spiritual exercises. My wife is fairly well. Some days very well. Until now no *tangible* effects of the

…vaters! Agathe is very well. Claude only half. Paule, this-
way, that-way. These times are overwhelming. . . .

Your P.V.

Valéry to Gide]

June 14, 1917

My dear André,

My states of mind are stupidly almost those that I had
foreseen.* You know them better than I and have known
them for a considerable time. And you know that *being*
responds to eulogies by surliness (a sentiment that eulogy
addresses to someone who was yesterday), to silences or
almost silences by the irritation of being irritated. To the
whole—alas!—by the fatal increase of nervousness. I recognize that I have but one very pure diversion. It is the people
who don't understand, and who tell me so with a frankness
such that I want to do what one must not do: eat the morsel.

. . . Lie! . . .

But know . . .†

Your letter did me great good, a while ago, and in this
way: you would not believe to what point my work has
been done with the precise, personal idea, always present,
of a few recipients. Three or four imaginary hearers have
been the instruments of my work.

And you may well think that I have chosen only the
good and the better (as they say at Cette) for these essential
roles.

(I don't say that a few lines may not have been entrusted
to secondary actors.)

* *La Jeune Parque* had just been published by Gaston Gallimard,
Éditions de la N. R. F. It is dedicated to André Gide.
† Cf. *La Jeune Parque.*

Pierre did his part and you yours and I mine; and something more.

Here is a curious confidence. To clarify it again, imagine the immense duration that separates 1892 from 1913 to 1917, and what was needed for me to build the bridge of reeducations and peculiar solutions. I add (without much connection with what I am adding it to) that I found afterwards in the finished poem a certain air of autobiography ("intellectual," is understood) and set aside the piece on La Primavera, which was improvised in great part towards the end.

I am quite aware that I have lengthened and disproportioned the apostrophe to the serpent only from the need to speak, myself. . . .

The technical history of this fragment is, moreover, among the most curious. It is also a shortened version of the history of the whole poem, which is summarized by this strange law: an artificial fabrication, which has taken on a sort of natural development.

This would take me too far. These remarks however are my little gain. . . .

I am also very much aware of Larbaud's fragment. Indirect evidence is the most precious. I regret that he has not communicated a bit more of the Spanish version—*Deslizate, barco funebre*—which is a great deal more beautiful than the French.

I was waiting—we are still waiting—each day a word from you inviting yourself to lunch or dinner. But even your letter of today says nothing about it. Notify. We are seeing each other Saturday at half-past twelve *chez* Georges-ville.*

* At the salon of Mme Lucien Muhlfeld, who lived in the rue Georges-ville, Paris, near the rue de Villejust [now rue Paul-Valéry].

I am beginning to find this street very close to mine. The last breakfast! I was dreading it. All has happened as it was written.

I was invited to come back Tuesday afternoon to make the acquaintance of Edmond Jaloux. And this Tuesday engendered next Saturday which engendered. ... *Zut.*

I did not send to Ruyters, for lack of address.

As for Suarès, this is very grave. I take my head in both hands. Before doing anything, it is absolutely necessary that I confer with you.

Henri de Régnier wrote me the classic word: "I received. Thanks, I shall read with pleasure..."

He was wrong, I fear. ... But after all, this is perhaps ... a restitution.

Until Saturday,

Your P.V.

[Valéry to Gide]

Cuverville [July 27, 1917]

Dear André,

I have just gone barefoot to make my devotions to the Hêtre Supreme.*

It would well deserve—this tree that attenuates somewhat the mystery of the feminine for the names of trees in Latin— it would deserve that I add a few verses to the little ode. But those lines have not yet come. I do not call them nor rebuff them.

Moreover, I am quite convinced of the kindness of Monsieur Ingres' advice: "Copy ancient engravings, and

* One of the most beautiful plane trees on the Gide property at Cuverville. Valéry wrote the poem "Pour Votre Hêtre 'Suprême'," which he dedicated to Mme Gide.

draw very often *from memory*." To work from nature is
thing generally misunderstood. That is how realism came in
It confused two moments of the artistic act. The work *fro*
the life is necessary, but it is not enough. It is completel
incapable of making up for the personal mastery; and th
latter, from inventing it all.

I limit myself then, at the foot of the Hêtre, to looking a
it, to feeling it with the mind without trying to make i
speak.

It will speak by itself, far from here, one day when it wil
have found in my substance a territory, an air, a sun non-
present, less present, and more actual.

I am not yet used to your departure, which arrived before
the maturity of our reunion.

I remain vague in a brain where nothing ends. I don't
know even whether we should have talked any *more*? Me,
at least. I am completely without strength these days. So I
have begun this letter with the intention of telling you a lot
of things . . . and I am about to make of it a perfectly useless
bit of writing. It seemed to me that I ought to talk to you
about what you have read to me.*

But it is strange; I cannot think about it clearly yet,
without your presence, and I would even say outside the
place where I have heard it read by you.

Besides, it is a piece of writing of such a kind that the
immediate impression (I gave it to you) is certainly the good
one; since the genre itself is to express these things which,
either by their delicate nature, or by their relation to memory,
sunt ut sunt aut non sunt.†

* The first pages of *Si le Grain ne meurt*, which was published in
1920.

† Are as they are or are not.

The portrait of others has all the more resemblance when he first glance makes us cry out the resemblance. There is no use seeking the art afterwards. It is much too late.

Don't deduce from it, not exaggeratedly, that I advise you to file and use somewhat more those signal passages where the art is still responsive. My quite paradoxical opinion would be to conserve them in an expurgated publication, and to weaken them in a future *complete* edition.

Note. The word *resemblance* inserted above does not signify, here, from you to You (that would have no meaning for the unknown reader), but resemblance and probability of resemblance of You—to him—to the Man.

One must not hide from himself that the reader with an honest heart laid bare (Poe again, taken up by Baudelaire) must be honestly dulled. This is someone whose fixed idea is that one is hiding something from him again. Whatever one *says*, the confession seems to him incomplete.

That is why the virtuoso pieces are not without danger here. To spin words to one's confessor is grave: it is enough to make him forget to absolve you. He imagines in his penitence a composure incompatible with sincerity: a purely stupid idea, but an idea that really comes to people.

You see, I am talking to you stupidly and theoretically about the notebooks in which you wanted, no doubt, to be able to write: "This is my flesh, this is my blood."

But I cannot *yet*, cannot *today*, cannot *in writing*, say something useful and of more importance about them.

In me—this is a peculiar trait of my person—"objective" remarks easily precede the others. I am quite aware that further developments will arise. You are posing an enormous question: "Where does literature begin? Where does it end?" I won't go into that today. I see only that this work

will necessarily be the key to all your work; someone wil
search through it, someone will always find the explanation
of what you have written. You must not lose sight of this
point. In a certain sense, you are doing here all that you have
done already and all that you will ever be able to do. This is a
book which *will have written* your other books. . . .

But (I am repeating myself), all that I am saying today is
idiotic, foolish. Marcel is sleeping and I want to do like him.

The cannons are more formidable, endless, rolling up
waves nearer and heavier.

Jeannie with Mme Gide and the children are at Le Havre.
The echoes of your recital come back to me.* Claude, red or
pale, seizing what he can of his father's strangeness. What is
he thinking?

Jeannie has again repeated to me how much you have
stirred your world, the prestigious performer of my poems.
I regret my private audition, but I don't regret having
absented myself from the seance.

I would like now to thank you for so many things. And
yet, to a certain degree of intimacy, I don't like the words.
I find that they diminish that degree itself. Don't say a word,
then.

When shall I see you? You don't know. Rue de Villejust
at your return, would you say?

Your P.V.

[Valéry to Gide]

Tuesday [February 5, 1929]

My dear André,

Jeannie having given me your letter from Algiers to read,
ten days ago, it seemed to me that the delicacy of the debate

---

* Gide, before his departure, had read aloud *L'Aurore*, a recently
written poem of Valéry.

and the exquisite knowledge that it requires of You and Me, from antiquity to now, authorized me to let it go. As I was about to write to you, heavy anxieties concerning health came up. All the young are sick, including Claude and the complications due to his military condition. *Me*, still very poorly recovered, obliged to take part, etc. All this is still going on; but, finally, one must find the quarter of an hour to brighten oneself up.

Jeannie and I found ourselves in accord concerning the little anecdote-recital that you related in the *Nouvelle Revue Française*. Each of us has read it, and each by chance. But the same reaction, or almost, in each one.

Yet, she—it is the *fact* that touched her; with me, it is the *principle*.

The *fact*—this is the little shock—which is translated or substituted for the following question: must one publish, withold, expose, underline, a friend's lapse; draw public argument from an accident, and note a word that escapes? This is fair in war. No doubt. Is it then fair in peace? (The friend in question being, moreover, fairly surrounded with spies and machine guns.)

This is what must have surprised Jeannie, annoyingly.

As for the *principle*... (I do as everybody else does: I elevate my temperament to the dignity of principle...).

My temperament—principle consists in a profound horror for the confusion of the *As for Self* and the *As for All*.

This sensibility became extreme in so far as I was becoming a public man. Between my name and *me*, I make an abyssal distinction. Between the public and me, that is to say, between the unknown in bulk, the unknown Bloc and the very particular case that is the Self, I find it necessary to interpose "form," the demonstration, the will to objectivity —all that sends the others back to themselves. The *other* have a right to it, since we print—and our duty is to give them this elaborated substance utilizable in its *generality* as well as to refuse the rest.

But friendship is something quite particular. To the point that, having two friends or three makes two or three *institutions incomparable* one to the other. But who have this in common: the friend has a right to our stupidities, to our escapades, to our weaknesses, etc.

(It is not that *this* may be more *true* than *that*. The common error is to believe that a man who *gives in* is more *true* (or more sincere, as one says rather stupidly) than a man who *holds on*. It is believed that there is a foundation of truth which appears when one abandons himself; that the man in pyjamas is more true than the "monsieur"...)

But the fact is that the friend is *liberty*. Sensation of safety and delicious repose, or of vitality exchanged, etc.

And then—you see the rest.

If you give away to unknown persons what I give to you, known, you go outside your definition, you are no longer you, you are a hindrance. I want to talk to you, but I see at once the hand of the writer, the page of your *Journal*, and the *N.R.F.* with a pink band.

I don't know whether all this will make you understand that even the magnificent things that you have written about me several times over may have at one and the same time delighted and annoyed me... to that strange point that I have rather seen than *read* them, and have found myself incapable of word for word or phrase for phrase. Since however beautiful they might be, it seemed to me that you were speaking an exterior language. And no doubt you were writing for the public; but me, I could not put myself in the skin of Paul Valéry *for all*. Impossible!

And this—of which I do not defend the peculiarity—is in accord with an impossibility of mine still more tiresome. I cannot praise my *intimate* friends except by intimacy itself. Not long since, someone asked me to write about you. I wrote some essays that disgusted me. The time was lacking for me to insist, and also at that moment I was having great troubles in the head!... But even at leisure and free of mind, I know that for me you are almost impossible to treat according to the public and its presence.

What can be done when one distinguishes as essentially as I do the person that I know from the person suggested by the works?

Et cetera.

In short, I cannot "reproach" you (to come back to the origin), except for not feeling what I feel, that is to say, not to judge as *private* what I consider such. I do not believe, at all, that you have failed in friendship *in abstracto*. But in the particular case, you have astonished mine. Just imagine what someone may have drawn from your recital (or what someone has perhaps already drawn).

There. And then, at bottom, I don't hate you at all...!

P.V.

[Valéry to Gide]

In May 1927, Valéry, after the death of his mother, began a letter to Gide who had just then sent his condolences to Valéry. The letter was not finished and it remained in a desk drawer, where it was found by Mme Valéry after her husband's death.

Friday [May 1927]

My good André,

Someone has written about me, for good or bad, thirty or fifty times more words than I have traced myself in all my life. I am lost in all these *Moi* that someone has made for me, and who resemble me as best they can.

But finally you have painted—with the fidelity of an artist of the time of Van Eyck, and of a friend—what you have seen and heard, witness that you are of this bizarre and diverse career. You are a witness that I have never done what I wished (and besides I have always wished very few things; the minimum is part of my tastes). The circumstances have for a long time kept me in the dullest of conditions, and the most favorable for judging everything simply; afterwards they exalted me; but *nothing*, unfortunately, *goes to my head*; and I do not feel the enjoyments that might be thought to inebriate me. You know me well enough to imagine the bottom of my feelings.

When I want to explain to myself all this noise that has risen around me and the astonishing extension of my name (which gives me the effect henceforth of being a foreigner), I find three kinds of causes—of which the first and the most effective is no other than the great misery of our time in the matter of intellectual values. I have profited, no doubt, from the remarkable rarefaction to be observed. When we were 15 years old, how many men of the loftiest greatness were still living and breathing. Today, we are reduced to making a statue of the servant. . . . On the other hand, I have been served by a long absence from Literature, during which I have seen, from rather far away, so many modes and carnival chariots filing off to be acclaimed, to disappear, and even reappear. . . . The disinterested observer could instruct himself in the many causes of fragility.

And finally—a capital thing and my true pride—*I owe to my friends almost all that I am.* They believed in me, who did not believe in myself. They have designed me, modeled despite me a personage worthy of their friendship, of their quality, of their talents. And then they have taught me so much and so many things.

My pride is to have drawn this great and inestimable interest, which they brought to me.

The next time you write about me, old friend, you must not forget this, nor forget yourself. Moreover, I still hope to make for my friends a little temple. But when? I am discouraged by all that separates me from my true work. You put your finger on the wound, at the end of your article. In truth, I am devoured alive—and I feel my ideas crunching beneath the inevitable tooth of pressing things. I was a hundred thousand times more free at the period when I was not so. I would cross the avenue, I was doing my duty; I passed it again, and found myself again, just as I had left me, between my notebook and my thought. . . . But now you no longer see me. It is because I no longer see myself. I arise between five and six. I find a confused mass of "necessary" things, of promised and claimable foolishness, and I work without stopping, against these works of boredom and command. At eight o'clock, the cursed mailman. The mail of a prime minister, but with no desk, no secretaries. If I had begun to get excited about my work, this shock of letters would stun me, pulverize my mind. The visits begin at 10 o'clock. Until 1 o'clock, I must receive, talk, talk, talk. By lunch time I am dead. One must run, afterwards, since one must "live"—and I fly from publishers to libraries, etc.

At this point I am *finished*, and it matters little whether I go into society. I am no longer good for anything but that, towards evening.

Lectures serve to make me run away, to exchange one fatigue for another. I would have liked, by the way, to see you on my return from Germany. Odd impression . . . but I must leave you, time is pulling me by the arm.

Thanks, my old André. And this little word about my mother—it is discreet, perfect—two lines in depth, which pierce me to the soul.

In Marcel Prévosts's Time

FROM 1892 until about 1898, I rarely missed paying Heredia a visit on Saturdays in his large sunny apartment on the fourth floor at the corner of rue Balzac and rue Lord Byron. The poets, and those on the same footing, were shown into the master's study; the ladies went to the drawing room.

There you found (in the poet's camp) a more or less intimate mixture of dolts and talents, bores and wits, marathon talkers and mutes, the diverse types of bumptiousness, acerbity, and good nature brought together by any gathering of literary men. Heredia, affable and stuttering, passed out cigars, their quality corresponding to the respect he had for the talent of the guest. On his table were quill pens (those he would use to inscribe with a flourish of violet ink the two vast strokes of his signature), 'presentation copies,' periodicals, and under this pile, no doubt a sonnet slumbering in gestation. He went from one person to another, from the known to the unknown, from the old to the young. Those who were published by Lemerre and those published by Bailly—graying Parnassians and Symbolists budding or already full blown—argued about free verse and regular verse, with passion, with scorn, and with smiles of three or four kinds. Blunt pronouncements provoked incredible subtleties in return. It was hard not to feel a kind of literary nausea among all the smoke and all the talk. About poetry, only the master of the house occasionally expressed the views and counsel of a craftsman—about a craft even then in dispute, and one which would soon rejoin the crafts of manuscript illumination and stained glass window painting. ... On certain days I had the impression, valuable to me, that Heredia had provided me with specific instructions, the result of experiments handed down orally for two or three hundred years of French poetry.

Now and then the door between the study and the salon would open, but close again at once; only a very few of the privileged were allowed to pass from master of the house to mistress, from mistress to master. The common run of poets dared not cross that theshold. Between the opening and closing clicks of the door, we would hear a sudden burst of feminine voices; then the door would close again, having delivered some fashionable young man, or (after 1895) a candidate for the Academy. One day, Paul Deschanel came to pay his respects. He thought to win over the smokers and the talkers by announcing that he was thirsting for literature, that politics bored him. This could not help seeming rather strange coming from a man who had recently given all those strategic luncheons which had made him President of the Chamber of Deputies. ...

One day, the same door let someone pass who, I was told, was a famous novelist, and none other than Marcel Prévost. He was smartly dressed, in a frock coat with silk lapels. Was Paul Hervieu with him? This is something I cannot recall. Was he venturing into the rhymers' precincts out of duty when he would rather have lavished his time and wit on the ladies in the salon? I did not yet know (and learned only much later) that he was a great lover of poetry. That is entirely possible, without one's being a great lover of poets. We are most likely to be insufferable when we are several together. In any case, Marcel Prévost's preference for the ladies' drawing room came from his preference for young ladies. One, still very young, with long hair falling free down her back, and a remarkably delicate profile, seemed to interest him particularly.

I do not believe that anything passed between us. I was the one called *the stern little man* by the poet's daughters. I was passing through a kind of crisis of intellectual rigor and almost of cruelty. My life without a definable future, my situation completely uncertain, my peculiar ideals made of me a curiously contradictory human being. I saw almost no one but writers, yet I wrote nothing and had no wish to write. A swarm of curious notions were at work in my head; I jealously guarded a few of my own truths as if they were state secrets, but I was very talkative between five and seven with the friends in whose company I spent the early evening. The novelist Prévost, like Hervieu and various others, seemed to me men belonging to another universe, living under another 'sky' than mine. Popular success, newspaper articles, the kind of ambition defined by decorations or the Academy seemed to me devised for the living and thinking systems of an inconceivable species. I seemed to myself positively *insular*.

Who could have told me, forty-five years ago, that I also would belong to the Academy, receive decorations, and not only have Prévost as a friend but as one of my sponsors for the Academy?

I was ingenuous enough at that time to wonder that a man who had made a brilliant beginning in the field of the abstract sciences would condescend to write love stories. This shocked me and almost set me against him. Twenty years later, I remember upbraiding Painlevé roundly for abandoning analysis for politics. It was inconceivable to me then that you could put into love whatever depth of mind you wished. As for politics, my opinion has only hardened.

Time passed. Beginning in 1897, a job at the War Ministry put me out of touch with humanity in general, and the rue Balzac in particular; then came the Dreyfus affair with its radically divisive effect.... It was enough to make one rush to the ends of the earth to escape Paris salons and gatherings. Time passed, by which I mean that I did not meet Marcel Prévost again, or rather, did not meet him until after many events, some of which, insignificant in themselves, were to be considerable for me.

In 1917, various accidental circumstances having driven me back to poetry, I published a work which caused rather a stir. Its obscurity put me in the limelight; neither the one nor the other was intentional. But this had something to do with taking me into society, where I wore myself out regularly. Ordinarily I frequented the salon of Mme Muhl-feld, who was my neighbor. Marcel Prévost was often there. He was interested (which always surprised me) in new poetry and the experiments then being made. Sometimes he would ask the mistress of the house: 'What has become of your *rare* ones?' And he revealed so informed an interest in the experimentations then being made in poetry as to seem, in him, rather astonishing. It was at the time when my relations with him became closer. We met occasionally on Sundays in the salon I just mentioned. I was as interested in the sciences as he was in poetry. Our interests caused mutual surprise. But these rather infrequent conversations were not without influence on the subsequent development of that game of chance which it amuses me so much to call *my career*. Mme Muhlfeld was ambitious for her friends. She liked to see them established in high places. Sometimes she scolded me for the verbal liberties I took in regard to honors of all kinds, and particularly the dignity of belonging to the Academy. Yet she had grave doubts about the success that might await me and often discussed these mysterious questions with Prévost. He too was well aware that the known obscurity of my poetry, my natural unconcern, and the feeling I myself had and had expressed of being unassimilable by the Company of the Immortals, were not exactly in my favor. In the same salon I used to see René Boylesve, whom I had known for a long time and who, although he also found me rather obscure, tried amiably to communicate to me an ambition I did not have, while on the other hand he did his best to elucidate the mystery of my merits to some of his colleagues. Finally, in 1924, M. Hanotaux (whom I did not know at all) summoned me to his house and tried with friendly authority to convince me "to think of a chair in the Academy." Henri Bremond and others came to back me up. In short, I had to set sail. Having first aimed at the chair left vacant by the death of the Comte d'Haussonville, I was led by various circumstances to transfer my candidacy to the chair of Anatole France.

At that time, the Academy, image of the nation, was divided into two parties—a right and a left. Their courteous but most real and active antagonism, rarely revealed itself in all its force except on the occasion of elections. I hope I will not hurt anyone by saying that most of the writers belonged to the faction of the left. Marcel Prévost was the leader of this group, which included Brieux, Boylesve, Barthou, de Flers, Henri de Régnier, Henri Bremond,

Henri-Robert. . . . This faction, necessarily more liberal than the other, was also one which saw no threat to the social structure in literary boldness and even in a certain so-called hermeticism. This was at the time when Paul Bourget, who was the recognized leader (that is, the head) of the other faction, had generously called Gide, Claudel, and me "bad teachers." I would not have liked to be included among the good.

Prévost, therefore, was to play a most important role in my election. At the moment when I was going to withdraw my candidacy, sure of my fate if I persisted in trying for d'Haussonville's chair and furthermore having decided to renounce the Academy forever, Bremond and Barthou independently enjoined me (the word is not too strong) to transfer it to the chair of Anatole France. They informed me that a large academic dinner had been given by Marcel Prévost, and during the dessert all the guests had acclaimed me as their candidate. In this way I knew that Prévost would support me in the fracas, although he had never formally promised his backing. But henceforth I felt as if I were the candidate of his party. I think the outcome pleased him, for I was sufficiently informed of the annoyance my election caused on the opposite side.

It was at our meetings at the Academy that I learned to know Marcel Prévost better, and our more intimate acquaintance revealed in him a kind of intelligence that I prefer because of the balance of mental powers it presupposes.

I knew very well that Prévost had the rigorous preparation in the sciences with the aptitude for mathematics required to pass the examination of the École polytechnique with honors, but I confess that I knew nothing whatever of his taste, I might even say his indulgence for poetry. I will ay outright that *this taste is exceedingly rare*. My experience has shown me that a true predilection for poetry is very uncommon among us, for whom that form of language is felt to be tainted with the ridiculous, or incompatible with serious mindedness, and is generally confused with the oratorical expression of tragedy, with its ingenious rhymes, or sentimental effusions weak in form.

Consequently, I was somewhat astonished to find in Marcel Prévost, engineer and novelist, a completely just sense of what I myself believe to be true poetry—a sense that has nothing to do with culture. Those who possess this noble and exceptional passion of the mind are rarely misled about the quality of poems. I often talked with Marcel Prévost about questions relating to my own poetry and I clearly saw that he had a most discriminating idea of what constituted its essence and perfection. At the same time I learned something else so much in keeping with the other that they have fused: my colleague was "nourished on Greek and Latin," and to a degree that always amazed me. Whatever the defenders of the humanities may say, one can be an excellent engineer and a popular novelist without having read a great deal of Euripides and Virgil. But Prévost had a profound knowledge of these fundamental languages of our culture, and could dazzle the pedants who were always of our company. But yet, all the learning in the world is not enough to give a poetic bent to a mind that would not have invented poetry; it can greatly develop what is there; it cannot create what does not exist. Marcel Prévost felt what he knew and knew what he felt. He was remarkably well versed for an amateur passionately fond of poetry, but *the sensitive are unhappy*. His exquisite taste did not fail to make him as difficult as it is appropriate to be in such matters, and he suffered from the mediocrity or thinness of poetry in two ways, as a love of the Muse and as the editor of a review. He talked to me several times about the problem of finding poems which would not dishonor his review. I had the pleasure of providing him with one or two works that certainly did not lack talent. But it must be said that a concern for providing the readers of a review with a frequent and good selection of good poetry is hard to fulfill today. His was in fact a large and important review which could not venture to print those works I will call experimental, works still unsuited to not very daring readers. And moreover, whether daring or not, the reader should not find in the review, in the guise of poetry, the revivals, repetitions, and empty imitations such as any editorial office receives in countless numbers. Even so, Prévost was indulgence itself. . . .

May I add a reflection which, for all of being ingenuous is nonetheless somewhat captious. *I have spoken of Marcel Prévost and I have not mentioned his novels.* What I have said about him gives the singular impression of being, as it were, the definition of as complete a mind as one could wish, without my having mentioned what is taken to be the most important part of his work. Are there many novelists who could stand up under such a test? I am inclined to doubt it. . . . That one can at will separate from someone's activity what had consumed most of his time and work, and after such a deletion find that he remains a man of undiminished value and rare quality, seems to be a most remarkable outcome for the subject of such an operation. I have always thought that the wealth of a nature consists in its possibilities, while the happy success perhaps crowning an undertaking depends chiefly on circumstances, that is, on chance.

But it is not absurd to imagine that Marcel Prévost's career as a novelist could have been determined, to the detriment of whatever gifts he might have (and he certainly had them) for poetry and geometry, by the "novelistic atmosphere" that existed at the time of the decline of the Naturalist school. He may have been tempted by what was then developing under the influence of Alphonse Daudet and Paul Bourget, even of Maupassant, in reaction to the brutality, the descriptive excesses, and grossly simplified humanity of Zola's imitators. . . .

Finally, it must also be said that the novelist's art exhibits, demands, and develops a particular taste for matters having to do with love.

Graduation Ceremonies at the
Collège de Sète July 15, 1935

YOUR PROFESSOR of philosophy, in a few excellent paragraphs, has reminded us that the simplest, most profound and most general function of our being is to create the future. Not just our minds but our whole being is concerned with what is to be, since it proceeds only by acts, more or less prompt and more or less complex. To breathe, eat, and move are to anticipate. *To see* is *to foresee*. All our sensations and all our feelings, and even our memories and regrets, involve us in what is not yet: to think that something *has been* is to define a future time that necessarily excludes it. In each of us the future is indistinguishable from the act of living itself. A being is alive inasmuch as he will continue to live, if only for an instant; and, on reflection, this signifies that the circumstances surrounding us will not change very much in that next instant. In short, life is no more than the conservation of a future.

Our mind, which is life, opens out before us according to its resources of knowledge, logic, and analogy, the always changing image of the possible. But what we know best and what constitutes the power of that image is what we wish and what we fear. Our momentary future is an invention of our wishes, our needs, our rejections or our dislikes, which we try to adjust to the knowledge we have of our milieu and he larger world around us. The better we know these surroundings, the more our perpetual creation of the future —the inner poetry produced naturally in all men who come into the world—limits itself, confines itself in becoming more precise. That is why this inner activity, which depends on our epoch, our culture, our situation, and our strength, depends so largely on our *age*, as your professor clearly demonstrated a while ago. A man's real age could be measured by the exercise of the *Future-function* of his mind.

In short, we cannot prevent ourselves from foreseeing. Our organism is like a system of mechanisms designed for automatic foresight. Each breath is a hope. *Spiro, spero.* Each living act has its consequences as its only incentive. And our mind is constantly transforming and shaping itself according to what can be, what must or must not be: it desires, draws back, goes ahead; in some way it moves like a bee around the flower of the moment, which Horace advised us to pick: CARPE DIEM.

But here is something quite remarkable: if foreseeing is of our essence, if our action requires it, it is nonetheless essential that we cannot foresee exactly. We must foresee, but this foreseeing must be dubious, and we must know that it is. We cannot imagine ourselves without the idea of a time to come, and we cannot imagine knowing with certainty the train of events in our future and living our life before actually living it, as one reads a musical score before hearing it. The very idea of such foresight is absurd. Can one imagine a man without *hope*, without *hesitation*, without all the combinations of the certain with the uncertain, of hypotheses, doubts and differing probabilities, which make up the greater part of our mental activity?

275

I assure you, dear young men, that I did not foresee, long before you were born, that I would one day return to thi school in the braided garb of a Member of the Institute.

I certainly had no notion of that illustrious State Institu-tion when I climbed this hill on October 2 or 3, 1878, with my hand in my father's; rather anxious but also rather curious about what would come of this great adventure, ready to laugh but not far from tears. I still remember the first sensations of my schoolboy life: the special odor of the new notebooks and the imitation leather satchels, the mystery of new books, stiff and at first almost impenetrable in their armor of glue and cardboard, but soon turned into albums where life is inscribed in the form of blots, strange drawings, notes, check marks and underscorings, even an occasional curse. I am not claiming that books have to be marked up to make them look as if they had lived. I would not for the world fall out with the bibliophiles. But let me say that nothing so touches a writer's heart as to come across an underscored, broken-backed, dog-eared, note-covered copy of one of his works—even if the notes are not complimentary. The true reader, we must admit, respects only the mind.

So I have come back again, *fifty-seven* years after I first came as a schoolboy, and I seem to recognize in myself not only these sensations produced by the beginning of formal study, but the deeper emotions and corresponding reactions of a child confronted with the incidents of the classroom and the schoolyard. As soon as he enters he receives his first lessons in psychology, politics, and sociology, in a milieu that has its own laws, rites, customs, and a curious diversity of hierarchies; one, for instance, that acknowledges a muscular authority and an intellectual authority, values

assigned by the teachers and other values assigned by the
opinions of classmates. They do not always coincide. ...

I remember also my gropings among likes and dislikes in
the midst of so many new faces, which are our first experience in our knowledge of men, and those very private
impressions, which we learn to repress and which govern us
so imperiously. We experience the anxieties of infraction,
the anguish of competition, the torture of unintelligible
problems, of unfathomable texts, of words that refuse to
come to mind, and all the agitation of sensibility caused by
circumstances which are no less powerful for being childish.

Even an inner life creeps (or once did) into the schoolboy
soul by way of a certain punishment which has perhaps
been abolished in the general relaxation of your codes. I will
not conceal from you that I sometimes spent several hours
here with my nose to the wall and my arms crossed. Such a
cure by silence and immobility in a vertical position is
probably no longer in favor, for all good things are disap-
pearing. Yet being stood in a corner had its virtues. What a
lesson it is to be silent! To control the leaping and bounding
born of a young energy, which the mind must reabsorb—
what more immediate notion is there of *duration*. ... And
what better occasion for daydreaming than when contem-
plating the unevenness of the whitewash on a wall!...

Thus, ghost that I am come back to this hill, which is
dear to me because of you and sacred to me because of the
dead, I should find here the mixture of permanence and
change which allows me, as I have said, to foresee to some
extent—enough to be able to act, and not enough to reduce
us to automatons.

But among the things that have profoundly and terribly
changed since my time I find the capital condition of the

life of the young, which is precisely the idea they have ha
of their future.

This leads us back to the philosophy I expressed a whil
ago, but viewed in another way.

What are you doing here, comrades? You are preparin;
for life. But a preparation presupposes a conjecture. Al
teaching implies a certain idea of the future and a certaii
conception of the beings who will live that tomorrow.

And here is where the matter clouds over. Your situation, and I tell you without joy and without sparing you
feelings, is far more difficult than ours ever was. Your personal destinies on the one hand, and the destiny of civilization
on the other, are more puzzling and obscure than they ever
were.

In the past, education led fairly regularly to careers in
which the majority managed to establish themselves. Starting to school was in a way like taking a train that, barring
accidents, took you somewhere. You attended classes, you
passed the examinations, even if you had to repeat them.
You became a notary, a physician, an artilleryman, a lawyer
or government clerk, and an almost certain future was
offered to anyone taking one of these well laid out paths.
In that day, diplomas were worth their weight in gold. You
could depend on the social milieu, which changed very
slowly and tended in an easily foreseeable direction. Then it
was possible to waste a little time at the expense of your
studies: this is not always time lost, for the mind feeds on
everything, even leisure, provided it has the appetite which
I see as its principal virtue.

But now! Never has it been so hard to imagine the future.
We have only to sketch it out for the outline to blur, for
ideas to conflict with one another; we lose our bearings in

he disorder characteristic of our modern world. You are
aware that the most learned and subtle minds can say nothing about it that they are not tempted to retract at once; that
here is not a philosopher, politician, or economist who can
pride himself on assigning an end to this chaos and a final
return to order and stability. This critical situation is the
combined result of the human mind's activity. Within a few
decades we have in fact created and destroyed so many
things at the expense of the past—by refuting it, disorganiz-
ing it, creating new ideas, methods, and institutions—that
the present seems to us a concurrence without precedent or
example, a conflict without resolution between things *that
cannot die* and *things that cannot live*. That is why I have
sometimes made the paradoxical statement that tradition
and progress are the two great enemies of the human race.

Within a few years the world has become unrecognizable
to those who are old enough to have seen it far different.
Think of all the new facts—altogether and prodigiously new
—that have become apparent since the beginning of the
last century.

Wait, let me tell you a little story to emphasize the
thought I am proposing, and which is, in short, the entry of
the human species into a phase of its history where all
prevision—only because it is prevision—becomes a chance
for error, a suspect production of our minds.

Just suppose that the greatest scientists who existed before
the end of the eighteenth century—Archimedes, Newton,
Galileo, and Descartes, for instance—were gathered together
in some place in Hades, and a messenger from earth brings
them a dynamo to be examined at their leisure. They are
told that this apparatus is used by living men to produce
movement, light, and heat. They study it; they turn the

mobile part of the machine. They dismantle it, questionin
and measuring each of the parts. In short, they do all the
can. . . . But electric current is unknown to them, inductio
is unknown; they scarcely know anything other tha
mechanical transformations. "What is the purpose of thes
coils of wire?" they ask. They have to admit their helpless-
ness. Thus, all the knowledge of these human geniuse
assembled before this mysterious object fails to discover it
secret, to guess the new fact discovered by Volta, and those
revealed by Ampère, Œrsted, Faraday, and others. . . .

(Let us not fail to notice here that those great men who
were unable to understand this dynamo fallen from earth
into Hades did exactly what we do when we examine a brain,
weigh it, dissect it, cutting into thin slices and subjecting
those lamellae to histological examination. This natural
transformer remains incomprehensible to us.)

Notice also that in my example of the dynamo I chose
minds of the first magnitude, minds reduced to impotence,
to the radical impossibility of explaining an apparatus whose
workings and use are today familiar to a great many people
and which has become indispensable, moreover, to our
social organization.

Imagine what an effort of adaptation is demanded of a
race so long restricted to the contemplation, explanation,
and use of the same phenomena always immediately
observable!

In short, we have the privilege—or the great misfortune
—of witnessing a profound, rapid, irresistible, and total
transformation of all the conditions of life and human action.
No doubt a certain future is in preparation, but a future we
absolutely cannot imagine. This, no doubt, is the greatest
innovation of all. From what we know we can no longer

educe an image of the future to which we can attach the lightest credence. We see nothing, anywhere on earth, but rials, experiments, plans, and gropings in all orders of life. Russia, Germany, Italy, and the United States are like vast laboratories where experiments of a scale hitherto unknown are being carried out, where an attempt is being made to fashion a new man, or to create a new economy, new customs, new laws, and even new beliefs. Everywhere we see that the action of the creative or furiously destructive mind, multiplying material means of enormous power, has engendered modifications on a worldwide scale in the human world, and these unheard of modifications are imposed without order, without restraint, and above all, without regard for living nature with its slow adaptations and its natural limits. In a word, we can say that man, in departing farther and farther and ever faster from the primitive conditions of his existence, has come to the point that *all he knows*, that is, *all he is capable of* is strongly opposed to *what he is*.

What then do we see at present? What does each of us observe in his own existence, in the difficulties he finds in maintaining it, in the growing uncertainty of tomorrow? Each of us is well aware that conditions are becoming more and more cramped, more and more brutal and unstable—to such a degree that, in the midst of the most powerfully equipped civilization, the richest in usable matter and energy, the most knowing in the organization and distribution of things and ideas, the life of the individual tends to become again as precarious, as restless, as tormented, and as uneasy, as the lives of the remotest of primitive peoples. Do nations not conduct themselves like strangely exclusive and childishly self-centred tribes?

All this makes sharper and more dangerous the existin
contradictions in man's diverse activities; material nature i
more and more compliant; he has profoundly transforme
his notions of time and space, matter and energy. But h
has been able to reconstitute almost nothing in the spiritua
and social order. The modern world, which has prodigiously modified our material lives, has been able to make fo
itself neither laws, nor customs, nor a politics, nor ai
economy that would operate in harmony with these vas
changes, these conquests of power and precision.

The present malaise, then, seems to be a crisis of the mind
a crisis of minds and the things of the mind. Our minds are
permeated with habits that the rapid upheavals of recent
years have disturbed without destroying, and we also bear
the weight of mistakes about the future committed by those
men who preceded us and who perhaps could scarcely have
avoided committing them.

Here is an example that seems very significant to me.

In 1881 Bismarck was at the height of his fame and
authority. He was in fact the arbiter, almost the master of the
political universe. He convoked a congress at Berlin, attended by all the ministers of foreign affairs in Europe. Its
purpose was to settle the fate of Africa and divide up the still
free or disputed territories there. *Bismarck asked nothing for his
own country.* He suggested that France extend her dominion
over Tunisia. He gave the richest morsel, the Congo and
Katanga, to Leopold II, king of the Belgians. It did not occur
to Bismarck that in a very few years Germany would
demand colonies and would embark on a policy of worldwide expansion leading inevitably to war and to the ruin of
all his work.

Whatever his genius and foresight, Bismarck was

unknowingly dominated by a vision of the world formed, and as if solidified, by his education. He saw Europe and the world in the light of the political science and economics he had learned in the first half of the nineteenth century. He was acting as he would have acted in his youth.

But this reflection brings me back, my friends, to the College and you. May I be allowed to imagine for a moment what you are doing? And may I also make some reflections on Education?

What will the minister of education say if I dabble in his affairs? Alumnus Roustan is, to be sure, an old friend of alumnus Valéry. The minister and the academician meet fairly often on those solemn occasions whose solemnity does not prevent them from smiling at each other. And in that smile, dear comrades, I assure you that the memory of this old school has its part. We see each other together again here.

May I then very timidly put forward certain bold views? May I think aloud without risk of shocking either the Rector of the University (who has been kind enough to come from Montpellier for this ceremony), or the Deans, or the Principal of the College, or the Mayor, who took the dangerous initiative of inviting me here to speak?

But no . . . rest assured that I am not going to call for far-reaching reforms in our education system. That would be the opinion of an outsider, an amateur, and we should be wary of those people. One should never listen to any but competent men, those who make mistakes while following all the rules. Here you have Bismarck again.

I will simply say on the delicate question of Education what I think about all current questions. Everything depends, or should depend, on the idea we have of man, the man of

today—or rather the man to be, the man who is in you, m
dear young men, who is growing and forming himself i
you. Where is this idea to be found? If it exists, I confess
do not know about it. Is it the fundamental principle of th
programs in use? Does it constitute the soul of our methods
Is it (if it exists) the guiding light of those who educate ou
professors? This is my wish. This is my hope. But if it is no
so, if (as some warped minds claim) our education shares ou
general uncertainty and dares not consider that its purpose
is to educate men who will be ready to face *what has never
been*—well then, should we not think about the fundamenta
reform I mentioned, discreetly, a while ago?

Let us not forget that the keenest competition is one of
the cruel conditions of the present time. Even in science and
sports, nations are constantly competing for preeminence.
This contest exists also in the education of the young, and it is
beyond doubt that this kind of education will have far-
reaching consequences. In Europe the men of tomorrow
who are now children and adolescents are divided into quite
different groups. In three or four large countries, youth is
subjected to a treatment and a training of character quite
varied as to doctrines but very much alike in the intent to
form men adapted to a specific social structure and to clearly
determined national ends. *The State forms the men it needs.*
I do not think that culture will be the better for this. But we
cannot, it seems to me, fail to observe that our children will
soon be faced with these new men, moulded, trained
according to systematic plans, and constituting populations
uniformly educated and adapted to the economy and
conditions of modern life. I very much fear that intellectual
freedom and the refined productions of culture will suffer
from this regimentation of minds, but this is a considerable

act which I cannot help seeing and which we French would
do well to think about.

Nevertheless, do not imagine that I am in the least
despairing. I know our resources, which we demonstrated
not long ago. I simply wish that we would use them with
more consistency, and not only under the pressure of danger.

I would wish for you, young men, that you be aware of
your own strength. Your education will have produced its
finest fruit if you are able to give to the varied knowledge
taught you, to the writers analyzed for you, a completely
personal value. It is not so much the quantity of learning that
matters as the place you give to it in yourselves. Your business and your interest is to bring all that intellectual matter to
life. A little knowledge and a great deal of mind, a great
deal of mental activity—that is the essential.

And now, look out over the rooftops. You are very
lucky in this school. If you raise your eyes from your books,
they rest on the sea. As for me, I owe much to that prospect
of my first school years here. I also was lucky in having the
view of this sea and this port turned toward the east at the
disposal of my wandering eyes. I sometimes talk about it a
long way from here, in my lectures in far countries, and
fairly often I am asked: What is Sète?

The question annoys me for a moment, but I soon take
myself in hand.

All right, I tell myself, I am going to instruct them in
what is Sète. And I begin a long sort of descriptive poem,
sparing them nothing of what we see and what we love in
our town. I tell them that we inhabit a remarkable island just
barely attached to the continent by two shoals of fine sand.
That on one side we reign over the sea; on the other, over a
salt lake which the Phoenicians probably called THAU, and

that we drink (when we drink water) a water that come from afar, from a spring whose name is incomprehensible no one having explained the mystery of the Issanka; that here we have the consummate art of producing the best wines in the world, by magic; that in all the Mediterranean there are no fishing boats as sturdy, as beautiful as ours; and that nothing anywhere is more graceful than the clusters of horns on our oxen when they are gathered along the quai bordering the old port as far as the breakwater.

I tell them many other things in the style of Herodotus. But you know them as well as I do. You know them, but perhaps you do not think about them often enough and attentively enough. I was like you. I did not see what I saw. But circumstances having kept me far from Sète for many years, I have often observed that when my thought begins to deepen a bit, I always find in the depths of myself an impression that came from Sète. You may well believe that every thought has its home port, and however old an academician I may be, I have only to reflect to recapture some early and decisive moment in the formation of my thought. . . . I do not mean that you need only to reflect in order to grow young again. . . . That would be too good. I say only that if, from event to event and from idea to idea, I go back along the chain of my life, I find it attached by its first link to one of those iron rings driven into the stone of our quais. The other end is in my heart.

Remarks about Myself

FOREWORD

THE TEXT of these "Remarks" brings together without order or system a few jottings and fragments from my notebooks, having to do with many things other than the author himself. Could it be that in these remnants his *moi* most clearly takes shape?

They are no more than moments caught and set down as they came from time to time in the course of some forty years, with the repetitions, the gaps, the fluctuations of mood or of ideas that might be recorded by the meter of any life.

It seems advisable, by way of introduction, to point this out in cautioning the reader against the effect of "unity" that a text might produce were it the consequence, as one would naturally imagine, of a concerted effort constituting a WORK. This is not one.

I do not keep, I have never kept a record of my days. I jot down my ideas. What do I care about my biography? What do my used-up days matter to me? Nothing of the past should be retained but the true wealth, the bounty snatched from time, which increases our power to act and which necessarily loses at the same time its attachment to its source. Language is a good example. Language is outside time. How

287

could we think, how could we talk, if each word recalled the circumstances in which we learned it? Its history would shackle it to the past, which is impotent.

No, I have no fondness for memories, which to me are images already used, a dreary useless waste. Bad memories remain bad, still wounding and confounding us; the good ones are atrocious. Long ago I wrote this verse, which is redolent of that far away time:

> *Nos plus chers souvenirs mordent nos cœurs dans l'ombre...*

The Hades of the Ancients (a true and noble compound of psychological symbols far superior to the monstrous contrivances of our foul Hell) lacks a sufferer, akin to Tantalus and Sisyphus, who would be condemned to re-witness (which is not the same as reliving) the happiest moments of his life. Hades also lacks another miserable creature whose torture would be a memory constantly unfolding to him the tableau of missed opportunities. . . .

No, no! It is no pleasure to retrace in my mind those old paths of my life. I am not one to pursue remembrance of things past! Even less would I approve of those absurd analyses which implant in people the most obscene riddles, supposedly concocted in their mothers' wombs.

*

My memory, moreover, is rather peculiar. It retains only isolated impressions; or, rather, ideas; or, *preferably*, ways of treating the ideas that come to me. These I retain fairly well. I also remember two or three hundred lines of verse, which forced themselves on my memory *by their own authority*. This spontaneous recording in me, *who have never been able to memorize a lesson*, made me suspect some exceptional virtue in the form of these verses. Those I *absorbed* in this way perhaps taught me in consequence something about the *real* conditions to be required of the art of poetry. Most of the theories about it are nothing more than *intellectual views*; the urge to supplant a system currently in fashion, according to the rules of literary politics; or the childish desire for novelty, which has tormented and weakened our arts for at least a hundred years; or even some theoretical notion, which does not reckon with experience, theory having a larger part there than the observation of experience itself. But that a certain structure of speech should act upon the mind's organism, harmonizing and uniting with it, and that such action is desirable, is an independent fact and destroys all theories.

*

My memory! If you asked me on pain of instant death what I did last evening, I probably could not answer.

Besides...I do not like memory, which is often as deceiving when accurate as when treacherous, for what *one has really seen* is ... unusable—when it is not unbearable.

*

A bad memory or, rather, a peculiar memory—selective—irregular in the extreme. It does not retain facts, or scenes, or in general what is of no interest to my own sensibility and my own personal problems.

For example, a "lesson" or a text chosen at random— events which could have happened to someone else, and could appear quite different to each of us. Few childhood memories ... and doubtful ones at that. ... The past, then, is more obliterated for me in its *chronological* and *narratable* development, so it seems to me, than it is for most. My being tends to forget what is nothing more than a picture, and to

retain what can be assimilated so intimately that it is n
longer the past but an element of potential action, a resourc
for the future, and to the least possible extent a *tota
recall*.

(The "Proust phenomenon" shows that, in this respect
beings of my kind are denied a great literary reserve.)

Fundamentally, my *essential self* resists receiving what i
not sufficiently divided up, sorted out for the combination
of its group of inventions. . . . It does not find *its* requirements in the raw recollections called up by chance and place
before it. I react in the same way to landscapes, which are,
after all, *natural accidents*; I sense the arbitrary in their forms.
But on the other hand, I find what I need in the perception,
and then in imagining the *substance* of things: water, rock,
pulp of leaves, fine sand, flesh.

*

I *know* that I have lived through a certain period. But almost
nothing about it comes back to me. It is impossible for me
to reconstruct a single day.

My mind exists only for—the exact opposite. The past
is not at all its climate, and what I feel most acutely about the
past is its *nullity*.

*

Far from evoking the past, my tendency is never to encourage it.

The necessity and the ability to forget. Should we not
blot out what was not strong enough, not stimulating
enough to survive?

*

Another trait (and I think an unusual one) of my character:
vents bore me. People say to me: "What fascinating times!"

And I reply: Events are the foam of things. *It is the sea that interests me.* We fish in the sea, we sail on the sea, we swim in it. . . . But the foam?

Events are "effects." They are products of sensibility, sudden precipitations or simplifications that announce the beginning or the end of some specific duration; and they are either single accidents from which nothing can be drawn, or they are consequences whose principal interest lies in their preparation or in their after effects.

History can record little else than "events." But reduce a man to the facts that are the most striking and the easiest to perceive and define—his birth, his few adventures, his death—and you have lost sight of the texture of his life. Reduce a life to a "summary"! It is just the opposite that might be worth something.

Thus, the "beautiful line" is an event in a poem, but we must admit that it tends to destroy the poem; its value isolates it. It is a flower picked from a plant to ornament the memory. A highly refined taste might disapprove of such beauty—too jealous of its own conspicuous power—might even suggest self-denial when it offers. Such renunciation would require a singular strength of character. . . .

*

I find no unity in my nature. I do not know its "essence." . . . But what is the essence of my nature, and what is my nature itself? I simply mean to say that I know only what I like and what I dislike, and that *only for today.* But in this choice, which my nature has made and imposes on me, I see nothing but a "result of chance." *To be self-aware—is this not to feel that one could be quite different?* To feel that the same body might serve as many characters as circumstances demand,

and the the same ME might confront an infinite number of
combinations, among them, all those automatically formed
by the kaleidoscope of dream? Are we not born of an
encounter, not of two persons but of two potentialities, each
of which is the biological sum of an innumerable quantity
of *others?* Therefore, I am easily prone to consider as
accidents (which are essentially rather foreign to me) my
tastes, dislikes, opinions: all that spontaneous output of
inconsistencies which, nonetheless, makes me what I am in
the eyes of others, and in the end determines my general
behavior. This interior alienation appears forcefully to any
being who suffers; what is more *ours*, more indivisible from
me than my suffering, and yet what is more alien? But this
feeling is usual enough in me.

My decided feeling of a profound difference between
myself and me tends to reduce this *myself* to the capacity of
living a number of different lives, of which I have just
spoken. "Fate" decided the one I have lived. By degrees,
and from incident to incident, and from reaction to reaction,
"fate" makes our life resemble a game played by *what we are
at that instant* against *what happens to us.* I knew a famous
novelist whose custom or method was to consult the cards
for each of his characters, to determine by fortune-telling
their personalities and destiny. Nothing could be more
reasonable and proper.

*

In this way I explain my natural distaste for any opinion on
any subject, once I have thought about it. My own opinion
is the first to declare itself as useless, purely expedient.
Opinion calling itself conviction seems to me a grave
matter, and I am driven to despair of the intelligence of
anyone who bases a strong stand on a foundation of initial

disorder and irregular variability, which is (and even must be) characteristic of the mind. But this is an opinion.

*

It seems to me that no one has ever influenced me directly. More than one has interested me to the highest degree or has taught me, but only as an agent transmitting the kind of knowledge that does not devolve upon the opinion of one man, no matter how superior. Language always reminds me, and rather quickly, that it is language—someone speaking. *Speech* and *someone*, these two constituents of all discourse, are at the outset two objections, which must, on reflection, temper the immediate effect of things said. I can scarcely give more value to remarks than can be granted to a mortal; and, if he fails to endow what he says with a power independent of his own self and of language, he has said very little to me. I have never been able to conceive how anyone can be convinced, converted, swept away, transformed, profoundly changed by eloquence, and moved by it to action. This sort of insensitivity cannot but affect what I say to myself. Furthermore, any rigorous train of reasoning makes me examine the definitions and postulates on which it is based; and there is no metaphysics, however well reasoned, that is not imperiled by such scrutiny.

*

Nevertheless I recognize in myself a certain way of being influenced by others. It might be that another's act or thought so exactly conforms or is so directly opposed to some disposition or preoccupation of my inner self that it is stimulated to react strenuously, as if for reasons of security, against the declared threat. An opinion that strikes me as being too much like my own causes me to doubt mine.

*

All this might lead one to guess that I am no thinker when it comes to History. I am taken for the declared enemy of this kind of occupation. I am an enemy only of its pretensions, its ignorance of its own real value, and of those famous lessons supposedly to be drawn from it. The stupidities and misfortunes propagated by these stimulating images are clearly evident. There is no doubt of that, but who can prove that they even taught anything else?

My intention of studying and clarifying what I call the *true value of History*, isolating its never stated postulates, making up for the lack of unstated definitions, making known the crude mechanism of the Worship of the past—all this will probably never be accomplished. I will say here that *History teaches us only the historians*: if they have style, wit, a talent for the craft of making us believe in "causes" or "laws"—that is, in whatever they have taken here and there from their fellow-historians—that will suit our penchant for order and explanations (for after all their books are made out of books). The writing of History is an art—nothing less, but nothing more.

*

At the age of twenty, I was driven to take upon myself a very serious course of action against "Idols" in general. At first I was obsessed with only one among them, and it made my life intolerable. The power of the absurd is unbelievable. What is more humiliating to the mind than all the harm done by a mere nothing—an image, a mental element doomed to oblivion. Moreover, even the intensity of physical pain does not depend on the vital importance of its cause; a toothache can drive one crazy, and it is nothing in itself.

This crisis set me against my "sensibility" insofar as it worked against the freedom of my mind. I tried, without much success at first, to set off my awareness of my condition against the condition itself, and the observer against the patient.

I became the theater of a strange drama, which I think no one has ever described fully or dispassionately enough. I began to make note of all those traits which, in our inner irritations and torments, our apparent hesitations and re-sumptions, the frenzy and stupor of our phases of anxiety, showed some resemblance to physical phenomena, suggested certain laws, and allowed me to consider as disturbances or defects of a *local* function all that our simplicity attributes to self-engendered forces, or to fate, or to contrary impulses, as when a dreamer transforms a pillow into a monster, or a cold uncovered leg into a voyage to the North Pole. All our emotional storms dissipate our energies enormously and are accompanied by an extreme confusion of values and func-tions, with the production of pictures and scenarios in-definitely renewed and recharged with violence or with resources of alternate gentleness and bitterness, and perhaps they result from incidents as trivial as a poorly insulated wire in an electrical apparatus. Such a trifle can cause wild disorder in the functioning of a whole machinery, or it may set fire to a house.

This led me to outlaw all Idols. I sacrificed them all to the one that had to be created to subjugate the others, *the Idol of the Intellect.* My *Monsieur Teste* was its high priest.

*

HOMO QUASI NOVUS

Who are you? "I am what I can do," I say to myself.

*

Forcing one's thought so far toward an awareness of its own naïve, natural mechanism (and of the way of reacting peculiar to *itself* equals *Monsieur So-and-So*) that anyone's opinion, even one's own, no longer counts except as a document on the speaker.

*

I don't like writing.

I read but little for the sake of reading.

As for literature, I rarely look at anything but form and composition; the rest never seems "serious" to me—that is, worth absorbing.

Descriptions, in particular, are useless (always excepting the search for form, which they sometimes exact of their authors).

As for "psychology," what does it have to say? That is a problem it has never resolved—nor even stated, as for that.

*

What do you like then?

I like to believe that I see things no one has seen in the things that everybody sees. . . .

*

I try to hold my opinions as opinions—that is, to consider *at the first possible moment* what comes to my mind, on any subject, as a production or a formation which, coming *from me* or taking place *in me*, is not to be trusted.

I respond, therefore, to my original response, etc. . . . In this there is a certain contempt for the mind, considered as purely spontaneous.

*

Apologia.

All that I am reproached with (*nihilism* and other stupidities of the *ism* kind, *antihistoricism*) amounts to blaming a man for using the mind he has—or blaming me for insisting on its being used (*obscurantism*). The various beliefs are incompatible with the legitimate exercise of the mind—and its demands—or *simply with the recognition of its most immediate findings*.

This legitimate exercise consists in deducing from what is alleged, what is actually contained in it; either in bringing it together with the facts, or in questioning, etc. . . . In short, I feel a kind *of instinct to maneuver* whatever comes to me.

If I am to be criticized on this point, then, it should be admitted that no one wants my freedom.

How can we say to the mind: this is where you stop . . . unless we are God Himself.

But God Himself would be of the same opinion.

*

As I was ruminating and reviving a certain annoyance, a certain disappointment (*sense of injurious injustice*), I folded my arms and stared fixedly at *a point.* . . .

And something like a voice in me said: "Genre painting: Man nursing his rancor." And I saw myself, and gnawed myself like a man wronged, offended, hurt by some mortal, or by myself. . . .

*

Self.

From the beginning ('91), I have (instinctively) disparaged all literature that failed to give me the impression of *mental work carried to the extreme.* . . .

The probability of a series of lucky finds is very unlikely in poetry because of the simultaneous independent requirements. Language, being composed of separate and complex elements, offers only accidental solutions to those who adopt the conventions. . . .

The almost inevitable triviality in poetry made me bristle. That is why Mallarmé impressed me.

*

I cannot write a *normal* literary work. For that, I would have to diverge too far from my own nature, which is non-literary.

There are sacrifices I cannot, do not know how, do not wish to make—and the first sacrifice to get viable literature is the *sacrifizio dell'intelletto*.

*

I find against myself, as a writer, that I am not interested, am even annoyed by writing what I have seen, or felt, or grasped. For me, that is finished. I take up my pen for the future of my thought, not for its past—to advance, not to turn back. But circumstances have brought me to write something other than notes.

I write to test, to clarify, to extend; not to duplicate what has been done.

But what do I care for what is, has been, will be?

I suffer, I dread, I even desire; but with contempt. *You* frighten me. *I* tremble, and yet—I still feel that *we* are unimportant. What is the importance of a nervous reaction? It is infinite and nothing.

*

For me—whatever requires no effort, being of no value— it happens that I spare no pains for those who might read me. (In this, my "public relations" is at fault.)

Whatever requires nothing of me fails to give me the sense that I have lived it. Begetting comes easy, and the pleasure it gives has nothing really "creative" about it. But bearing and giving birth to a child are of quite another order of power and meaning. The female is more "profound" than the male, who serves after all no more than a moment, a spark—perhaps not an essential one, according to present-day biology. . . .

*

Some false notes.

Certain words in a thoughtful text, or one that could be thoughtful, strikes me as false notes. For instance, the word *soul*, the word *reason*, the word *nature*, *life*, etc., seem to me external, useful for chatting.

When I hear them I have a sense of insufficiency, of the provisional or the unfinished. Everything said is weakened by them. From a state of *musical* precision and coordination, I fall back into the state, or the moment, when the instruments are tuning up.

These are what I would call *absolute* false notes. There are also relative ones. For example, a certain facial expression, or a word that escapes inadvertently, shatters the system of appearances that a man has assumed in relation to me. He must have been playing a role, since he has just stepped out of it. His apparent character collapses from a want of harmony. It lacked the ability to exist in all circumstances, to live outside the theater of the moment.

Like those characters in novels who are never seen without their resources, are never involved in earning a living, and exist only in the story.

*

I know very well that my friend *must* at times want to strangle me; *must* necessarily call me stupid and annoying, ridiculous and unfaithful, yet this does not alter the need we have of each other, the reciprocal recurrence of the desire to see each other.

And yet the *wrong note*, the reactions and inevitable variations among the harmonies of friendship are always a thorn, a pain, rather like those produced by the body.

We must admit that there is no affection, however deep or strong, that can prevent the freedom of thought which, however regretfully, must observe what it observes and create what it creates that is shocking and irritating, inimical to what it loves.

*

I love real thought as others love the nude, which they would sketch for a lifetime.

I see thought as the utmost nakedness, like a person who is all life—that is, in whom we see the life of the parts and the life of the whole.

The life of the parts of a living being overflows the life of that being. My elements, even the psychic ones, are more ancient than I am.

My words come from far away.

*

If I desire that happy shore, that power of seeing, of re-creating—such plenitude, such a delightful intoxication of the mind will lead me back to where I am. . . .

To complete any happiness, we must add this awakening, the light that finally shines through and evaporates it. "Coming back to oneself" is a quite terrifying expression.

*

EGO SCRIPTOR

It is in my nature to impose rather harsh *conditions* on productions of the mind—that is, to set off in opposition to all formations of this kind the idea of the whole group of possibilities of transformation or variation that define the mind itself. I respond immediately to whatever offers itself, by trying the changes I could make in it. And this is the basis of my feeling about literature, history, philosophy, etc. —all such things entail the *authors' maximum of arbitrariness exposed to the maximum arbitrariness of readers.*

*

Writing (in the literary sense) always seems to me a sort of *calculation.* That is to say, I refer what comes to me spontaneously to the idea of problems and operations; I recognize the proper domain of *literature* in a certain kind of combinatory work, which becomes conscious and tends to dominate, to model itself on this type; thus I distinguish sharply what is given from what it can become through work. This work consists in transformations, and I subordinate (all the more when I am closer to working at *my best*) the "content" to the "form"—being always disposed to sacrifice the *former* to the *latter.*

I justify myself by the example of the musician who works by computations of harmony, who develops and transforms. This comes from working with verse, where *words* must be disposed quite otherwise than in ordinary usage, that is, under the pressure of a thought that sees nothing but itself in its haste to be expressed.

*

I have a strange aversion—a *fastidium* to writing what I have seen.

This repels and bores me.

I sense all the crudeness of approximation in any description of men or things. I am aware that, once my pen intervenes, I can make whatever I like out of what was. Take it or leave it. Or else, write a full report, and what a bore!

The novel is possible because the *true* costs *nothing*, and is in *no way* distinct from the spontaneous creation of a barely disguised memory. I mean, of course, what is *true for all*, the real common denominator.

This *truth*—like air and sun—costs nothing. It lends itself to an infinite number of compositions of equal likelihood. And this is how what *was* is indistinguishable from what *might have been*.

*

In me, a work does not come from an inner need.

It is the *mental labor* that, for me, is a *need* (after the initial stimulus). This stimulus spurs me to the labor itself, and not to its *product* (unless the idea of a *product* is one condition of the labor, but not the only nor even the principal one).

To my mind, then, the product is *application*, whereas ordinarily it is the principal object of desire.

So, the *Great Work* is for me the knowledge of labor in itself—that most general transmutation in which the works are local applications, particular problems; these are the problems into which, as more or less given conditions, the characteristic of the Other come in—the idea I conceive of the external effect of the works on that Other who is part of the problem.

*

"My thought," written down, put aside, picked up again, has by then become "a thought."

*

I have always feared doing what I could do best.

And what I could do best, I have done, fearing to do it.

*

Profiteer.

This man listens and profits. I give him ideas and I am sure that he will make something of them.

But the strange thing is that, if he knew my thought even better, if he had penetrated it as I have done, he could then not use it.

He would find in that depth exactly the same reasons that I found: *my own reasons for not acting*.

He profits from me to the extent and for the reason that he is not me.

And this may be true—even between me and me.

*

Characteristics and peculiarities of My Honorable Self— (not in order and only partially expresssed).

A very odd conviction of the "relativity" of knowledge —that is, of the power it confers—or does not. For me, spoken words are not enough. Impossible to believe anyone on his word—when I can imagine what the one speaking may know, and when I feel that I could write or forge speeches and stories of the same kind. . . .

Whence my distaste for convincing others. I am least of all a proselyter. I have contempt for anyone who tries to convince me. Apologetics is impurity. A mixture of reason, passion, self-interest. All means are good. It is then that the subtle is vile. It is an insult to man to want all men to think alike.

Impurity is my antipodes. Politics, religions. Use of grandiose words (truth, God, justice) and the face that goes with them. There is a decency in *exalted Things* which I believe more profound and more substantial than the decency that is shocked by sexual terms and manifestations.

"Opinions," "convictions," and "beliefs," to me are like weeds—confusions. Offering the provisional as something established. It is quite enough to have to endure these compromises with convention, the order of the human world, the functioning of organized life. . . . It is a dreary necessity having to hear and sometimes even bear the expression of seeming ideas, which no one can believe that someone would have thought of when he was alone with himself.

*

I am writing to L——, a bad day; I see everything with a passive eye—the eye that quite recently *made* what it saw, more than *received* it, and never turned *inward* without observing there some entirely new problem or some sign of a treasure of universal value.

*

What you think is worth no more than the one who thinks: You!. . .

But only in so far as it is *You* thinking it.

For it is not certain that your thought when expressed will not *yield* more than you believe or can believe, in another mental milieu. But it may be quite the reverse.

*

Whereas for the common lot, as for the philosopher, a *certain word* signifies a *certain thing* or *something*, for me it signifies *someone* (with all that this term carries in the form of acquisitions, creations, etc. . . .) *thinking of that thing*. (Myself, for example.)

This being admitted, I am no longer concerned with the indeterminate problem of the *word-thing* but with the functioning of the *counterpart* (*Myself* being the *nearest counterpart*).

This is similar to what the physicists did when they substituted ideas of instruments and acts of measurement for the ideas or categories that served to speak *universaliter* of phenomena.

Time equals *clock*; *Space* equals *measuring rod*; *Force* equals *contracted spring*.

*

INTIMACY (degrees of)

Listening to a tall strong man and seeing him in his robust person, with his gestures and his coarse tone of voice, I realize that there is very little in common between me and him. (I don't know him at all.) Prodigiously dissimilar. *Immiscibles.*

I feel myself involuntarily striking him off the list of human beings, classifying him among the least attractive animals. Yet he is of my kind. But not my true kind.

In our minds, we spontaneously destroy those who seem to make all effort toward a free interchange, those who make us feel the impossibility of *divining* them or being *divined* by them. Despair of divination.

What gradations there are in this classification of others in relation to oneself!

But You, the closest, or who would be—and that is why... *Yourself* drives *Myself* to despair.

Suddenly there are distances from nebula to nebula, between you and me.

*

I like everything that extends the mind to the limits of its power, but brings it near while organizing itself and assuring its progress.

*

APPLICATION OF FORCES

Having discovered and recognized Application of Forces *for myself*, at about the age of twenty, that man is a closed system in relation to knowledge and acts, Monsieur Teste's question: "What is a man's potential?" became my whole philosophy. That was a good base for the *application of forces*. I have not used them as well as I might. Nevertheless, I have tried to treat myths, words, and mind, as they deserve.

*

I *feel* that I am falling asleep, that I am going away. I drop the book, turn off the light, *I obey*, I give way. . . .

Consciousness again says: you must turn out the light, mark the page. . . . You are going to change.

I obey the need of not being, as one obeys the need to drink and eat.

*

I see clearly only at a *certain level*, in a certain light, according to a certain focus, so I was obliged to redefine the common notions for myself—just as I had to consider and acknowledge to myself that they correspond very poorly to those I would have formulated and adopted for myself. Particularly in the system of abstractions, I would not have invented many of the entities that now exist—and are very important —and I would have invented others which do not, but should, exist.

Although my sensitivity and exacting temperament regarding language are not the most favorable to literary production, nonetheless it is in the world of Letters that I could most easily *exist*. This explains my career and its eccentricities.

*

I have tried to create for myself a "philosophical" language based on my own observation and my real personal needs, rejecting problems formulated by others and seeking an organization of ideas useful to me. After all, my *constants* are my needs.

In my own observation I find very few of the things that bedevil the philosopher, and I find many others that worry him not at all.

I would say the same of the physiologist. He does not know how a man stays upright on his legs, nor what takes place inside him when he suddenly has an impulse to walk faster, or to change direction. . . .

*

Looking back at myself, in terms of the number of hours of my mental work, I see that I have spent almost all my conscious life in creating a sort of "philosophical dictionary" for my own use—perpetually revising it, more or less successfully.

*

I can love nothing deeply but intelligence. . . . Or rather one of those "sensibilities" that astonish the intelligence.

*

My imagination never moves on the common average human plane, that is, by taking its place *in medios homines*, in the world of exchanges.

What interests me most is not at all what matters to me most—or *should*. This *should* is an anticipation.

That is why I would begrudge the effort expended in writing a novel. (Not that I write any, even in my mind, except for *pure amusement*.) For this task seems not to lead to any betterment of my . . . kind! It is too easy, too quickly done, to compose for oneself another life than one's own.

*

If I select these fragments from my notebooks and publish them, separated by asterisks, the collection will be something. The reader—or even I—can give them a *unity*.

And that arrangement will make *something else*—unforeseen by me, in another mind or in my own. With a bit of fable to bring together a few observations, one can create a fairly viable character. In this way, I wrote *Monsieur Teste* in '94 or '95.

*

CONCERTO FOR UNACCOMPANIED BRAIN

Sometimes, with a surge of energy to my brain, I feel all the pleasure of thinking for the sake of thinking—pure thought . . . thinking as if it were the free movement of a swimmer, in water at body-temperature, thinking with the awareness that these are only the natural forms of my ability to think, without believing that such compositions, such figures, conform to a reality, to certainties, foresights and explanations, applications, utilizations, etc., of these transformations. . . .

Aside.

The force behind all this is the *reality* of that condition (also its *perfection*) as impossible to achieve as absolute zero. Only a *sort of death* could give access to it.

It is obvious that a pure musical composition means nothing—proves nothing, exists in itself, like a body. Pure reality means nothing, says nothing. *Coeli non enarrant quidquam.* "What is has nothing to say." Contrary to the philosophers, etc. . . . Pure sensation is whatever it is. *Pure*, meaning the sign of nothing.

But what restrictions can be *given* to this activity of the mind, which refuses to *accept* any? If there are no restraints whatsoever, nothing distinguishes this combinatory process from a digression. *Now it ought to be the contrary*—it ought to digress infinitely less than a *reasonable thought*, one that does not take itself for a thought—for what it is.

*

I scorn *what-is-worth-nothing-when-I-am-alone*, when I am really *alone*—that is, without even the idea of another person, and when nothing is to be hidden. *For all non-real values result from this*: that someone does not see everything. Credit requires that the walls of coffers be opaque, and the interchange of human things between men requires that brains be impenetrable to one another.

True solitude aims to leave nothing to be imagined: *a presence, and nothing more.*

*

There is no end of *human things* that are alien or antipathetic to me.

Among them, *essential* things.

Some of these I did not accept or understand or feel until very late, and even then after great changes. Others, which for many are natural and easy, are for me impossibilities, oddities, etc.

I can scarcely believe or understand something I would never have invented.

I do not know how I came to be such an . . . *outsider*?

It also seems to me that no one owes me anything, and that I owe others only what I am forced to ask of them.

*

I have just read a book that is almost exclusively abou "me." It has been here for at least five or six years, and I hav never opened it; its title did not tempt me. I opened it b chance, saw my name, read it. Very conscientious an scrupulous—a bit moralizing, etc.

But I observe in this what I have observed in othe writing on the same subject—a variety of things—*interesting* things.

First of all, the general impossibility, when "judging," describing or defining "somebody," not to construct—that is, not to forget the part played by *accident*, or *chance* in the successive accretions which, heaped together, appear to make a certain *shape*. But this heap is composed of bits and pieces that have never coexisted, that are in fact things handed down—that is, impure—a mixture of "mine" and "thine."

I have also observed that the unknown and missing parts are supplied by conceptions of *least action*. For example, as for me, I know very well that what I value and what means little or nothing to me—or rather, what I consider to be easy and unimportant and what I consider to be difficult and desirable —is quite characteristic of me.

If the absence of certain genres or themes in my literary production is surprising, it may be that I have found them sufficiently well treated by others, or perhaps they displease or bore me. It happens at times that I am praised for things of no value in my eyes. Moreover, people seem not to understand or believe—and yet I have said it often enough— that for the most part my "work" is composed of *responses* to requests or to fortuitous circumstances, and that without these solicitations or external necessities, it would not exist. I have not obeyed my desires. My nature is potential. But we

ttribute to some imaginary person what is due to the
regular effect of unforseen circumstances on a momentary
eal person.

I have worked at *literature* as a man who, fundamentally,
does not much like it for itself—since he finds in it the
necessity of producing "effects," using means of startling or
stirring the surface of the mind. If one tries to go farther, the
reader gives up, and the writer himself is in trouble. The
quality of one's response to literature is not of the kind that
beguiles me. It excludes the *alert reader*. Besides, people talk
about everything when the subject is literature, except its
true substance—the *immediate effects of discourse*, and the
relation of the means of language to the production in each
mind of what is aroused by those means.

I suppose that I have made for myself an idea of literature
rather different from the usual sort, one that seems to me a
bit more precise or verifiable than the latter. From this
comes a change (which may be profound) of the *values* I
attribute to products of this kind. *I no longer seek, I no longer
reject, I neither urge nor neglect* all the same things as most do.
My indulgences, my prohibitions, my manias and phobias
derive from a sort of ideal not to be found in a book. The
line that I write, then, is at the intersection of my way and
the highway.

*

When I was about fifteen years of age and someone scolded
me, I used to think: "This is nothing but association of
ideas," and I would rise by way of this childish awareness of
my adversary's mechanics. I had contempt for him in his
authority, and this gave me the pleasant sensation of regarding him as an animal observed in its automatic behavior,
and therefore lesser than myself and *contained* in my observa-

tion of him. I was changing him into a predictable phenome non. It must be admitted that a reprimand diminishes th one who utters it. He loses the initiative.

A bit later, I used the same defense against circumstances or rather against my torments and obsessions—*love-pride*, fo example—and all "sentiments" in general, when the became painful. But this time my success was much disputed precarious. . . . The mind must acknowledge that it is human

The method of seeing or imagining the mechanics o *living evil*, of predicting its moods, its anxiety, resonance repetitions, etc., of devaluating an object by means of a knowledge of its common substance or its too simple structure, etc., has never produced quick results. But there is no other way.

But the tendency is essential in me—constant.

*

There are only two things that count, and ring pure gold on the table where the mind plays its game against itself.

One I call *Analysis*, which has "purity" for its aim; the other I call *Music*; it arranges this "purity" and makes something of it.

*

What I have most desired was not outside me; it was inside— but not within my power.

*

Occasionally I find myself (at dawn) in a state of intellectual freedom and general readiness. Like a hunter ready to pursue the first prey that appears. At such a time sleep and lucidity merge one into the other. And something to dream, and something to observe and combine (that is, not to lose). But as yet no *object*. . . . Delightful sensation of readiness.

*

What is more productive of thought than the unforeseen?

That is why I became used to accepting those jobs I had not planned but have performed by the hundreds.

He who does only what he wished, conceives only what comes from one part of himself.

One is unaware of oneself in all that the non-self has not asked for and required that one produce.

Who would guess the suffering he contains, without the shock that draws this spark from him?

*

This evening I feel alone, gloomy, sad—to the extreme.

Suddenly at about 8 o'clock this overcame my *soul*, as a fog suddenly comes over the sea. For no "cause."

Nonetheless I must dine and try to talk, despite a state of abstraction so pervasively lodged, blocking all speech and even all positive thought. As one fears to move even the slightest bit the part that hurts, *or that might hurt*, so *One* foresees the thoughts that might come, and are *here*, and this *One* settles into a sort of stupor, at the heart of a *forest* of impending, *ultrasensitive* ideas, that no one wants and that anything can set going.

I feel impulses to whimper—nebulous oaths—ghosts of screams—bottled up rages.

And then: the next moment wonders *what is more stupid than melancholy?* But the sensation of that stupidity is added to the bitterness of the ruined evening, to round it off. . . .

*

I don't go in for *metaphysics*, that is, I take care not to endow words with more force or scope than I have. I have never been able to believe in human speech when it expresses things that no man has managed to see nor conceive. Even

as a child, I felt that a person who speaks can speak only 〈
himself.

*

I wonder at those who speak of the *universe*, of *time*, of *life*-
as if they had no doubt that something corresponds to tho:
splendid names and will answer to them, and as if they had ;
their disposal some other domain than the range of the:
arms and the duration of their attention!

There is a sort of dissimulation or falsification in specula〈
tive thought.

Thought of a practical order, thought that is an ingredien〈
of our acts, must merge *instantaneously* with the reality int〈
which it is leading us and apply its results or forms o〈
coordination.

But speculation, which has no act to prescribe nor any
reality to submit to and restrain, can only unknowingly
simulate resistances and accomplishments, which would be
completely illusory if the conventional difficulties it makes
for itself and the real pleasure it derives from itself did not,
after all, justify its use.

*

Here is something that is really mine—that is really me!

Everything "dramatic" in life, in history, etc., seems to
me of minor interest. . . . They are accidentals, things that
call attention to themselves and consequently are likely to
diminish or depreciate the will and ability to observe—*to
direct one's astonishment where one wishes* and be as little as
possible subject to it.

Whether or not the heart beats fast, the fact that it beats
is what interests the mind. Fast is the modality. The mechanism of the heart is more interesting than its irregular
rhythms. This is a criticism of novels.

This antipathy to violent or theatrical incidents explains me insofar as I am nonnovelist, nonhistorian, nondramatist. would not be one; I would not attempt to be one unless had to.

*

POETIC OBSERVATION

watch the smoke of the cigarette I have put down; it is a oft ribbon with delicate ravellings along its edges; it widens, wists back on itself, uncoils, becomes a sheet with different planes, with swirls, etc.

And I am wonderstruck and humiliated not to be able to conceive how this fluid transformation is perceptible to me—this stream of successive forms and figures begetting one another so easily and freely, with a grace, a fantasy, an indolence, a continuity and a progression like inventions of a lazy man, like seaweed under water. How can my eye follow this progression? I am here, as if listening to music. It is the same state.

How do these variations pursue each other, deducing themselves one from another so gracefully before my eyes, revealing figure and motion to be inseparable, as a voice does which is tone, action, substitution, enchantment, and living arabesque?

*

I am not sure that the entity Mr. P.V. is anything but a "convenient notation."

*

It occurs to me that in these notebooks I *never* write of what pleases me, and *very little* of what distresses me, nor of what is purely transitory—descriptions, memories. . . .

315

But of what seems likely to increase *my* power of trans formation—to modify by combination—my *implex*.

This implies a kind of belief in some sort of *construction* by additions and successive corrections. A belief that has only the value of a belief.

*

I wrote to M——. In me there is always *reason for not* preferring a solution. This is an odd kind of fecundity, prolific in negative consequences. We see examples of it in what we call "Nature." We usually attribute nonproduction to "sterility." But that is nonsense. Besides, I see no major disadvantages in not doing—if exterior results are equated with zero. Malthus is a great man, even in the intellectual order. Think what becomes of this realm as books accumulate!

The sight of the bookstalls on the quais, and of the Bibliothèque Nationale, made me seasick even at the age of twenty.

*

I detest fixed fantasy.

Nothing tires me more than the temptation it inflicts on me of adding and inserting, at every turn, the unexpected in the work of an author. Everything must be in its right place, and fantasy in the mood and the matter.

Moreover, *fixing*, in this genre, is an odd occupation.

*

History.

Having observed that philosophy, psychology, and history were useless in the problems that thrust themselves upon me *personally*, that were *born* of *me*, I have considered them as alien—and their values as conventional.

Moreover, their characteristic problems seemed rather

arbitrary to me. Their difficulties were not mine; I would never have invented them. And to me, their solutions were without force.

For example, it would never have occurred to me to discuss the *reality of the sensible world.* For I never would have thought of giving the word *reality* any but a finite and observable meaning, which would leave no room for any hypostasis.

*

MEMOIRS OF ME

I could write a book of my ideas just as they came or come to me, not as truths or purposes (in the manner of the philosophers) but as the most ordinary facts and events of life, and almost as one writes a diary, with no more regard for what is remarkable than a barometer or thermometer gives to the value of the air's weight or its temperature, registering the extremes along with the rest.

The production of ideas is for me a normal, almost physiological function, and any interference with them is a real torture to my physical regimen; their outflow is necessary to me. I am literally ill all day if, just after waking and for two hours or so, I am unable to let my head have its own way.

The ideas that come at these moments are not ones which utility or circumstances require and use as means; they do not figure in my external actions and designs, nor are they ones that have some literary work as object or recipient. I distinguish the latter from the former *by their nature,* and even *by the hour* of their production.

*

ABSTRACTIONS

My profession obliges me to use a great many vague *word*
and to give the appearance of speculating about them, b·
way of them.

For me they have no value. I do not really think witl
these philosophers' words—which are generally expedient
of everyday language to which a specific importance is given
and from which we try to draw some superior knowledge—
attributing a meaning to them, considering them as problem·
in one attitude of mind while using them as adequate means
in another.

For instance, what is Time, Beauty, etc.? Your *pause*
is not promising. A can understand B, who uses these words.
But *A does not understand A.* In this realm there are only lexi-
cological—that is, *exterior* problems—*which refer to something
other than my real, interior, active experience.*

*

I am *Mind,* which is to say, an incomplete or asymmetrical
man—*A Man of Mind*—incapable of living by his own
resources on the most fertile ground. The enticement of food
is not strong enough to make me rise above the labor of
digging and hunting and a disgust for killing and cutting up
animals. The cycles of natural life bore me, for the mind
does not tolerate repetition. For this kind of man, love also
must be transmuted, transfigured. All instincts and customs
are either condemned or disguised, or must be justified by
some practical necessity.

*

like the flesh of animals only when it is disguised in stews, ransformed as much as possible from its bloody state and organic semblance.

*

How I detest writing about my "feelings," making note of what gives many so much delight to set down on paper! In the first place, there are no valid words for these *intimate feelings*. Whatever is said about them, even to oneself, suggests *a third person*. I have never been able to write except to shape my own thought or to influence the thought of others—which is very different, a mode of calculation or preparation for an act. But never do I write to relive—what a weakness!

And this is in keeping with my sensibility, which has and has always had a holy horror of itself. Without it, I could have been a novelist or a poet. But my sensibility is my inferiority, my cruelest and most detestable gift, *because I do not know how to put it to use.*

*

I have just lit the fire. I am *nervously myself* between this August chill and the fire, in my early dawn state of extreme anxiety—gnawed by myself, by ideas, my mind taut, as if on guard; the rest still wrapped in loose-fitting wool and linen. Over there, the rumpled bed is growing cold. Cadaver of my night.

Lighting the fire is full of ideas. Building this little pyre. The part played by the brushwood, the catching delineated by the thinness of the twigs; it is a question of producing *one step after another* until the big log catches. The spirit of war, or revolution. Propagation of a faith. Love.

*

One of my first steps in the direction of my Self, which
developed from 1890 to its maturity in 1910, was the dis
covery in 1892 of the immense interest invariably aroused by
every resistance to an effort of the mind—when the question
of understanding is clearly put. *Not to understand*, when thi
is rightly acknowledged and somehow redefined, should
bring on an activity and a lucidity exactly like a *stroke of luck*
We must be trained to find these resistances. But these must
also provoke us to require of ourselves an extreme precision
in their expression, and they must stand up under it.

I have often been reproached for not constructing a
"system." I have no wish to do so. A man's thought is not
a poem, a finished work with a precise form, and I like only
well-finished works.

A system is a work of art or nothing. Every work of art
is a choice. Every choice excludes this thing or that. But in
this case it happens that *choosing* would exclude *what interests
me*. A man as such is not a choice. *I am merely a "result of
chance"*—that is, I consider myself in no way necessary, and
I have the impression that all the controlling events in my life
could have been quite different.

I do not mean that the ideas I have used, not to mention
those left unexpressed in my various writings (which tell
sometimes more and sometimes less than I think) could not
be collected and even arranged as a *summa*. It would only
remain to complete this *summa* in the manner of the philosophers.

A true philosopher would consider himself beneath his
ideal task if he did not add to those parts of his structure,
which came to him by way of luck and circumstances,
everything necessary *to close the square*; and, as an architect
may, for beauty and ostentation, add to the main portion of a

building, which he constructed according to need, other symmetrical or complementary buildings according to his aesthetic sense; so a true philosopher brings in, for example, a certain "theory of knowledge" from Ethics, Aesthetics, Psychology or Sociology, which in the beginning he had not wanted, and this makes what is called a System. But who can fail to see in this a kind of faking? I recognize that faking is useful in teaching philosophy, since after all philosophy *is* *taught*.

*

But I am not a philosopher, true or otherwise. There are problems which have thrust themselves on me, and which I find *real* in what concerns *me*. Others seem to me empty or meaningless, or belonging to semantics or lexicology. Several of these problems astonish me *to the limit of astonishment*, seeing that supposedly thoughtful minds can fasten on them at length. How can we not feel that to be concerned about the origin of the world or even of life itself, including all our present knowledge, and expending the resources of the subtlest and most rigorous thought, can only lead to a certain imaginary view contained in the possible imaginings of an actual head, and which can only be distinguished from so many other possible combinations by its identification with an observable *original*.

Moreover, everything that is verbal, either logical or not, and that can be exchanged only for something that is verbal, is worth no more nor less—pleasure apart—than any other combinations of words. I do not say that the pleasure may not be extreme.

*

Nevertheless, making myself a philosopher in my own way, for a few moments, and again taking up the question of constructing a system, I shall say what comes to my mind in this connection.

Let me suppose then that I begin to form a "philosophy" after I have agreed with myself to give that illustrious word the following categorical meaning: *Philosophy is the art of making a system of everything that enters the mind,* that is, of giving order to a constitutionally total disorder, in which the very order that pretends to contain everything forms a part.

This is not without analogy to the operation of making a map of Paris in Paris. That map would consequently be reproduced on itself and this reproduction would contain another, and so on.

*

If "constructing a system" means introducing a certain order, it implies that a certain disorder is attributed to the initial state of "all those things that come into the mind." Now *all that comes into the mind,* this is the mind itself; and consequently my orderly reproduction excludes the mind itself. My philosopher, I suppose, is a determinist. He can be so only by conceiving the opposite thesis and refuting it. (Otherwise, he would be simply an ordinary "believer," since his "reason" or his inner strategy would not have to show itself. . . .) He is, then, an antideterminist for a certain time. But instead of regarding both opinions as changes in his inner plasticity, or perhaps as two arrangements of terms in his language, he assigns values: nil to one, total to the other. And in this way he will have *explained.* . . .

*

It follows that *if there is to be philosophy, there can be no possible verification.*

*

This reminds me of a famous swindle that worked out wonderfully well a few years ago. A woman of very good family had the "genius" to make people believe that she had inherited hundreds of thousands, but from an inheritance which she situated overseas. She managed to have the ownership of this fictitious gold contested by fictitious co-heirs, and the whole working out of her fraud depended on the contesting of these phantom rights by phantom litigants. Accomplices then brought a succession of suits against her, each of which, with its points of law, its appeals and petitions, its legal documents and the crushing weight of a flood of arguments and decisions, lent support to the fable of the American uncle's fortune. *Its reality was never questioned.* Neither the Court nor the Tribunal dreamed of questioning its existence. But on this nonexistent foundation, which day by day became more solid juridically, the lady could establish all the credit she wanted. People vied with one another to lend her money. Finally, some petty incident occurred to ruin this marvel of applied mythology and knowledge of laws as of men, and it all ended with prison cells, dupes, and laughter. . . .

*

Some "memoirs" of me.

By nature I tend to neglect all that my nature finds of no use to its own permanent growth—those things I call *accidents* or *individual cases*. I say *my nature* because I have observed that my memory does not retain certain things and cannot forget others. It is an automatic classifier. No doubt it has its reasons. . . .

Now, what does it forget? Whatever could be quite different, without hindrance to the interior action of me in me on me.

It retains what could be useful to me in the struggle against inner monsters and in forming a freer immediate self that is, provided with more effective doubts and more available solutions. Many *models* and few *documents*. I am antihistorical. My impulse is generally a *defense through change of axis* and *number of dimensions*. I am always searching for a further degree of freedom of mind. ...

To be sure, I forget more and more the names of people, even of those I know well; I have very few clear images of the past, and these losses can be annoying and sometimes harmful. But what can I do about it?

*

The novel is an unsophisticated genre.

I regard poetry as the least idolatrous of the genres. It is the sport of those who are impervious to the *fiduciary* values of ordinary language and who do not speculate on the kind of fraud called *truth* or *nature*.

I have just used the word *sport*. This comes from relating all that I think about art to the idea of *exercise*, which I find the most beautiful idea in the world. The real amateur of poems looks on them as horse lovers look on horses, as others look on the handling of ships. They notice a revealing detail. They appraise the animal's equilibrium, the economy of grace in its movements, the elegant and effortless movements in its gaits. ... For me great art in poetry comes from training the animal known as *Language*, and leading it where it is not accustomed to go, but leading it with every appearance of unrestricted freedom. The thing is to conquer this freedom, carry it to the point of grace; and not only does the work profit in beauty and intrinsic life by these efforts toward perfection, but the author himself becomes more

ndependent regarding words—that is, more the master of
his thought.

*

I very rarely have the idea of writing a book. I very seldom
feel the need; pouring out my thought and having others
share it has little appeal for me. Think as you like! However,
more than once I have been taken with the idea of writing
a kind of "Treatise on the Training of the Mind." I called it
Gladiator after a famous race horse. I have already written
a number of its parts.

*

Can I, in 1943, give to a few people far younger than I some
notion of the effect produced on a certain young man in
about 1891 by his sudden encounter with the poetry of
Mallarmé? This young man must be imagined as somewhat
preoccupied with poetry, sensitive above all to inventions of
form and the many solutions possible in a line of verse,
consequently from his rather close reading of the Parnassians
having but little respect for Lamartine and Musset, and
observing in Baudelaire a disconcerting mixture of an extraordinary magic, defying analysis, with lamentable bits,
ordinary expressions, and very bad verse. I insist on the
imperfections I found in Baudelaire mingled with his full
harmonic power, for that impression created in me, as though
intentionally, the need or rather the *necessity* of Mallarmé.

From my first contact with his poems—whatever their
initial effect of obscurity and complexity—I had no hesitation
about the exceptional importance I was forced to admit they
had for me. From that moment, all other poetry seemed to
me reduced to awkward beginnings and pleasing fragments,
preceded or followed by insignificant or prosaic passages.
I noticed that the strange verses of this poet I had just then

discovered possessed above all the singular property of fixing themselves in my memory. To me this was particularly remarkable. My memory is deplorably undisciplined. I was never able to learn a lesson by heart. Now it happened that Mallarmé's poems imprinted themselves, without the least effort, on that same memory.

A few months later I felt the shock, overwhelming at the time, communicated by the work of Arthur Rimbaud.

I was as if bowled over intellectually by the sudden appearance on my spiritual horizon of these two extra-ordinary phenomena. The mechanism of my defensive reaction against the assaults of two such offensive poets would be worth analyzing as closely as possible. . . .

*

Yet these impressions of power and surprise affected nothing in me but my sensitivity to the resources of an art which the two inventors in question had strangely developed, each according to his own nature. I would vaguely compare Mallarmé and Rimbaud to scientists of a different species; one creating some sort of symbolic calculus, the other having discovered some sort of hitherto unknown radiations.

But three or four sentences of Edgar Poe gave me the capital sensation that awakened the *creature of desire*, the demon that possessed me.

*

It came to me in about 18– to consider as vulgar and trite all natural or quasi-natural feelings—or rather their ex-pression. The preaching of virtue, justice, and humanity, or the talk about the love one felt seemed shameful—indecency or hypocrisy. It always sounded false and stupid to my ears, whether as shamelessness or exploitation. *How can one not hide in order to feel?* I made every effort to be and to seem *unfeeling* at a time when I would have done better to display —and hence finally to simulate and exaggerate the feelings of my inner self.

Clearly all these emotional reactions have no connection with what we find as their cause, and they seem possessed by nonsense when we wake from them and the tide of energy flows back into the living mass where what has just happened is recast.

*

There are moments (toward dawn) when my mind (that very important and capricious personage) feels the essential and omnivorous appetite which it turns against the All, like a tiger against a flock, but feeling a sort of uneasiness as well from not knowing what to go after, what particular prey to attack and seize. It seems to my mind that any particular object exclusively fastened on must diminish the divine sensation of its awakened powers, and it can foresee throughout the coming day an embodiment, and thus a diminution of that illusion of power in a pure state, which my inner sense places above everything.

*

During such a period of tête-à-tête with the only thing that interests me, I experienced a delightful freedom of mind, without thinking of any future except that of the idea just come into being, or of any work but myself... *having to be created.*

*

There was a time when I could see.

I saw or wished to see schemata of relations between things, and not things themselves.

Things made me smile with pity. Those who were

327

attached to things were idolators in my eyes. I *knew* that the essential was *schema*. And this was a kind of mysticism, because it made the world that is apparent to the eyes depend on a world apparent to the mind and difficult of access, implying revelation, initiation, etc. . . .

*

I dislike events, exaggeration of facts or words. Events are exaggerated facts. I despise effects. Very early I found that all these "big problems" are simplistic.

My pleasure is in organizing and functioning, and this is revealed even in my quest of poetry.

Everything related to sensibility No. 2—sentimental songs, Musset, beggars, Hugo's poor, Jean Valjean, etc.—disgusts me if it doesn't infuriate me. Pascal playing on death, Hugo on poverty, virtuosi though they may be on these moving instruments, are fundamentally antipathetic to me. The calculated drawing of tears, melting of hearts, stirring people by the too beautiful or the too sad, would make me ruthless. Emotion seems to me a forbidden stratagem. Playing on weakness is not a noble act.

I have been reproached for not using such base weapons.

*

I confess that I would exchange many novels and histories for one paragraph of noble architecture.

I find in a certain formal quality a kind of sureness and immediate delight which I prefer to the illusion of living another's life.

Such an intellectual sensation develops me, while the involvement and excitement produced in me by stories leave me merely amused.

*

As for writers, I like only the thoroughbreds.

*

Not since 1891 have I been able to think of the art of literature without comparing it and setting it up against an ideal
of work which would be somewhat comparable to that of a
composer of (learned) music or of an author of a physico-
mathematical theory. A musician is permitted to wear himself out over combinations of harmony. The poet is denied
the pursuit of a deliberate and organized development of his
means. . . .

Spontaneous production did not seem interesting enough
to me. It did not allow me *to feel* the full use of the mind
when confronting a problem to be solved. I am convinced
that facility must be acquired, not accepted. I mean that
there are two kinds of facility. The basic one, which comes
from presumption and unconscious ignorance; and the other,
which costs dear but which must be sought and obtained at
any price.

Perhaps I went astray on this path, for such exactions are
far-reaching, and this one led me to an endless study of the
mind, a study, that is, of the possibility systematically
stimulated and explored in regard to expression and the
permutation of language, of its values and its effects.

That is why I could do nothing that depended solely on
my pure and simple discretion (such as novels). For me, either
conditions of logic or harmonic conditions always had to
be produced in support of whatever was written. Both
conditions are opposed to the possibilities of substitution
that a reader may be inclined to make in the text, if he
is left free to think of modifying the form, denying a consequence, or simply finding in the statement of the writer

329

only one combination among many that are equally think-able.

*

Confessions, memoirs, and diaries generally have to do only with facts, anecdotes, or monologues of a moral order.

There would be a more sustained interest in simply drawing up a list of a person's likes and dislikes—a list like those we used to find in young ladies' albums: "What is your favorite flower?—your favorite color?—your favorite poet?"

Such a catalogue could be made up for many a writer. A table or questionnaire could be composed of all the "valences" of the sensibility. The blanks would be filled by a thorough reading of his works.

All this, it must be added, would serve no purpose. But what use does literary history serve?

It would amuse me to make a list of my own tropisms. I dislike violet, and green, and blackish brown. I cannot endure solemn people. I cannot abide even the idea of kidneys, tripe, or inner organs in general; I like meat only when it is disguised.

Here we must distinguish between the phobias we feel a priori and the distastes resulting from experience. I remember the horror I had of cod liver oil.

As for the people I have known, I should have to examine myself carefully in order to recall the effect really produced in me by X, Y, Z—my attractions, repulsions, mistakes, presentiments.

It so happened that two or three people who became my intimate friends aroused in me at our first meeting an intense dislike that I thought insuperable.

I should also make up a table of what I understand and what I do not understand.

I ought to note my somewhat difficult relations with time. I am always in a hurry. I cannot take time to . . . for example, put things in order, organize things around me. It gives me a feeling of wasted time. Later on I suffer from having neglected this or that. But the rather interesting point in this self-examination, not of conscience but of functioning, is that I am often intellectually opposed to what I am organically. I eat too fast, I talk too fast, and I think too fast (which produces quite different thoughts from thinking slowly). But I rethink very slowly—and I could rework endlessly!

Another trait of my character: I do not see what is around me; I have no need for any setting whatever and I work best in a hotel room as impersonal as it can be. But if an object catches my attention, my eyes bore into it and exhaust it. . . . In some way it seems to me that *I do more than see it as I look at it.*

Another trait: I do not like to make books out of books, or make books out of "my life" as it is—or out of the lives of others.

*

I have just said that I talk very fast. At least that is what everyone has told me. Pausing to think about it, I observe that my rapidity of speech tends to equal that of my thought. This might be pointed out to anyone who expects thought from poetry. It must not be forgotten that meaning in poetry is something quite different from thought, since poetry is subject to a mode of speech in which speed is somehow burdened with time intervals, accents, and intensities which define the phonic rhythm characteristic of poetry. While tempo plays only an accessory role in the expression of direct thought, and vanishes with understanding, in poetry on the contrary it is an essential ingredient inseparable from it, which might impose definite conclusions as to the very nature of how much thought can be granted to, or imposed on poetry.

I come back to myself and my rapidity in speaking (but when I write poetry, I say it to myself in a low voice, and listen to it very slowly in myself).

I have noticed the same rapidity of speech in Foch and Keyserling—they speak even faster than I. In his *Journal*, Gide mentions and condemns my rapid talk, and this is what made me think about it.

The mental haste that governs this verbal haste has its advantages and disadvantages for the mind's productivity. I lose and I gain. On occasion I instantaneously rid myself of transitional ideas and worthless appendages; I rush toward the essential. I mean *my* essential. But again, I dash into an idea-mirror trap, or I fall and come down on an obstacle that should have been circumvented or taken apart bit by bit. I know this danger and that is why I am so slow to accept from myself a definitive conclusion, that is, *a final form* (since *concluding* is a matter of form).

The limit of the mind's function is a form. Experience has warned me against improvisation. Because of this acquired experience, I exact of myself the step-by-step, the word-by-word, much as my temperament and my inborn nervous nature resist it (as my handwriting shows . . .).

*

What is there of mine in what comes to me? What is there of me in what comes from me? Here the ridiculous problem of inspiration converges with the ridiculous problem of responsibility.

In both cases the self is searching for a self. Who has done what I have done? Who found that pearl? Who killed that man?

One *self* produces and acts; the other receives and sometimes judges.

—But why in the devil do you have to *introduce* this self? And this *introduces* a new question.

*

I see my reflection in this remark of Father Hardouin (166–): "Do you think I got myself out of bed at 4 o'clock in the morning every day of my life in order to think like everyone else?"

I have got up at that same hour almost every day, since I lost the habit almost forty years ago of sleeping through the night. And to think otherwise than everybody else (simply by recasting everybody's observations) comes almost naturally to anyone who feels uncommonly wide-awake when most others are asleep. From this I formed the habit of considering the common view of things as an expedient, always untrustworthy. *Each one of us must perhaps do his utmost to find, or render false, everything that is accepted as true by all*—at least in his private usage.

That maxim is scandalous, I confess. But here is another, less immoral, which seems to me to express a kind of duty of the intellect: *Try to make obscure everything that seems clear or evident at first glance*. As for the opposite reaction, it is natural to the mind.

*

Many have felt obliged to attribute to me some sort of "metaphysical anxiety." Unfortunately I know anxiety well

333

enough, and it is a deplorable state of mind. I would be quite willing to have some metaphysical problem as "cause" for my tormented nerves; I would put it to good use. But I am not interested in problems whose terms are easily seen to be nothing more than a misuse of language—and their solutions, whatever you please.

My Work and I

THE USUAL practice of critics, and even of readers, is to go directly from the work itself to the one who must have made it—that is, beginning with the effect produced, to reconstruct a living and intelligent cause for that effect. In this way we create for every work of the mind a corresponding man whose act produced that work. By the same naïve operation we neglect, first of all, everything that belongs to ourselves in that invention, and in the second place, everything in the work that does not belong to the author, including what he conceals from us, consciously or unconsciously, of his real personality. When we say Shakespeare, Molière, Balzac, or Victor Hugo, we are creating myths, begetting monsters whose fabulous children are Hamlet, Tartuffe, or Père Goriot.

But that is not all. It happens that authors fabricate for themselves a character who little by little takes the place of their own authentic SELF, and who explains to them, by his imaginary qualities, what they have created or produced that is *real*.

It is notable that the more rigorous the intellectual effort going back from the work to the author, the more precisely it is founded on observation and comparison of the characteristics of a work, the more scrupulous the interpretation, the more careful the reading of the texts, the more complete the investigation, *the more fantastic the result is likely to be*. It would be easy to demonstrate, by glaring examples in the field of the sciences, to what point observation strictly interpreted and confined to itself can lead to egregious errors, as we see by Aristotle's famous analysis of the laws of motion.

In a more familiar realm, nothing is more instructive nor at times more amusing than to witness either as observer or participant the encounter of an author with a reader. Between the author just as he is and the author produced in the reader's imagination by the work, there is usually a considerable difference that never fails to cause the greatest astonishment. The man one imagined to be stern is jovial; the jovial author presents a melancholy face and an icy reception. But a very simple analysis of the real conditions of literary production shows that the difference is both more profound and necessary than most writers imagine.

Every work is the result of a sum of efforts, of psychic moments, at times quite far apart. The time taken to elaborate a work, not to mention the extent of time when the author is preparing himself for it, is always much longer, and is even time of a quite different kind from that required by a reader to appraise the work as a whole. A very simple image will illustrate what I mean. Suppose that every day you carry a certain weight to the top of a mountain or a tower—one stone, for example, weighing one pound—and after a year, when all the stones have been put in place and cemented together, you push the entire block from the top of the tower where you built it to the bottom. Each time you carried one stone you felt that you were carrying only a small weight to a certain altitude, and you cannot even imagine the energy expended by the block's fall from the top of the tower. This is the block that falls on the reader. In the space of an hour or two of reading, he is subjected to the shock of a total aggregate compounded by impressions and stimulations. The author has almost no way of gauging that effect. The parts of the work which act almost simultaneously on another person were conceived and formulated by him gradually and at very different times. In a certain sense, one might say that the author does not know his own work. He does not know it as a whole; he cannot judge its *effect*; he has experienced it only in that he is its *cause*, and only in detail. Thus, if we were to attribute to the author the total power of the shock received, we would be prompted to consider him, as I said above, a kind of intellectual monster whose powers and means are out of all proportion to our own.

This is not all. Between the fictional character and the real person there are other causes of difference. Every writer, in addition to having the particular intention that led him to write one work instead of another, necessarily has a general intention, an aim, an ambition. The poet's object in his work, *in particular*, is to succeed in writing a specific poem on a subject he has in mind, and, *in general*, to arrive at results that designate him a *great poet* by the largest possible number of his readers. Many other conditions are involved, consciously or unconsciously, in the work of a writer: his own ambitions, his interests, and circumstances peculiar to him (as, for example, a wish to please certain people). These are elements which enter into the genesis of his work and which are generally very difficult, if not impossible, to reconstitute from the work itself. In a word, *the author* in his work *is always impelled either to round out and enrich his personality, or to falsify it in part*—or rather *to do both at the same time*.

We see what difficulties, what possibilities—or rather what certainties—of error exist and are imposed on a critic when he tries to imagine the real living being who produced a work, whether literary or not.

These thoughts have often come to me in regard to myself and my relations with what I have been able to give to the public. My case, my own individual case, seems to me amazingly clear, for I imagine that there are very few writers who would consent or would even want to remain different from their work. I should say here that my fundamental aim, or rather the natural tendency of my mind and character, did not incline me to follow a literary career and would even have caused me to shun the literary profession. To be sure, between the ages of eighteen and twenty, I yielded to the pleasures and torments attached to the disinterested exercise of poetry, but its importance for me was no more than episodic. I saw no necessary connection between this activity—to me almost a sport, a refined and sometimes skillful game of combining the musical and plastic resources of language—and my most intense desires and feelings. Never, in my heart, had I conferred on myself the magnificent title of poet. I saw no relation between the poems I scribbled and occasionally published in little reviews and the imposing volumes of consecrated verse found in libraries. Moreover, the sense of my shortcomings, and the inability I felt to accomplish the more complex works I had begun to conceive, only confirmed my instinctive feeling that I was not made for sustained and important relations with the public. My mind, after two years of such efforts, being still only too well aware of their insignificance, turned inward on itself, and I made a fine gesture of renouncing everything related to any attempt whatever to stir or persuade anyone else. I even came to judge harshly those who devoted their lives to an art in which I saw, and perhaps exaggerated, all it requires of idolatry, all it exacts of intellectual sacrifice and, let us admit it, of partly voluntary and partly conscious falsification. I then set myself to explore the possibilities of my thought, and I wrote only for the benefit of my solitary thought. I wrote only to aid, spur, define my thought. I gave my mind its full freedom, in the sense that no considerations of present or future publication and no conjecture about the effect my notations might produce on others intervened, intruded between me and myself. It was a strange state in which I passed some twenty-five years, all told, and one I often regret. The object of my attention was not, strictly speaking, philosophical, for I refused to grant any universal value, or total application, to the ideas I retained among those that came to me. It seemed to me that one should have a complete system of tested, perfectly personal ideas, which is, in sum, a sort of negation of all philosophy. It seemed to me that one ought to pursue an inner organization of all the experiments one had made, or of all the knowledge one had accumulated, and that such a *perfectly and precisely personal* organization must, if it is to attain to its own perfection, be valid and suited to one person only: to the one who conceived it. Nevertheless, to use the term *philosophy* and to illustrate by a very ordinary image what I was trying to do for myself, I shall say that it seemed to me that one ought to have a system of ideas as proper to oneself, and as little proper to another, as a pair of shoes would be, or a suit of clothes.

Furthermore, the absence of any external production kept me in a condition of harmony with my temperament.

I have an instinctive horror of anything that defines me to myself. (This is not one of the lesser reasons why in the past I refused to call myself or let myself be called a poet, at the very time when I was writing verse.) I was bent on remaining, somehow, in *reversible equilibrium*—and I succeeded fairly well during the quarter of a century of which I was speaking. My ambition was to recognize and define the ensemble of my real powers. . . . I believe there can be no ambition more opposed to the ambition of becoming an author. *The underlying ambition of any man who addresses himself to a public is to confer on himself, or to allow others to confer on him, powers superior to those which come only from himself.*

So for a long time I remained on a sort of island, a Robinson Crusoe of the mind, where I tried to make for myself with my own means and, insofar as it was possible, with instruments of my own making, all that I needed to maintain and increase as best I could my mental vitality. I could have lived indefinitely on that island if external and quite unforeseen circumstances had not obliged me to do exactly what I was not made for, what I had always resisted, and what I had for so long argued against. . . .

Men and things having more or less compelled me, at about the age of fifty, to address myself to others than myself, I found myself in a truly singular situation. I had lost all habit of immediate production, and I did not know how to write without thinking of what I wrote as a simple means of clarifying or organizing my thought. Moreover, I had notions about many things and had made definitions for myself that presupposed a whole structure of unexpressed thought, and I had the habit of translating into my own language any question that came to mind. These were deplorable conditions for entering into relations with the public. Literary art, which I had sometimes thought about from a purely theoretical point of view, seemed to me a completely artificial enterprise, and I saw it only as a fairly interesting object of speculation and analysis. Yet I had to produce something more or less like ordinary production. It is common knowledge that I did not altogether succeed, my work in general having a reputation for obscurity, which perhaps is not completely undeserved. It can be seen from the preceding that if I often write a difficult work, it is not that I have the slightest desire to impose on the reader an intolerable punishment, but that I myself have the greatest trouble in not acting toward the reader as I had so long acted toward myself during that long period of problems and constructions to which I alluded.

In fact, the *true value* of literary work is a great question. By that I mean it is very difficult to constitute an ethic of this kind of labor that would be satisfactory both to the author (at least if the author is not indulging in the feeble exercise of pure and simple vanity) and to a clientele of readers—that is, that would in short satisfy both *noble egotism* and *altruism*. Is it possible to achieve from the exercise of literature a furtherance of one's self, a knowledge and control of one's intellectual faculties stimulated and made supple by the labor of writing, and, at the same time, a legitimate, powerful, and fruitful modification of minds, or at least a certain category of minds?

I do not believe this question has been posed, but I seem to see traces of this little-understood struggle in certain powerful and exceptional published works. At the beginning of this little essay I insisted on the difficulty, if not the impossibility, of going back from the work to its true author, and I must say that, of the evidence we lack, the most important is *the knowledge of the real and permanent aim of the author*. It is obvious from what I have just added that the question is even more complex when there is a question of dual objectives in the author's mind, of a real division in the man himself, which results in indecision in his work as to whether it is a means, or an end, for its creator.

The Avenues of the Mind

Two Hours with Paul Valéry
(An interview by S. Bach)

PARIS, March 1927. In 1921, the review La Connaissance *held a referendum to name the leading poet of the time. The majority of votes went to Paul Valéry, who expressed his thanks with modesty, wisdom, and a shade of apprehension. "I am aware of the full worth of this honor... but I am even more clearly aware of its danger."*

Modesty and a dignified caution, which keep him from being carried away by social or literary vanity, are the rare and likable qualities shown by Valéry in his first words of greeting.

P.V.: I confess that the number and boldness of my commentators frighten me and sometimes give me a kind of vertigo of ideas. I am at the point of looking for my thought in all those commentaries....

B.: Nevertheless that thought, so wary of itself, has made the rounds of Europe. Your essays and poems henceforth belong to the common heritage of literature and of cultivated minds in Oxford, Cambridge, London, The Hague, Salamanca, Brussels, Bucarest, Bologna, Rome, Berlin, Heidelberg. You are among those, as Abbé Bremond has rightly said, who are applauded by the literary league of nations.

The Master smiled and turned the praise aside. To these flattering perspectives, the reward of a ripe maturity, he brings up the period of his first fruitful meditations when he was unknown— a time, nevertheless, to be looked back on with regret.

P.V.: It was in 1890. I was only nineteen then. An anthology has mistakenly given my birth year as 1872. Tristan Derème one day wanted to know my age. He wrote to me, and this was my reply:

> *Tristan, votre cœur est de bronze.*
> *Je compte plus de jours que de biens je n'acquis*
> *Depuis le jour où je naquis*
> *Trente octobre soixante et onze.*

At the age of nineteen the poet was still to be born, but the thinker and essayist was preparing himself for his first works, " The Introduction to the Method of Leonardo da Vinci" having come out of that phase of youthful reflection!

P.V.: At that time I was drunk on my first intellectual encounters—Pierre Louÿs, Huysmans, Mallarmé. To me, Leonardo was a kind of intellectual hero standing far above the disorder of my feverish probings.

B.: And you chose him, as later on you chose Monsieur Teste, less as a likely subject for psychological developments than as a symbol, a region of your mind in which to locate your first exercises in philosophical mathematics and ideology.

P.V.: That is true. "The Introduction" and "Note and Digression," like "The Evening with Monsieur Teste," are pure mental exercises, like little novels of mental research and analysis.

B.: "The Introduction," especially, has a Cartesian ring. It is your own "Discourse on Method," and all the more because you were seeking the crux of the matter—the primary source of all mental and creative activity.

P.V.: Perhaps. And my friend Thibaudet was mistaken when he tried to establish a parallel between my modest effort in self-education and the magnificent unfolding of Bergsonian philosophy.

With a few exceptions, I pay no attention to the great traditional problems of philosophy. When some psychological or aesthetic puzzle comes my way I tackle it with my own means, following in general the disciplines taught me by the masters of ancient and modern thought.

The Master then confided to me the secrets of the development of his poems.

P.V.: As you know, I do not believe in miracles of inspiration in art, and especially in poetry and music. My *Jeune Parque*, which is my grand opera, developed in four years of slow elaboration, is a work of the will in which I amassed problems of prosody and poetry in order to overcome them. One can never exaggerate the importance of technique. In art, the scarcity of matter is one of the essential elements of perfection, whether it be plastic art, a musical score, or a poem. Wagner, who knew this, had carried the orchestral wealth and principal themes of *The Ring* and *Tristan* within himself for thirty years before arriving at a definitive adaptation and "realization."

At times, however, facility and ease in creation reward a long period of waiting and drought. It was thus with me that after the long penance of *La Jeune Parque* I was able to write "Palme" and "Aurore" at one sitting!

B.: Isn't this to admit that the creative impulse, as

Bergson has said, always animates and permeates, more or less, the subtlest "mechanical" calculations? You yourself have said that, in the morning on waking, the lines of your unwritten poems sang in your astonished memory. And thus, at the dictation of some divine dream, you came to write the finest lines of "Le Cimetière marin." Is it not true that inspiration is of another order, and no doubt of a higher order, than the dry combinations of the geometrical mind?

P.V.: I said and thought otherwise, if not the contrary, in my "Introduction," and you know that my aesthetics is purely intellectualistic. For my part, I believe in the essential unity of the mind, whether it be a question of intellection or of creation.

B.: As an essayist, philosopher, and poet, you are not fond of novels even though you are indulgent with novelists.

P.V.: Every day I receive ten or fifteen books, mostly novels. I am far from belittling the mental activity and invention manifested in this vast department of literary activity. I simply confess that this form of invention is completely foreign to me. I was not born a novelist. Nevertheless I do read novels, and those of the younger literary generations are sometimes very amusing and suggestive.

I have just reread Giraudoux's *Elpénor*, and I enjoy Morand as one of the brilliant heirs of the great cosmopolitan writers of the eighteenth century, especially Voltaire and Montesquieu. Let me tell you how much I admire Fabre as a poet and novelist.

B.: You wrote one of your finest prefaces for him, and dedicated to him the deeply thoughtful pages of "Au sujet d'Eureka."

P.V.: Mathematician that he is, he occasionally has the

verve and creative enthusiasm of a Balzac. His *Rabeval* is a youthful work, but it is vigorous and strong.

B.: What do you think of André Gide?

P.V.: That he is a great writer.

B.: And of Cocteau?

P.V.: I think he has a curious mind, and one of the most "diverting." I wouldn't hold his conversion against him. . . .

B.: Don't you think that Catholic literature has become a bit too encroaching, despite the great talent of such novelists as Mauriac, Deheil, and Bernanos . . . ?

P.V.: No doubt. And you know that I am a pagan, "like Maurras, and a pure Mediterranean. . . ."

B.: That is the friendly criticism made of you by Father Gillet, who loves you nonetheless and is consoled for your paganism by attributing "metaphysical anguish" to you. And yet Paul Souday has every reason to say that he finds no trace of it in your work. . . .

P.V.: I am of another generation, alas, than your young Catholic novelists, and neither do I fall into the German, Slav, or Scandinavian trap of "the unconscious." I believe that we must be on guard, in music as in literature and poetry, against these vague idols and emanations that can all too easily be taken for inner divinities, when they may perhaps be nothing more than an obscure awareness of our organic activities.

Doubtless no higher and finer creation has ever been accomplished than the mind, the mind itself, as Descartes and Spinoza understood it.

And works bearing the mark of *the mind* are sure to endure and flourish in every latitude, and to be recognized in all the intellectual capitals of the world.

The precious minutes were passing. Paul Valéry's conversation seemed to me a marvel of density and versatility. In it I recognized all the familiar themes of "L'Ame et la danse," "Rhumbs," and "Cahier B.". I lingered with the Master in his half-Parisian, half-Provençal drawingroom, in the rue de Villejust.

But suddenly all the bells of Paris rang out like a reproach on this Sunday midday. At the end of two hours I took leave of Paul Valéry, both ashamed and happy to have beaten the record of Frédéric Lefèvre at his most indiscreet.

Reply

MY VIEWS on poetry are those of a man of sixty who has seen any number of schools, tendencies, and works come into the world and perish; many an enterprise exhaust itself; many a reputation fade; many enthusiasms reduced to ashes, and many personalities to shades.

But, from the time of my youth, I expected nothing else. I did not believe it essential to attach a measureless value to external achievements, to make one's life depend on the effects one can produce on others. That is why, keeping to myself the results of my work, I long held aloof from literary activity, which I confess had come little by little to seem incompatible with the exigencies of precise and rigorous thought. Certain circumstances independent of my will having belatedly drawn me out of that closed state which was natural to me, *I had to choose*, to make up my mind (since I was obliged to write), and then to seem to propound an "Aesthetic." Nevertheless, I did not allow myself to aspire to prescribing or forbidding anything whatever to anyone at all in matters of literature, art, and philosophy—or anything else. What I permitted or forbade myself was only by way of convenience or of personal and provisional experiment. It was not that I did not have my preferences—tenacious, exclusive, and even violent—but the more pleasure

I had in certain systems that I had worked out for myself and the more attached I became to certain writers, *the more deeply I felt that, for the same reason, I was denying them universal value*. What I like most, what most illuminates me, being necessarily that which is most in conformity or most in harmony with my nature, must therefore suit my needs as well as the clothes or tools made for an individual suit his. In any case, awareness of this peculiarity is acute. It excludes any temptation to proselytize, to persuade, or to teach. It excludes me from doctrines and parties, and causes me, moreover, to consider my own opinions as I consider those of others—that is, *as purely accidental in the eyes of a third person*. Finally, I feel an instinctive antipathy for any attempt to win anyone to any cause whatever, and if in a sort of fit of abstraction I catch myself trying to convince another person —trying to make him like something he does not like, or to hate what he likes—the sound of my own voice soon becomes unbearable to me.

I say all this in an attempt to explain the nature of my relations with poetry—which in themselves are very simple, but something less than simple if they are interpreted according to the idea ordinarily held of poetry.

I began, like everyone else, with the desire to produce works which might possibly charm me, and which might cause me to value and appreciate myself a bit more than my customary relations with that self had led me to do. Thus a certain poet took shape, encouraged by a few friends, Pierre Louÿs and André Gide among them.

But in my twentieth year I had been as if transformed by various torments of soul and mind, or rather by the extreme effort to overcome them—for nothing alters or transfigures us more profoundly than the struggle against those of our powers that have turned against us. Finally, I was led by I know not what daemon to set consciousness of my thought in opposition to its products, and thoughtful action against spontaneous formations (even when beautiful), against chance (even when lucky)—in a word, in opposition to all that can be attributed to automatism. This desperate choice of inner defense, which divided me against myself, led me to extremely rigorous judgments in regard to what I had admired, piously cultivated, adored, beforehand. All spontaneous productions of the moment appeared suspect to me, and I took a cold look at what I had previously held to be of infinite value. Poetry reveals itself to us through marvelous accidents and very remarkable interlinkings of our inner states of mind. I came to consider the accidental or mechanical character of that fabrication more highly than its value as delight or marvel. I went so far as to question whether what I had most divinely felt or most ardently desired in that category of spiritual events might not be interpreted as discards or rejects of mental activity, as effects of local stimulation, powerless to attain to the fully developed form of the considered intellectual act.

This amounted to throwing into question all literature, and particularly modern literature. It was to decree that *gold* is a base metal, and to evaluate everything *by its quantity of conscious labor*.

As a consequence of this attitude, I resolved to deny any importance whatever to considerations of innovation and tradition, originality and banality, to speculations about surprise and contrast—which for more than a century have been the upshot of almost all the strategy of creators. All this, along with manifestos, insults, and polemics, is of little interest to a man who is *sufficiently alone*. It seemed clear to me that nothing has been more tainted with automatism than taking as a criterion what others have done or not done, than *living to imitate* or *to outmode*—which in the end is the same thing. The wish to become more "advanced" or the wish to conform to a preexistent type comes from the same principle of "least action," which, in the realm of life and of the mind, has as analogue our tendency to react to incidents by a reflex, sometimes fortunate, and always local.

When I came back to poetry after more than twenty years of non-literary studies, that is why that strange undertaking presented itself to me only in its "absolute" aspect—that is, of deriving whatever its value by *intrinsic* qualities only, independent (in so far as possible) of the prevailing taste, of presentiments of the taste of the next epoch, and the modern setting and "sensibility." Among other forbidden things, I did not wish to play upon systematic surprise or unrestrained enthusiasm, for it seemed to me that this was a matter of reducing the effect of the poem to a dazzlement of the mind without having reached or satisfied its depths.

All this can be legitimately considered as paradoxical. However that may be, I have been led by these views and particular deductions to impose upon my work extremely strict conditions, more numerous than "inspiration" usually allows. And I have placed a particular value on all arbitrary conventions, which, by limiting the choice of terms and forms, have become almost intolerable to the moderns. I have a weakness for the formal.

It is not altogether impossible to justify in others' eyes my mental approach to poetry. I confess that I applied myself to poetry insofar as it seemed to me a superior exercise and a quest for freedom through restraint. Man is so made that he cannot discover all he possesses unless he is obliged to draw it from himself by severe and prolonged effort. One comes close to oneself only by going against oneself. A poet, moreover, may well impose upon himself what any singer or performer imposes upon himself, and what all artists have imposed upon themselves when there was still the leisure to mature and the desire to last. . . .

This sort of confession exempts me, I hope, from making any oracular reply to the question posed. I do not know what poetry *should* be. I cannot and do not wish to know what it will become.

Memories of Paul Valéry

by Pierre Féline

It was at Montpellier that our friendship began, a friendship that was to last for half a century. Paul was studying law, and I, a schoolboy, was preparing for the École polytechnique. We lived in the same house, at No. 3, rue Urbain-V, a steep, winding street bordered by gardens, dilapidated houses and shops, and also by an ancient and substantial three-story house with a monumental doorway of carved oak and a stairwell more spacious than the rest of the building.

The Valéry family lived on the ground floor, in an apartment surrounding a rather dank garden where everything grew wild. A squeaking gravel walk cut through this little oasis and led to the room where Paul worked. From my window on the third floor I looked down on my friend's worktable. His table! Every day, early in the morning, I would see him walking towards it, slowly, his head bent, like a young priest going to meditate before the altar.... And when Paul reappeared he was completely changed: standing up straight, singing, taunting me. I would call out to him ironically: "To work! Get to work!" He was on his way to the Law School.

The room where he worked was dark and narrow: a single window with a table pushed up against it—a kind of desk with shelves, piled with papers in great disorder, but *his own personal and familiar disorder.* As for the bookcase, it was kept in fair order, but beside it was a sort of bench where certain books had been thrown to jostle each other off onto the floor. Afterwards these volumes wandered unimpeded about the room.

The walls were completely covered with clippings from old illustrated magazines. Why this lurid collection? These stupidities had been there for a long time. He paid them no attention. Anything else would have uselessly caught his eye. Later he said to me: "What I would really like to have for wallpaper is a set of maps from the Hydrographic Service of the Navy...". Their never-ending sinuous lines would not have distracted him.

Sometimes my friend beckoned to me to come; sometimes, waiting for a favorable moment, I called to him. Occasionally I would go with him to the Botanical Garden, his favorite walk. And in the evening, after dinner, we would wander in the narrow streets of old Montpellier.

One evening on our way home we were talking about Hoëné Wronski's theory of Messianism. I took a piece of chalk from my pocket and drew Wronski's pentacle on a door near our house. Paul took the chalk then and added a few words: "I am Alpha and Omega...", etc. The next day, the newspaper *L'Éclair de Montpellier* reproduced our drawing with a long article. . . . For several days the police watched the house. Those were the times of the [anarchist] Ravachol, and a banker lived nearby. In a letter written in 1938, Valéry alluded to these pentacles.

His silhouette! How can I evoke it without being confused by more recent memories? It is all the harder since nothing about him attracted attention. It was his kind of coquetry to pass unnoticed, in dress as well as in behavior. However, I remember his bow tie, sometimes badly tied, and his too-long shirtsleeves, which he pushed back with a mechanical gesture.

He was always calm in the midst of the exuberant people of the "daoû Clapas." However, if our conversation grew lively, Paul would stir himself a bit, substituting other and more forceful words, talking close to my ear as if I were deaf. Then suddenly he would move away and his idea would spurt out in a new rhythm. I hung on his words. . . . (*Only the passersby seemed free.*)

At home, at his writing table, he was completely different: this face—sometimes mobile, at other times strangely set— and his slightly protruding eyes seemed at times troubled by the anguish of the word that would not come or was slow in coming. Then his hand would begin to undulate, shaping the nascent thought. . . .

*

He never talked to me about his courses at the Law School, nor about his plans for the future. His sole ambition, I well understood, was to write and continue to write. ("Narcisse parle" was published in *La Conque* in 1891.)*

His silence extended to his adolescent love affairs. Was this the modesty of a beginner? Or rather a delicate and deliberate attitude toward a comrade who was still on the benches of the lycée? To my knowledge, no sensual or

* On this subject I would like to rectify the error made by the journalists who attributed to Valéry certain poems that had appeared under the signature of Michel Féline. This was not a pseudonym but the name of my older brother, who also published a sonnet in 1890 in *La Plume*. Later on, Léon Vanier published a collection of his poems, *L'Adolescent confidentiel*, some of which have also been attributed to Valéry by certain critics. [The footnotes to this chapter are by Pierre Féline.]

sentimental attachments interfered with his early medita-tions.*

I can say the same of the "romantic sickness," which afflicted so many of the young intellectuals of the time. My friend was spared this spiritual crisis, unless he had already passed through those turbulent waters.

Paul was *strong in his boundless desire for precision* and, at the same time, strong in the enchantment of poetry, drunk on the promises of the Muse.

He recited Mallarmé in a calm melodious voice and a fairly low tone; then he went back over the poem, inter-preting it line by line. What a marvel! *Hérodiade*, "L'Après-midi d'un faune," commentated by Valéry! Alas! I did not understand the value of such words. He not only explained Mallarmé, but Heredia, Edgar Poe, Verlaine. His commen-taries were extremely precise and were not encumbered by any sort of banality. They were directed toward clarifying the words by poetic thought and the structure of the poem as a whole.

In particular I clearly remember his reflections on *Le Cygne*. He used Mallarmé's sonnet to show me certain methods of Symbolism.

Sometimes I would have him hold forth on our classic and great Romantic writers. To rouse him, I told him one day that Victor Hugo had made his poetry ridiculous when he tried to mix it with metaphysics. At first Valéry pretended to agree with me, and began to declaim:

> *Que fait Sennachérib, Roi plus grand que le sort?*
> *Le roi Sennachérib fait ceci qu'il est mort!*

* However, I learned much later that in about 1891 or 1892 he fell in love with a lady belonging to one of the best families of Mont-pellier—an almost violent love which came to nothing.

Then he decided to confess his admiration for Hugo, but I cannot recall his words.

Another time I tried to tease him about his dear Racine. How could so sensitive a poet not have sung the beauty of the landscapes of France? "I have often asked myself that," he said. "And in fact I've found only one verse on the subject in all of Racine":

La nature, Madame, est fort belle aujourd'hui.

Then he took it upon himself to explain to me the profound reasons for the absence of Nature in the work of Racine.

Every day he would come and sit beside my piano. I played Wagner for him. I played through all of Wagner, from *Tannhäuser* to *Parsifal*. In spite of my faulty playing, the Wagnerian formulas enraptured him.*

Was this really the music that he needed? Certainly not. Music of more subtle variation, less grandiloquent, would have been better suited to him. Mme Valéry, later on, understood this and tried with great talent to initiate him into Bach, Schumann, and Debussy. But in vain. The impression produced by Wagner on the adolescent had been so strong that he gave scant attention to the spiritual dialogues of Bach or the moving melodies of Schumann.

What interested him in Wagner was, for the most part, certain of his methods of composition. In particular, his way of developing musical emotion. Wagner excels in preparing

---

* At the end of each session he tried to recall the principal motifs by picking them out on the piano with the index finger of his right hand. Later, in Paris, he amused himself by playing Wagner's leitmotifs for me by the same rudimentary method. The only progress he had made was to have learned to read the notes, provided they were not too encumbered with sharps and flats. A Wagnerian score was always on his piano.

it, then in intensifying it, until it attains its paroxysm at a moment fixed in advance, after which, calm is brought on by degrees. This schema, found in a number of the Parnassians' sonnets, was well known to my friend.* What captivated him was the art with which Wagner put it to use, in particular, in the Prelude to *Lohengrin* and in the second act of *Tristan*.

Found in his old notes: "September '91, 10 P.M., I leave for Paris in an hour. Féline has just played for me the Prelude to *Lohengrin*, the end of the *Walkyrie*, and *Tristan*. Sadness. I reread Poe (Colloquies)."

Mathematics was the most frequent subject of our conversations at the rue Urbain-V. Not, certainly, at the beginning of our friendship. For that reason Paul had graduated from the lycée without the slightest tinge of science, and he seemed scarcely to care.

However, I was finally able to interest him in mathematics. I give all the credit for it to my professor of "Spéciales." That eminent scholar, philosopher, and mathematician,† had taken it upon himself to make me admire the transcendent constructions of pure science.

In order to become a mathematician, he told me, you must familiarize yourself with the language of algebra; make your

---

* In this way the intensity of emotion is achieved at the end of the second third of the Prelude to *Lohengrin*. The same is true of many sonnets. But in Heredia's poems, on the other hand, the maximum intensity comes in the last verse. The effect is a dazzling finale, rarely sought by Wagner.

† M. Gaston Milhaud. About 1895 he was in charge of a course in philosophy at the Sorbonne. He published various works on metaphysics: *Descartes savant*, *Essai sur les conditions et les limites de la certitude*, and an *Étude sur les sophismes de Zénon d'Élée*. In these titles we recognize Paul Valéry's essential preoccupations. However, the works of Gaston Milhaud were never in my friend's library.

own the concepts and symbols of the calculus; subject your mind to the disciplines of geometry. Three exercises of very different sorts, but all to be pursued equally. Such was the counsel of my eminent professor.

This is the method that I followed strictly with young Paul. With no preliminaries, I put him to work at algebra. Fairly soon he was able to handle polygons, and later on he set himself to pursue his training in that matter.

At other times I would demonstrate to him the structure of mathematical reasoning by "dissecting" for him some theorem of elementary geometry, or of the theory of numbers. Then, after several weeks I presented the fundamental symbols of the calculus. The theory of functions made a profound impression on this young twenty-year-old poet.

From that time he was keenly interested in mathematics, and set himself to probe each of its three domains.

Nevertheless, each day I was more and more demanding of him. I remember that I had to go back three times to a certain theorem in the second book before I could induce him to follow the reasoning strictly.

To follow, more or less, a line of reasoning in geometry is not to follow it at all. Either you do not understand it, or you understand it as well as Pascal or Henri Poincaré did. To reestablish all the links in a logical chain, to unfold it slowly, stopping for a moment over each element to verify the connections, is to think in exactly the same way as Euclid thought two thousand years ago, according to an unchanging order. At the lycée it is impossible to proceed with such purity. At each class meeting, a dozen theorems are presented. If the students remember the terms and learn by heart certain simplified demonstrations, this is enough to pass the examination!

With my comrade, our enterprise was of a different order; we were not restricted in our use of time, and we could reflect at considerable length on a single theorem. Paul took the habit of distrusting everything that seemed evident, and he understood that any effort to simplify a line of geometrical reasoning was to risk destroying it altogether.

His mind was most drawn toward the speculations of the calculus. To create symbols without apparent connection with the real, and to give them life by defining their modes of variation and combination; with these symbols to form groups and consider each form of transformation as a new abstract entity, and to set to studying the groups they can constitute by their structure. . . . Paul showed keen curiosity for all these degrees of transcendence. When I saw him again later, I found him quite at ease in this domain, where thought sees only transformations and combinations of abstract concepts.

The hold that this art was to have on his mind cannot be better expressed than by the following lines:

"Mallarmé, in this, joined the attitude of the men who have deepened the science of forms and the symbolic part of the art of mathematics. . . . It is the ensemble of possibilities and the variations of thought which define the mind itself. . . ."

It is interesting to compare these lines with the following by Gaston Bachelard, in *Le Nouvel Esprit scientifique*:* "It is in poetry that we should find aesthetic values comparable to mathematical symbols. In thinking of these beautiful symbols, where the possible and the real are blended, one can evoke Mallarmé's images."

*

* This work was never in Valéry's library.

There came a time when my comrade proposed that we meet once a week to discuss a theme decided in advance and chosen from the subjects that had most interested us in our daily talks. These were our *amicales*, our "club meetings," as Paul called them. I remember some of the topics: Parnassians and Symbolists, Mallarmé, Wagner and aesthetics, the theory of the leitmotif, one supreme law for each of the sciences,* the modes of geometric thought, the creations of mathematicians.

We each prepared our thesis and read it at our "seance."† Then our dialogue began. Grandiose theories were developed, connected by their contrasts; and extremely abstract arguments collided with simple images. This would go on for three or four hours, but we interrupted our debate with some interlude or other—a poem, a mathematical diversion, and always a bit of music. These pastimes had no connection, of course, with the subject of our meetings. Paul insisted on them. He enjoyed observing the effect produced by the resumption of our topic in the atmosphere created by the interlude. These *amicales* were always held in my room, where there were two chairs, a table, and a blackboard three and one-half meters long. Before Paul arrived I would amuse myself by writing in chalk at the two ends of the blackboard some fragment from Mallarmé or Poe, or again one of Paul's sonnets, playing the trick of changing it slightly by omitting or adding a word. There was an old Erard piano

* Hoëné Wronski set himself to discover a supreme law for each of the sciences: one for physics, another for chemistry, etc. The law for mathematics he wrote down in a hundred or so lines! His demonstration is rather intricate: how is it possible to treat the science as it should be treated since it is the supreme law!

† For the Mallarmé *amicale* I confined myself to presenting several requests for explanations.

in the next room which my family had consigned to me.*

Each *amicale* allowed us to confront two opposing theories, and to go from one to the other, accentuating their difference. And thus a new antinomy was erected, which Paul delighted in making concrete by some formula written on the blackboard.

Although I took great pleasure in these friendly jousts, I had a vague feeling that the two parts of our dialogue were not well balanced. Young student that I was, I was able to make my older comrade talk about mathematics, but that comrade failed to enrich my mind very much with Mallarméan symbols. In other words, the exchange of intellectual values worked only in one direction. Later on it amused Paul to say to me: "After all, I am the one who is indebted to you!" I could easily show him that it was the contrary: the best way for me to develop a mathematical mind was by demonstrating to him all the rigors and all the subtleties, but the one who sets out to explain a poem risks dulling its most beautiful images, even in his own eyes. ... Thus, I was the gainer, I told him, while he might have warped his poetic talent.

Was it true that in our conversations in the rue Urbain-V, Paul was really trying to make me share his own enthusiasms, or at least teach me to understand certain formulas of Poe and Mallarmé? At the time I was convinced that this was his purpose. Today, in thinking back, I am led to believe that his eloquence was fed by another ambition than that of

* One of our *amicales* took place on a Good Friday, so we called it "the enchantment of Good Friday." It included the traditional visit to various churches, and when we returned I played the famous selection from *Parsifal*. Paul read several of his poems, among them "Le Jeune Prêtre."

convincing me. In reality it was nothing more than an exercise for himself. These improvisations gave him the opportunity to develop his own ideas without forcing himself to give them a calculated form. And as for our *amicales*, they probably had no other purpose than to "consolidate" our daily offhand conversations.

Paul had other friends. No doubt in his talks with Pierre Louÿs and André Gide he used another language than with me. His admiration for Mallarmé found in these two a sympathetic response. And his theories about aesthetics were clarified by confronting the ideas of these poet friends. On the other hand, in relation to me, a young student at the lycée, Paul felt freer to sketch out his "poetics," and he would put it to the test at our *amicales*. If in this way he passed on to me all his thought in the realm of literary art, he confided very little of what might have been troubling his inner life. It was only much later that I heard even an echo of the crisis he passed through in 1892.

Nevertheless it brought about a rather strange incident in our relations—an incident the cause of which I could not fathom. Paul left for a trip in August 1892, and gave me his address. I wrote to him. He answered immediately, but to tell me . . . that I must not write to him anymore! I pretended not to be hurt, and sent him a wire: "All right, henceforth I will telegraph you."

When he began to write to me again he gave no explanation, and I never asked for any.*

*

* "Is it possible that one reveals himself most fully to the one he loves best?" Rather a tardy consolation!... It is true that one has friends from different sectors.

I never failed to see him when I went to Paris. During one of those years I was his guest in the rue de Villejust for a whole week. He would wake me every morning when he had finished his meditations, for he already had the habit of setting to work at dawn. He wrote as his thoughts came, and without regard for future publication. Nevertheless, the first sketches of his work were there beside him, and they already formed a voluminous dossier. "What will I do with all that?" he often said. But I saw that he was little concerned with their fate. He was in good form, happy to be free to pursue his intellectual exercises. Their difficulties, ever increasing, marked in some way the successive stages of his speculation.

Paul continued to work at mathematics. Beside his table there was a revolving bookcase containing books on the calculus, chosen from among the most recently published. We had long talks about the theory of groups and groups of transformation.

Two anecdotes, which may interest some amateurs of Valéry's work, date from that period.

Being in Morocco, I amused myself by translating an Arab poem that I heard in the Moorish cafés of Casablanca. I sent the literal translation to my friend, who found something in it that pleased him. He remembered a line and put it into *Eupalinos*.

En le voyant, on se sent devenir architecte.★

★ In *Eupalinos*, there are these lines: "Un de mes amis qu'il est inutile de nommer disait d'Alcibiade: en le voyant, on devient architecte." [One of my friends, whom it is useless to name, said of our Alcibiades who was so beautifully made: "Looking at him, one feels oneself becoming an architect'..."] In the Moroccan poem, it has to do with a cup-bearer who pours the wine for the guests at a festival. [See *Collected Works*, Vol. 4, p. 75.]

The other episode is the following. In 1912, Berger-Levrault published a fairly obscure technical book that I had written on our military campaigns in Chaouïa. I sent the manuscript to my friend and asked him to revise my preface. He rewrote it completely and sent back some very fine pages which appeared under my signature!

To finish with the period 1894–1914, here is the complete text of a letter he wrote me in January 1914. His habitual irony is given free rein; however, for the first time he complained to me of his intellectual work "which is dragging along," he told me.

Paris, January 20, 1914

My dear Pierre,

I have received your graphics with the usual pleasure, and I have made an appointment with myself at some favorable and unburdened time to study the system of your signs. An arduous question, certainly.

But I have so little time, this time! I have just spent five weeks in my bed or my bedroom, and am still feeling rotten, feeble, dizzy with weakness, and all my long overdue work before me.

And I am frozen! The cold is unbearable—age has skinned me, and a man from the South re-emerges and shivers with images of the Sun. My "intellectual work" drags along—I am so done in, without appetite, that I'd rather not talk about it.

Let us speak, O Muse, of that Oranian park* where you claim to languish. . . .

I shake your hand, man of the park.

P.V.

* The Parc d'Artillerie at Oran.

366

During the 1914–1918 war, I made several short visits to my friend. Then, in 1919, I spent my time in far distant countries: Japan, Siberia, the Levant, Constantinople. We wrote to each other regularly.

Valéry's letters of 1919 to 1923 are very curious to read for anyone interested in the development of his genius.

It was during that period that he decided to present his new works to the public. His silence had lasted for twenty-five years! What, in fact, was known about him in 1920?

From 1891 to 1896, these works had appeared:

A few poems, among them "Narcisse parle."
La soirée avec Monsieur Teste.
Introduction à la méthode de Vinci.
Une Conquête méthodique.
From 1897 to 1917, nothing.
In 1917, *La Jeune Parque* was published (in 600 copies).
In 1918, nothing.
In 1919, *Note et Digression,* to serve as a preface to a new edition of his *Introduction à la Méthode de Vinci.*

*

Beginning in 1920, Valéry decided to make something of the "stock" of notes he had amassed in twenty-five years. He selected, assembled, consolidated, and began writing the masterpieces to be called *L'Âme et la danse* and *Eupalinos.*

He also conceived the publication of *Charmes,* which would contain his collected poems.

In addition, he consented to write articles and prefaces and to give a few lectures.

This departure toward his destiny is touching. What a crisis of conscience, with its hesitations and bitterness! But also what fidelity of thought lies beneath his lamentations! And through his ironic scorn for "literature" one can glimpse a profound faith in himself.

Here are a few of his letters to me, written between 191c and 1923. I have transcribed the one written in 1919 to show that he had not yet made his decision.

> Paris, August 30, 1919
>
> ... I have just received your cards from Indo-China, which mark your itinerary very well up to now. I wonder if you have received my replies? As for me, I'm a fixed point, and *BA* is easier than *AB*.
>
> ... Nevertheless, travel attracts me, and the planisphere is not distasteful to me.
>
> I am fed up with my self, with my habits, and the fatigue of piled-up work leads me to believe in the attractions of a complete physical change.
>
> This is an illusion. I give way to the wish to be a mero-morphe, multiform and polydrome. I give way psycholo-gically, to be sure, for I have neither the means nor the leisure to go even to the seashore. ...
>
> I look forward to your news. As for me, I have nothing to report. You see that my small life is bounded by 400 meters of territory.
>
> The best to you.
>
> > P.V.

So, Paul Valéry had not yet made up his mind to publish anything at all. He was hesitating, and perhaps in the end he even blamed himself. That is, he blamed the very form of his meditations.

The following letter, undated, was written towards August 1920:

Wednesday

... I hope to see you before you leave for Syria. I would like to go with you, because I am worn out, exhausted, a prey to disgust and extreme depression. Impossible to work, with work piled up before me.

Alas! I have a chain around my neck, and I must pull the oars of my own galley.

Literarily, I have nothing to complain of; and yet the old contempt I have for that sport and those poorly trained sportsmen (which made me cut myself off from them for so long a time) comes back to my mind. All that is nothing. It is infinitely far from an intellectual life. Furthermore, that life becomes and will become more and more difficult to manage. ...

P.V.

When he says "literarily, I have nothing to complain of," he is alluding to the successful publication in August 1920 of "Le Cimetière marin."

But Valéry was still hesitating; he still did not wish to insert into his favorite intellectual exercises the new work he had imposed on himself. The obligation to write articles and give lectures was perhaps the cause of his "disgust" and his "spleen." His anxiety seems to have grown worse in the following letter, written at the end of October 1890.

Paris, Wednesday

What has become of Syria? Are you an archaeologist, a merchant, a mystagogue, or engineer? Did you see Lebanon? That magic name evokes the idea of a marvelous landscape, rock and cedars.

You must study the Bible and the Arab authors. Down

there in the land of the Druses, there is something very important; there is a sort of mystico-political freemasonry, which dates from very ancient times, and is probably interesting.

As for me, I go from bad to worse—I spent a really hard summer, and the beginning of winter finds me with a very painful throat infection, with exponential worries, invaded by a sort of enormous lassitude. I can tell you that I have had far too much of my present existence. Coming back to Paris was nausea, disgust with living, and a total lack of interest in work, combined with forced labor.

I have stopped doing mathematics, and even verse; I am tied down to boring work that I was stupid enough to accept for the bit of money it will bring me. There is my financial situation. Not brilliant! I would be glad to hear that over there you see things with a more luminous eye. How many times I have wanted to chuck everything overboard and look around for another fate, I don't know where. In two days I will be forty-nine years old, and I know myself by heart. Goob-bye, old friend.

PAUL

We notice in the above letter that he speaks of his "lack of appetite for work" (this is related to those hours spent in writing without any thought of publishing), "combined with forced labor" (that is, the elaboration of work supposed to appear in the near future). If Valéry was discouraged in this way, it was because the idea of readers haunted his mind during his hours of pure meditation.

No day would bring joy to Paul Valéry unless he could give himself entirely to the exercise of his thought, at other times to consolidating certain points of his analysis, and finally to feeling the desire to write something purely literary. These were the conditions of his intellectual well-being, but they were never realized during those years.

The following letter is no less gloomy. Valéry did not have the strength to put the final touches to *Charmes,* a collection of his finest poems. But this letter is curious from another point of view: we see his thought roving in the realm of mathematics, where it felt at ease, and only there could it again find its old freedom.

Paris, October 17, 1921

... As for me, I am exhausted, foundered, at the limit of weariness with everything. I have spent a year of fatigue and worry, finished off by a holiday from which I came back sick.

Very little production this year! I would like to publish my volume of poems before the end of the year. But, though it is almost finished, I haven't the strength to complete it, and I don't know when I can get rid of this accumulation.

You poke fun at me, but if you saw what my life is you would find it unbearable. ...

The popularizations of Einstein are grotesque—in particular Nordmann's. No one can narrate a piece of music, above all to the deaf.

There you have men without the least notion of what is called *mass,* for example, who are trying to understand these theories. Not even to mention the mathematical part!

Now everything depends on that, for physically and intuitively, general relativity has not taken hold.

In short, this was our starting point: an experiment has

shown that the theory of the composition of speeds does not apply to that of light.

What must be upset for the theory to be saved? Or the notion of a solid body?

Or the form of waves, and therefore the ether?

There are no doubt other variables, more or less hidden, that could be brought in.

Minkowski's theory is the exciting one, giving the notion of *event* as the general invariable of all space-time.

But perhaps it is more seductive than really fruitful.

As for the question of absolute movement, I have never understood exactly what those words mean.

The idea of abolishing inertia and gravity is really splendid. These two concepts make only one, which is no more mysterious than their sun.

As to Einstein's continually varied and varying spaces, I am lost in them. The passage from one variation to another seems to me hard to imagine. But do not imagine!

My best, old friend.

P.V.

The following letter reveals a certain melancholy, but perhaps less extreme.

Paris, January 1, 1922

... As for me, last year was a bad one, with terrible worries, and it ended with a series of physical illnesses. I have reached my half century, which is tiresome enough; I produced what I hadn't counted on producing, and have not produced what I had counted on producing.

But what do you expect? Life is not an analytical function! Taylor's series is not the reigning mistress there.

I will probably go to Switzerland about the tenth of this

month. The University of Zurich has invited me to give a lecture. ... It is paying me. I will go running. I don't know exactly what I will say, or whether I will say anything. My voice is weak. My experience is nil; my fear is great, and the subject very delicate. It has to do in general with Franco-German intellectual rapport!... We shall see.

Mathematics is far off and difficult. Painlevé has often told me that you need one life to learn it, and a second to put it to use.

This is true of everything: language, music. Man's life is too short to make full use of the instruments he has created. ...

P. Valéry

In short, things were going rather better since he was able to joke about his so-called discouragement, and then rise above it a bit. But the Zurich lecture is bothering him. He talks about this!

Until that time Valéry had worked for Monsieur Lebey, director of the Agence Havas. In February 1922, Lebey died: Valéry was left without a job. Won't he be obliged to look for another? At the age of fifty! Several of his letters, written at the beginning of 1922, which I have not reproduced here, betray a certain perplexity.

In the following letter, my friend told me of the publication of *Charmes*. And, also, he seems to have decided to turn to account the rest of his "stock."

[Undated, written in 1922]

My dear Pierre, the Mosque of Eyoub ... a marvel to judge from your postcard.

Paris is less charming. I have no appetite for the life I lead.

My book of poems is out. I will keep a copy for you. I am disgusted with what is finished, and nauseated with what is still to do. But, one must live.

I have made use of . . . to drag from their slumber all my papers and notes accumulated in the course of thirty years.

What to draw from them? First of all, seasickness in the face of this chaos of my "ideas," which I feel are not usable, but must be used.

I need three eunuch slaves, intelligent and infinitely compliant. One to read my papers to me, the other to tell me if he understands, and the third, a secretary-stenographer. . . .

And, nevertheless, it would soon bore me to do this work with them.

I would need a black, a yellow, and a white secretary. You are at the confluence of all races. At the multiple point, of which the Levant is the resulting vector.

Find me a Greek mixed with an Arab, a Jew, and a Slav, thief, pimp, Doctor of Science, hopeless renegade, and a poly-polyglot. I need a shrewd intermediary to sell my soul to the devil, at the top price. Otherwise, the bugger will have it for nothing.*

Good-bye, Pierre, you are lucky to be a philosopher, an artilleryman, carefree, and at Byzantium.

Study Hagia Sofia! Eat melons!

Your old friend

P.V.

Is it not true that this letter has a more reassuring tone? This time his decision seems definitive: he will make use of his notebooks, which have grown in number with each year, and the project seems already to be in operation.

* These lines recall certain passages of *Mon Faust*.

The following letter is also less anguished; his comments are more ironic than troubled.

> [Undated, written in August 1923]
> Hôtel Restauration
> Châteauneuf-les-Bains
> Puy-de-Dôme

The article on Pascal is my current job; nothing worth passing on to any but the 40,000 readers of the *Revue Hebdomadaire*; I have also written a preface to *Eureka*—a limited edition and I have only one copy. In this preface I spoke of "matter" (another algorism, but faulty) and of the Universe—it was easy to demonstrate that it was a notion corresponding to nothing.

In the end, we must come to the point of sweeping away the dictionary and remaking all the nonconvergent ... notions.*

I am here for a few days: heat, boredom, annoyances, discomfort, all is here.

I shake your hand, O Turk!

> P.V.

Alas! In the following letter, which I received on my return to France in November 1923, Paul seemed discouraged again. One would conclude that he was overworked, that he no longer found the time to write for himself. Without any doubt, that was what overwhelmed him.

> [No date, written in September 1923]

My dear Pierre,

Thank you for your letter which came to congratulate

---

* "Définir, c'est établir la convergence de plusieurs concepts," my friend sometimes said to me.

me in the Auvergne, and to which I reply in Gascony.*
Decorated or not, I am still on the hook and fairly flattened
out in any case. People think I am content, and they are very
much mistaken. At bottom, I am always anxious, and even
more without any desire to work—which is the worst of all.
Work conceals one's life; as soon as you stop working from
disgust, your life becomes apparent, and that is not
amusing.

Perhaps I have overtaxed this powerful intellectual subterfuge—it no longer numbs me. ...

Writing bores me. I am obliged to regard it as a way of
making a living. But it is the worst possible profession, the
most exhausting, and one that does not feed a man—a man
who produces with difficulty—and who produces only
difficult things.

You see that my life is not rosy. I had best stop this, and
not tire you out with my reflections.

See you soon, then. ...

PAUL

When we read this series of letters, can we define precisely Paul Valéry's state of mind at this critical period of his
life?

At first sight, it would seem so; these letters are striking
in their freedom of style, their simplicity. The words pour
out freely. And they express nothing but weariness and
bitterness. Nevertheless, the leitmotif of his complaint
should be interpreted with caution.

When Valéry speaks of his disgust with work, what kind
of work does he have in mind? Is it the work to which he
strictly adhered every day from dawn; or is the work for

* I was congratulating him on the Legion of Honor.

which he had lost courage not, rather, the preparation of some article or other that he had promised?

When he says that some lecture or other is of no importance except for the payment, I strongly suspect that he was throwing out this remark in order to hide his true feeling: the "reserve" of the thinker who is about to speak in public.

We observe the mixture of an unusual modesty ("my experience is nil; my fear is great") and his exalted notion of his mission (his scorn for literature and for those who live by it).

Finally, I point out the following detail which has always interested me: in his correspondence, Valéry wrote to me about *Charmes*, and then about his article on Pascal, and also about his preface to *Eureka*. But there is no mention of *Eupalinos* in his letters of 1923. Now that is the year when this masterpiece, which marked a new stage in his genius, appeared.

Nevertheless, I trust my friend's confidences, and I realize that his mind underwent a fairly long and severe crisis at this time. But I admit that both its cause and its effects remain a mystery to me.

Is it not strange that his discouragement should have been most severe during the very year that he decided to publish his work? And that his discouragement persisted despite the success of his publications?

One might think that the death of Monsieur Lebey, in February 1922, had left Valéry at a loss and made him uncertain about pursuing his work. That explanation cannot be valid, for the letters written before 1922 are as morose as those of the following years.

How then can one penetrate this enigma? The following explanations pretend in no way to resolve it. And if I present them it is only in the hope that they will contribute toward defining the value of my illustrious friend's effort.

Let us then place ourselves beside the Valéry of 1920 and observe him in the course of his early morning's work, in those delightful hours when he was concentrating on transforming and combining the ideas that had come to him. Was he working without any afterthought, as he has often maintained? Was the idea of an eventual reader truly absent from his mind? Certainly it was, at the beginning of his meditation. But then, when he looked back over what he had written, the idea no doubt arose to do something with it later on. ... Later! An accounting he recoiled from every day. ... A secret desire, not yet acknowledged even to himself.

It was in 1922 that his intention clearly emerged. He must come to the point of using those many notebooks in which, for twenty-five years, he had written down the workings of his mind.

His friends were now insisting that *Charmes* be finally published.

At the same time, he decided to set about writing other things than poetry; he even consented to give lectures and to publish various articles. Mysterious coincidence! A sign of *the characteristic ambiguity and the high ambitions* of Paul Valéry.

For a long time he had neglected his Muse. He was no longer listening to her every morning between lamplight and the rising sun. The ideas he retained were those that allowed him to pursue to the best of his ability the analysis of his mind. Nevertheless, *Charmes* appeared. It was the legacy of the poet faithful to his literary group.

Valéry knew that this work would have success, but he

wanted his creative effort to reveal itself under various forms. During the year when *Charmes* was published, Valéry attracted the attention of the elite by his lectures and articles, and in secret he was writing *Eupalinos*. Prodigious mark of a universal mind! He had made his decision. He would take from his notebooks those pages he thought the most apt to beguile us. They were the material he used to construct those pieces of literary art in which the most abstract thought *sounds and glows*. That decision, endlessly put off, brought with it a considerable upset in his work. Until then, Valéry had *postponed to infinity the moment for the final writing*. Now time was intervening, and this disturbed the habitual discipline of his meditations. Could he now meditate facing only himself, as he had done with such delightful abandon? The Other has appeared. The Other was the public, the "Consumer." Henceforth it must be taken into account. This intervention of the "Other" could only trouble him profoundly, even in the moments when his thought exulted in jousting with itself.

It has sometimes occurred to me to compare his distress to that of an opium smoker who is interrupted every day in his reverie by the arrival of a visitor. This smoker would experience a certain nausea when he returned to his pipe. "Perhaps," Valéry wrote me, "I have abused this powerful subterfuge. It no longer intoxicates me."

Well, in reality, Valéry was intoxicated by the play of combinations in his mind. Without nausea, or lassitude, no matter what he says. I would not know how to define his state of mind. One might say that sometimes a kind of uneasiness possessed him. "Have I lost my way?" he would say to himself. The feeling of the complexity of his work would take hold of him, and this feeling would encounter his tenacious will to persevere. He was in the situation of a vagrant worker who, setting off along an unfamiliar road, asks himself if he has taken the right way, and he hurries on possessed by a sort of anguish. Panic. But this anguish would disappear as soon as Paul Valéry had clearly seen the new horizons opening before him.

He went through this crisis of 1922, remaining himself without relinquishing any of his freedom of thought. The reasons for his discouragement were more apparent than real. His thought, composed of a thousand and one combinations, would be used *to construct a work bearing the visible marks of the whole system it was founded on.*

> *Centre de ressort, de mépris, de pureté*
> *Je m'immole intérieurement à ce que je voudrais être.*

*

After 1928, I spent several months of each year in Paris; I saw my friend as often as possible. Every morning at 9:30 I would telephone him, hoping to make an appointment for the afternoon.

My memories of the Valéry of that period are very precise. His ability to work was magnificent. Gone was his weariness, the leitmotif that had saddened his letters in the past. His intellectual effort was again following *the way of his desires.* He was lavish with lectures, speeches, articles, at the same time setting up the most abstract of constructions. In particular I remember his enthusiasm for writing *Sémiramis* and *Amphion*, and, on the contrary, the trouble he had with his famous speech of 1931.[*] He drafted some of his articles in a few hours, while others required weeks of work before

* Reply to Marshal Pétain's Reception Address to the French Academy.

they satisfied him. As for his first lecture at the Collège de France, he concentrated on it for eight months; it provided him with the opportunity to revise his ideas on the subject of the creation of works of art.

He rarely talked to me about poetry. It no longer seemed to interest him. Sometimes, being curious about this renunciation, I would ask him to interpret certain passages of *L'Après-midi d'un faune* or *Hérodiade*, or even his own *Jeune Parque*. He would evade me, and if I insisted he would enlarge on his favorite theory, according to which a poem is reconstructed by each reader in his own way, and if these versions are many and various, that testifies to the richness of the work. This was not the way he talked in the past, in the rue Urbain-V!

Fairly often we talked about mathematics; he was still attracted by the theory of groups, and also of groups of transformations. His mind luxuriated in moving in this realm of speculation.

I often teased him about his difficulty in understanding an abstract proposition, or even in stating it without resorting to a concrete example. I made use of a fairly severe test for measuring his capacity for abstraction. It so happened that we both owned a work of uncommon transcendence: Georg Cantor's *Théorie des ensembles*. No vast amount of knowledge was necessary to get through this work; the elementary rules of the calculus sufficed. But alas! After reading a few pages the mind stops, exhausted. The next day we would try to go on, but each day we would advance less and less. ... "What page are you on?" I would ask my friend from time to time. He replied, "I have to reread such and such pages before I can continue. ..." As for myself, where am I today? To what stage of that transcendent construction must I descend to find the strength to advance anew?*

The scorn Paul Valéry professed for "literature" was real, at least for certain genres of literature. I found him very hard on young writers, poets in particular.

He received all the newly published books; he rarely cut the pages. These volumes, like new, lay on the floor in heaps. One day I witnessed a real ballistic exercise. The starting point: his table. "Trash! Trash!" he said, throwing the books into the middle of the room. When the pile grew too bulky, this literature was sent off to his daughter, and later on it was relegated to his studio on the Avenue Foch.

He talked to me freely about his latest publications and his plans, without any pretensions of language. But with what faith! With what pride in the purity of his method and the continuity of his effort! His passion for speculative exercises drove him to create ever new models for the operations of his thought, and that without at all modifying the principle of his work.

How can I say to what point I was embarrassed in talking about his work? I was confronted with the problem fairly often, and most of all when he showed me a copy of his latest book, or read me passages from his next public lecture. Then I found myself obliged to express my thought, and to do it by carefully avoiding any sort of flattery, banality, and

* In *Tel Quel* [see *Collected Works*, Vol. 14, p. 16] we read: "There are works, famous or otherwise, which for the purpose of triangulating the mental world are preferable to others; they provide us with guide-marks.

"For a long time I have owned a fifty-page pamphlet, dealing with a technical subject, in which what are called exactness, profundity, originality of approach, are constantly and admirably present."

Contrary to what I had thought, this brochure was not Cantor's *Théorie des ensembles*. I do not know what it was.

preciousness of language. How to squeeze from my brain
something personal, while relating it in some way to his text.
That was a problem in which the given data have no common
measure.

I felt that I was in a situation from which I could not dis-
entangle myself, and, to be sure, my friend enjoyed my
predicament. So much that he sometimes created the situation himself by directing the conversation to certain pages
of his work. But I was out of my depth in this contest to
which he invited me, and he dealt me some rude jolts. In
agreeing with him I ran great risks: I had not precisely
understood his thought and he did not fail to tell me so,
even to the point of demonstration. Besides, it seemed best
to take an opposing view. However, he would surmise that
I was doing that, and, waiting for this ploy on my part, he
used my remarks to improvise new combinations of ideas
which soon left me far behind.

In short, the difficulty of sustaining such a dialogue came
from having to portion carefully the amount of resistance
necessary to combat the thesis of the day. If my resistance
seemed insufficient, Valéry would quickly change the theme.
If it were too much, he would cut me off and quickly
administer a "knockout." In either case, the game was over.

I was no longer the one who demonstrated Euclid's
theorems, nor the comrade teasing the young poet about his
first efforts.

Here are a few letters to illustrate this period of well-being
in which Valéry expands without reserve or weariness.

I would even go so far as to say that he had passed the
stage of equilibrium between his different kinds of activity.
He had thrown himself into the hubbub of opinions and
systems which excite society and the community of con-

temporary minds. Changing many times a day the domain and focus of his mind excited his thought.

Sunday, January 3, 1932

My dear Pierre,

Your letter gave me great pleasure. It brought me an instant of the time when I had time.*

I spent the entire summer—working seven hours a day (this is not a rule of three) to fabricate a work payable at the end of October. But the "crisis" made it necessary for the one who had commissioned it to withdraw into a... meditative abstention.† I had to give some lectures in the Southwest and I have just returned. ...

I am not very competent in the matter of the radio. One must have dabbled around in these things to get one's bearings and above all have made electrical measurements. Moreover, I splutter all along the line. ...

In October, at a congress in Rome held to confer on the subject of the nucleus of the atom, one of the thirty illustrious physicists categorically stated that within the nucleus —*there can no longer* be a question of space or time.

The great thing now in fashion is called: Ψ. It seems that it envelops God in its depths. I don't know any more, but this is already quite a bit. ΔΨ.‡

Must one give up trying to understand? Renounce Math? Has quantity used up its resources?**

* Valéry liked these formulas in which the same word is repeated with a slightly different nuance.

† *L'Idée fixe*, which appeared in March 1932. [See *Collected Works*, Vol. 5.]

‡ This is a find. Valéry means that if this differential is known, the function is defined in its essence.

** *Has quantity used up its resources?* The word *quantity* may surprise some readers. I take it to be used here in its true meaning: quantity

As for politics, it's the same thing. Or worse. All the old dodges are worn out. Among them *war*, as efficacious or a solution. Do—written things—treaties, slogans, etc. At bottom, peace and war have no meaning!! This is super-intelligent! Hyperparadoxical! But there is some truth in it.

It is said that the financial crisis will ease toward the month of April! It is said—just the contrary. ... According to the English, everything depends on the *French* elections. ...

Conclusion: we must make music of the most ... mathematical sort, and math ... of the most musical sort.

I wish you a year without too many worries. ...

PAUL

Paris, March 15, 1934

My dear Pierre,

It is only too true that I am miserably late in answering you. With faultless wisdom you yourself indicate the cause of this "lag." My head swims a dozen times a day, and if I enumerated the number and diversity of things (and people) that devour me, you would shudder to the limits of shuddering. I am trying to leave for the coast in a short while. (I should have been there since December.) But I never leave except to go from one chaotic hubbub to another—and letters follow me.

And events. ...

In our time, seven-tenths of all events are created by the newspapers. For an event is only a fact "valorized," and that value is itself conferred by the vibration of publicity. This being said, there is something nasty, and *no* solution. Indivi-

is in effect that which can be measured or counted. In the quantum theory, the attempt has been made to try out data which cannot be measured or counted, at least in the continuum of space-time.

dual responsibility is, at bottom, no more than an empty pretence. This amuses the public, as has already been seen in many an "affair."

Everybody has ready-made remedies, in his head. To my mind, the worst of the worst is perhaps the diminution of professional conscience, found everywhere and in everything. We live by make-believe.

There is also a remarkable increase in general stupidity; the national skepticism is as stupid (to the limit) as the credulity of the people to the east of us. To tell the truth, *everyone does not have the right to be skeptical*. First point. Second point, those who are not, or should not be *everybody*, have no right to credulity. The result is great perturbations in the *system of inequality*, which is in the nature of things and men, and which is the fatal foundation of societies, and thus of politics. ...

P.V.

During the years 1936, '37, and '38, I organized a series of artistic and literary evenings in Morocco, for the purpose of instituting an exchange of intellectual values with Moslem writers and artists. Valéry followed my enterprise with interest, and I benefited by his support. Here is what he wrote me about the first lecture I gave at Fez on "the pleasure of music among Europeans and among Arabs":*

... Much interested by what you say about exclusive melodism. It is a capital point of technical difference. But have you noticed whether a Berber is more apt than a Semite in "understanding" our music? That would make a curious statistic.

* The text of this lecture was published in the *Mercure de France* (February 15, 1937).

Another melodic question. It seems to me that the *length* of certain of our melodies and the *complication* of the design of the *suggested arc* are greater in ours than in Oriental music. The phrase more developed?

And also what I call the structure of time. But I don't know how to explain what I mean.*

At Tunis I heard a great native concert at a theater—with pleasure for half an hour, boredom afterwards. It is true that this happens to me in Paris also. And then I am not a musician.

The chapter on musical pleasure deserves a formal discussion.

For example, I would say, contrary to you, that musical emotion is the most natural and almost the only natural one given by art. Music alone (in my opinion) allows us to represent the mysterious proceedings of nature equaling the development, the growth.

Natura means, etymologically, the "making grow," the generating-generator.

In sum, you have done a very complete and at the same time lively study of your subject. Everything is at least indicated—and neither the vague nor the boring have any part in this text. . . .

Your

P.V.

In 1937 I put to him the idea of presenting to literary Moroccans a few fragments of his work taken either from *Sémiramis*, or, preferably, from *L'Âme et la danse*. Here is what he wrote me on this subject:

* Valéry meant that Orientals and Europeans *mark* time in a different way. Their conception of rhythm is essentially different.

387

Sunday [no date], 1937

I am replying at once although I have no ink, and won't have until tomorrow. ...

Your idea of lectures, readings, even performances of my texts is amusing. In fact, the Moroccans might be likely to understand things that more than one among us don't understand. My brief contact with a few Arab intellectuals and theologians at Tunis, in April, gave me a strange sensation of the mentality of the Middle Ages.

But last year I saw partly-played some fragments of *L'Âme et la danse*, at the Salle Pleyel ... and it seemed to me that it was too carefully written and had too much "style" for the theater.

Amphion and *Sémiramis* require in principle a large setting, and they were murdered at the Opera. The music is complicated. But I leave you to make out as best you can. Whatever you do will be well done.

I am returning to Paris at the end of the week. We will see each other.

Your

PAUL [signed in pencil]

... After 1938, I never saw my friend again. ...

In 1944, the country being free again, our correspondence took on its habitual form. Here is one of his last letters.

November 11, 1944

... I received your card of October 27 with joy. Finally the way is open, after four years of pressure and privation. I assure you that between the occupation, the cold, the lack of food, the lack of everything—clothes, paper, cars, etc., and the feeling of constant menace—this has been a painful time. Nevertheless I have worked a great deal—the only remedy in that sad life. I taught my course, published a few small volumes and some fragments of a *Faust* of my own vintage. ...

I see that for your part you haven't been idle. I suppose you are still cultivating Arabic. And math? Can you imagine that a few days ago I found among my papers some poems and theorems from the Urbain-V times—analyses that you had corrected for me, formulas of derivation and integration? That was only fifty-two years ago. ...

It seems that my poor Sète has been severely damaged: Montpellier is intact or almost. Here we have had street fighting, and a strange Sunday, a mixture of the joy of liberation and the sudden bursts from machine guns, which made us run laughing toward doorways. ...

Your old

P.V.

Paul Valéry, in reviving his memories of that dear rue Urbain-V, and exhuming our old notebooks in mathematics, seemed to wish to evoke the cycle of our friendship and to emphasize its origins and its constancy.

NOTES

NOTES

I N this final Volume 15 of *The Collected Works of Paul Valéry* in English, no excerpts from his *Cahiers* have been included, except those selected by Valéry himself and published under the title "Propos me concernant." Valéry considered the entire twenty-nine volumes of his Notebooks, which he had kept from 1894 until his death in 1945 (now published in facsimile by the Centre National de la Recherche Scientifique, Paris, 1957), to be his real autiobiography—"where my *Moi* most clearly takes shape." In these he had jotted down, day by day, "certain very abstract studies," but with no order. A systematic account of these ideas would be a separate work.

However, during his lifetime Valéry drew from his Notebooks some of his jottings and published them under various titles. These have been collected in *Analects*, Volume 14 of *The Collected Works*. Other excerpts have been selected and published in other volumes of the edition.

3. AUTOBIOGRAPHY: "Autobiographie," a typescript given to the editor by Julien P. Monod. Unpublished and undated.

4. ...*great dictionary*: *Dictionnaire raisonné de l'architecture française du XIe au XVI siècle* (10 vols., 1854–1869).

12. MOI: pages sent to Pierre Louÿs with a letter dated

September 14, 1890, *Lettres à quelques-uns* (Paris: Gallimard, 1952). See *Œuvres II*, Pléiade (1957), p. 1430.

15. THREE WAKINGS: "Trois Réveils," *Paul Valéry Vivant* (Marseilles: Cahiers du Sud, 1946). The second and third "wakings" are taken from Valéry's *Cahiers*, Vol. 28.

19. MEDITERRANEAN INSPIRATIONS: "Inspirations Méditerranéennes," a lecture given at the Université des Annales on November 24, 1933, and published in *Conférencia*, February 15, 1934; reprinted in *Variété III* (1936), and in *Œuvres*, Vol. K, *Conférences* (1939). See *Œuvres I*, Pléiade (1957), p. 1084.

36. IMPRESSIONS AND RECOLLECTIONS: "Impressions et Souvenirs," *Maîtres et amis* (Paris: Camaïeux de Jacques Beltrand, 1927).

41. MY EARLY DAYS IN ENGLAND: *The Bookman's Journal*, London, December 1925. Published in English, by an anonymous translator; no known French text exists.

...*music by Suppé*: Franz von Suppé (1820–1895), Austrian conductor and composer of light opera. His overture to *Dichter und Bauer* (Poet and Peasant) is his best known work.

42. *Marcel Schwob* (1867–1905): a prolific writer of tales, novels, and essays, but best remembered for his brilliant researches into the literature, life, and language of France in the fifteenth century, particularly with reference to Villon.

43. *Mr. Gosse*: Sir Edmund Gosse (1849–1928), English poet and critic. Besides his critical writing on English literature, he was influential in bringing foreign literature to English

readers. He was a sympathetic student of the younger school of French and Belgian writers, some of his papers on them having been collected in 1905 and published as *English Profiles*.

44. *Meredith to Valéry*:

Boxhill, Dorking
June 20, 1894

Dear Sir:

A friend of Marcel Schwob is entirely within his rights when he expects to be received in my house. You will be most welcome, and I hope you will do me the honor of dining with me at seven o'clock. English cooking, unfortunately; but as for the wine, it is entirely French. I am at home every evening of this week at your disposition after four o'clock—on Friday, Saturday, and Sunday. There is a train that goes back at eight twenty-five.

Please be assured of my most distinguished consideration.

GEORGE MEREDITH

47. *Sir Frederick Pollock* (1845–1937): a member of a great English legal family. His own legal textbooks are standard works.

49. *Meredith to Valéry*:

July 11, 1895

Dear Mr. Valéry:

We are just now at the height of our travels, and perhaps you intend to visit in England for your studies. It may even be that you have friends who would invite you and help to find a few enticements in this rather dull country for a stranger. If that is the case, I beg you to count me at times among them, and to make me a visit. You will give me great pleasure. Sir Frederick and Lady Pollock, whom you encountered in my "hovel," recall that occasion with great pleasure. As for me, I scan the literary Gazettes to find your name and your works. I know that you work steadily and that you possess with ability that warmth which urges us to great results.

Mr. George Hugo spoke to me about a study concerning Da Vinci,—but please do not call me *Master*. I am no more than your elder brother.

Please be assured of my most distinguished consideration.

GEORGE MEREDITH

55. A TIMELY RECOLLECTION: "Souvenir actuel," *Marianne*, February 9, 1938. See *Œuvres II*, Pléiade (1960), p. 982.

59. *Now all peoples*: from "A Conquest by Method" (1897), *Collected Works*, Vol. 10, pp. 61–65.

60. VALÉRY–FOURMENT CORRESPONDENCE: *Correspondance Paul Valéry–Gustave Fourment 1887–1933* (Paris: Gallimard, 1957), with notes and a preface by Octave Nadal. Selected letters.

From a letter...: this passage was the superscription to the entire volume, *Correspondance Paul Valéry–Gustave Fourment 1887–1933*.

Gustave Fourment: Gustave Fourment was elected Deputy from the Var in 1910, and later Senator; he held this office until his death in 1940.

63. *Quemadmodum desiderat*...: "As the hart panteth after the fountains of water; so my soul panteth after thee, O God."

The quotation is actually from Psalm 42: Nadal is giving

the number of the psalm in the King James Version. It is Psalm 41 in the Douay Version.

65. *scripta volant verba...*: written words fly away, pleasing words remain.

Ce soir, comme d'un cerf,...

> This evening, the flight towards the pool, like a stag's,
> Has no cease till it drops in the midst of the reeds.
> My thirst brings me down on the very water's edge.
> But, to quench the thirst of this inquisitive love,
> I shall not trouble the mysterious surface...
>
> *(Collected Works,* Vol. i, p. 141.)

66. *Un Séraphin pensif...*:

> A pensive Seraphin leaning over my bedside
> Was shaking the lilacs from his light robe.

69. *...professors of philosophy*: In his "Souvenirs de la classe de Philosophie," published by the *Revue des Joyeux Escholiers*, edited by Marc Soriano, 1936, Valéry wrote:

My memoirs of the philosophy class? Well, I continued in philosophy to be the very mediocre student that I was in the preceding classes. I remember however a brilliant debut which had no success: the first dissertation assigned required of us, I believe, to compare common sense notions with the teachings of philosophy. Naturally I had no preference. Then as now, I was afraid of both, but I knew very well to which one it was important to give the advantage and I did not hesitate to compare *common sense* to the stick that warns and more or less guides our steps in the dark with *philosophy* and its torch that widely lights up our space. I believe I was *first*, and this disturbed my habits for only a short time. My professor was a fine man; I must say that he inflicted on me a final detention one day when we were talking about Descartes and the animal machine. A note that I had put into circulation in the class so as to spread a methodical laugh was caught in the hands of a blunderer, the one responsible being obliged to declare himself and be duly punished. In the end I was dismissed from the physics class by a future member of the Academy of Sciences, who recently died. Nevertheless I passed my baccalaureate at the end of the school year, the only thing important to me, and which moreover imported. [Included in notes by Octave Nadal.]

76. *La Vierge byzantine* . . . :

> The Byzantine Virgin, in solid silver,
> Remains hieratic in her orphreyed cope,
> Fixing her eyes of pearl on Heaven, as if dreaming
> Of the remote and luminous blues of Asia.

79. *Ces choses-là* . . . :

> Those things are crude.
> To understand them, learn how to be rude.

83. *Le Conte vraisemblable* [A Likely Story] :

Grief and fear hovered over him. At night, terrors shook him like a tree in the wind, and shivers passed over his flesh; he curled up in his sheets and watched the frightening shadow. Indistinct noises reached him out of the darkness—that froze him, or perhaps he believed that his body was breaking down. He held his chest between his arms, listening anxiously to the cadence of his alarmed heart and his rapid breathing. Often he thought he was dying and in his anguish would take the poses of a dead man, closing his eyes, joining his hands, tightening his muscles, and afterwards being astonished that he was still alive. . . .

Then the worry over *Woman* tormented him cruelly, and above all the desire for art, merely glimpsed, gnawed him like an eternal cancer!. . . *Woman*—he had at times considered her debauched, at times a mystic, or an aesthete. And his misfortune would have it that he had never found the union between the flesh possessed and the chimera of the moment.

He had never worked except with his head—enough to make a sonnet. He had possessed only through the senses and had never violated a single soul. *Woman*, in fact, is incomprehensible for those she does not understand, and he had always been for her a living enigma. He always found a *sainte* where he desired a beautiful piece of meat, since his mind instantly substituted for desire another one fulfilled.

All this soured him against women. He then turned toward combinations of style and the painful birth of rhymes. And there he suffocated more than elsewhere.

One ardent desire drove him and, for whole nights together, congested his brain. But nothing came. He was disturbed by the thousands of schools that suddenly appeared, influenced every day by a different author, but nothing of his own seemed to lodge in his mind.

When an inspiration came to him, a rare windfall, he would abandon it in despair of making it fit into the resounding meters and beneath the ringing skirts of rhymes. He was reduced to rewriting the works of the masters—he abstained either from thought as veneer for the style, or as style for the thought—and torturing himself to no avail for hours. When he read the great, the known, the victorious, his rages would take hold of him for not being *himself* a creator of masterpieces. In vain he learned curious words, strong details; he attained even to dreams, no doubt, in that he was an artist, but correspondence still failed him. And he said to himself, in dejection, that the glorious ones in art were all robbers like the others, for it is the same thing to rob someone with his strong muscles or with his genius.

Boredom meanwhile devoured him—boredom, the condition of man when he falls back into the rank of the ancestral brute, when under cover of the idleness of thought certain mysterious animal atavisms reappear in us and oppress us. This was his condition one autumn evening when he was thinking that art is a lure, that friendship lives on lies, love on cowardice, and that life is a great misery and very long.

Fleeing the lights of the city, the purplish electric flashes falling in livid sheets on the boulevards, the luminous tricklings from the cafés, he went off across the night, across the fields.

The stars turned pale, the heaven cleared and the Moon came out slowly, at first pale red, and *he*, haunted without respite, believed that he saw the enormous head of a man guillotined, at first bloody and swollen, then taken off by an invisible hangman and turning itself loose bloodless on a mortuary sheet embroidered with silver tears—which was the Sky and the Night. He was forcing his mind to notice that sinister rising of the star, to cling to those sensations like a drowned man to the branch of a tree. "Be quick, be quick! Look at this, look at that, be quick, if not you will *dream* of 'you know what' that gnaws your heart, and it waits only a second to melt on your soul!" And in spite of it all, the suffering came back! Suddenly, in that distracted brain a glimmer was seen and the beneficent desire for suicide was born.

Moreover, he saw death in a strongly raw light. He told himself quite clearly that with respect to the *beyond* nothing certain nor even probable is known and that it is a circle of perpetual occulation where all hypotheses come to be broken like helpless waves! One thing was certain: present suffering. Another was possible: change by destruction. His choice was made.

Everything then being resolved in his mind, his flesh pacified by the certainty that it would not suffer, he gave himself one whole day of grace and also the supreme pleasure of seeing and judging all the other pleasures with the new and special optic of a dying man in good health.

And coming back to his house at dawn, a flask of deadly alkaloid placed on his table, his papers burned, he said to himself, "I shall kill myself this evening!"

During those short hours this dying man tasted and enjoyed a modified and yet unknown soul, which he once carried unconsciously in *himself*—a new man lived in his body who incessantly returned to this standard: death, all that passed over the screen of his brain.

Certain Catholic priests, in the past, had noted and recommended this state of spiritual clairvoyance, of perfect calm in the face of contingent things, which comes from the endless contemplation of the final moment of life and, before them, the ancient philosophers. For him, it was with a still greater impassiveness yet that he observed the Rule made by himself for himself, for he had nothing to demonstrate, nor anyone to convince.

And it was truly a beautiful, a mad day.

The morning was clear and cool; he set out toward the rising sun in a fragrant vapor of cigar smoke, making his heels ring with a light heart, his mind sharp and ready to analyze the sensations of the day.

His first joyous astonishment was to feel so active and so strong, when just yesterday he was feeling his pulse and trying to find in his body an imaginary illness. How far away were the nightmares of last night!—the cold sweats and the horror of sleeplessness! And he enjoyed his health all the more in the exhilarating air that whipped him, for he did not lose sight of the final aim, toward which every minute brought him so much nearer! He was not afraid of the suffering to come after this passing excitement nor of the time lost by strolling in this way in the soft light of autumn.

Like all other days and all other men he experienced on that day a thousand of those little stings of life, which make it really bad by being numerous, and which the day before he would have considered mountains, but the persistent vision of death reduced them to their true importance. He didn't even notice.

He ate in a restaurant, never with a better appetite! In fact, the sleep needed in the morning, after the distressing nights, used to keep him from knowing the healthy walks in the early hours of the day, the lunches far from home, and the charm of trotting briskly on the asphalt.

And then everything seemed new to him, untried, unknown, as one finds his house when, before a long voyage, one goes back again to visit the smallest corners, to carry them away in his heart.

Everything seemed gay and diverting to him, the cares on the brows of the passers-by, the enormous scaffoldings woven by anthills of workers, a book that has just appeared, a clock striking. For nothing any longer touched him, of all this, neither money, nor time, nor renown!

He surprised himself suddenly versifying from habit, and tried to stop thinking about it, deciding that it was incompatible with his resolve to die. But habit was strongest, and he quickly wrote down his verses in pencil. But at the café an hour later he read them again as if they had been written by someone else and he stood astonished. They had been composed without a thought of any school and of any ambition, just as he had thought them, quite simple and human, and they were truly the best that he had ever written. Happy in his child's play, he tossed them in passing into the mailbox of a newspaper, giving them the title "Posthumous Verse."

However, the moments were flowing away. A friend he encountered called out to him, "This evening at X's house!" But he, smiling at death in his heart—"No," he said, "I am invited *elsewhere*!"

Then the idea came to him to visit the last woman he had encountered on the road of his life. Quite pink in flesh and dress, she was curled up on a blue divan, which delighted him. And this was the first time that he looked at her just as she was and did not dress her as Venus nor Héloïse nor Nana in his artificial mind. She was not an archetype of a poet nor an artist; she was merely charming. He realized this too late and, wanting to push the game just begun, he managed to be granted a rendezvous for the same evening.

So fast, someone will say? But that day he had forgotten his Byronic or sadistic mask of the days past; he was *himself* and worth the trouble then of being compromised.

And he found infinite pleasures in dreaming that on this evening he would embrace, instead of that delightful and enviable woman, the supreme and flat-nosed Lover to whom the rendezvous had been given!

The evening came. And he found himself in the presence of his verses, which he admired within himself for the exquisite sensations of the day, for the image of the beauty who awaited him and then the brownish bottle that contained the Unknown!

Then deluding himself, very comic but very human, he said to himself, opening the door again, "I shall kill myself TOMORROW!"

... *at the end of your letter*: Fourment had called Valéry "one of our greatest poets."

89. ... *I wrote to Joris-Karl...*:

Monsieur,
I lived for two years with des Esseintes in the country, with Usher also and several others very thin. We talked a great deal in a very close silence and we illuminated the evenings somewhat with liturgical formulas. At times the sentimental likeness showed itself for our distraction, the musical phantom of the dead Ulalume....

I have been in Paris for several hours; I am aware that the crowd is trampling in my brain and that the mad pyres of crystal called *cafés* dazzle it too much. This is why I have given myself the order to see you—interested in an admirable blind man who can elaborate at length a frail and delicious archetype—far from himself.

It is, then, an hour and a day that I dare ask of you.

P.-A.V.

91. ... *persevere knowingly in Stupidity*: a reference to his infatuation with Mme de R——.

... *on a certain date...*: Valéry saw Mme de R—— for the first time toward the end of 1889. According to Octave Nadal, *Valéry–Fourment Correspondance*, note 3, p. 233, Valéry transcribed into his *Cahiers* a conversation he had had with André Gide on January 12, 1925, revealing the role, in depth, that this encounter with Mme de R—— had for him. This entry is not included in the published *Cahiers*.

Valéry wrote of Gide: "I knew nothing about his life or

his habits until a short while ago [*Si le grain ne meurt* was published in 1921], which shows my blindness and my clairvoyance. (He approves.) For after all, we are completely different and all the same understand each other profoundly. But we have this in common: from the ages of 18 to 30, women, excepting Mme de R—— for me, played no role in our profound, essential lives. *Chastity?*—no. *Purity*, yes.

And he told me then that all the *feeling* he had was for his wife. Never had he mixed the least bit of intellect with his senses. Any intervention of the mind chilled him. But then, as for the senses, complete debauchery. He has practiced everything and *continues*. He insists on this word."

108. VALÉRY–GIDE CORRESPONDENCE: *André Gide–Paul Valéry Correspondance 1890–1942* (Paris: Gallimard, 1955), with notes and a preface by Robert Mallet. Selected letters.

111. ...*your book*: *Les Cahiers d'André Walter*.

112. ... *will blush with confusion*...: Pierre Louÿs, having given a poem by Valéry, "Pour la nuit," to Mallarmé, wrote to Valéry on October 15, 1890. "My friend, you are sacred. I wrote on Sunday to the poet you guessed, to ask him what day it would please him to hear some verses of one of my friends; and at his response, I brought to him yesterday your sonnet, "Pour la nuit," which is decidedly your *Vase brisé* (be it said with no insulting comparison to the sonnet). He read it slowly, reread it, and said in a low voice, "Ah! This is very good." And as I was forcing him to talk, he replied, "He is a poet, there is not the shadow of doubt." Then, talking to himself, "Great musical subtlety." And turning toward me, "Do you have others?" I had only that one, and I did well, I believe. You will send him others...

yourself. That would be much better. Write: Stéphane Mallarmé, 89, rue de Rome."

Valéry immediately addressed a letter to Mallarmé which began:

"Dear Master, a young man lost in the provinces, to whom some rare fragments discovered by chance in certain reviews have made it possible to guess the secret splendor of your works, dares present himself to you. . . ."

Mallarmé's response was immediate: "My dear Poet, the gift of subtle analogy, with the adequate music, you possess that certainly, which is *all*. I had said that to our friend Mr. Louis, and I repeat it before your two brief and rich poems. As for advice, only solitude can give it and I envy you that, reminding myself of the hours in the provinces and in youth which I shall never find again." (Letters cited by Henri Mondor in *Paul Valéry Vivant*, Marseille: Cahiers du Sud, 1946.)

112. *Your uncle*: Charles Gide (1847–1932), the younger brother of André Gide's father. At this time he was a professor in the Faculty of Law at Montpellier. Later he was invited to the chair of comparative social economy in the Law Faculty of the University of Paris. André Gide and his mother often visited him at Montpellier.

114. *A piano friend . . .*: Pierre Féline.

116. *One glance . . .*: his first sight of Mme de R——.

126. *D'azure au dextrochère . . .*: of azure with the golden gloved right arm holding an empty cup of the same, where a monster suffers.

140. *Coste*: Albert Coste, a friend of Valéry's from Montpellier who was a physician and the author of a thesis on the occult sciences.

181. *. . . an old friend*: no doubt Gustave Fourment.

187. ... *arme blanche*: cavalry saber.

201. *Mallarmé died yesterday morning*: see *Collected Works*, Vol. 8, pp. 412f.

The burial will take place: for Valéry's letter to Gide describing Mallarmé's funeral, see the *Collected Works*, Vol. 8, pp. 412–415.

... *these ladies who remain*: Mallarmé's wife and daughter.

221. ... *your wife is...free with her gestures*: Mme Gide, knocked down by a carriage, had a broken arm which required an operation.

259. ... *little anecdote-recital*...: in the number of *La Nouvelle Revue française* for December 1, 1928, Gide published several pages of notes under the title *Feuillets*. There he told the following anecdote: "Excellent verse is recognized in this, that not a single word can be changed nor displaced," writes Paul Souday (*Le Temps*, November 28, 1927), borrowing from Paul Valéry this formula, which the latter gave us during a lecture at the Vieux-Colombier. I was there and Valéry, anxious to provide an example as a kind of proof, chose these two lines from Hugo:

> Oh! quel tragique bruit font dans le crépuscule
> Les chênes qu'on abat pour le bûcher d'Hercule",
>
> [O what tragic noise is made in the twilight
> By the oaks cut down for the faggots of Hercules,]

but makes a poor start, which gave me an anguished sweat.

> Oh the tragic noise...

balances like a ropewalker on a tight cord, but catches himself at once:

> ... made in the twilight...

NOTES

which allowed him to say as he left: Well, my definition...
what f——! and the audience saw nothing but the fire."
[Included in notes by Robert Mallet.]

265. IN MARCEL PRÉVOST'S TIME: "Au Temps de Marcel
Prévost," *Marcel Prévost et ses contemporains*, 2 vols. (Paris:
Éditions de France, 1943); reprinted in *Vues* (Mayenne: La
Table Ronde, 1948).

274. GRADUATION CEREMONIES AT THE COLLÈGE DE SÈTE:
"Discours prononcé à l'occassion de la distribution des prix
du Collège de Sète," *Variété IV* (1938); reprinted in *Œuvres*,
Vol. K, *Conférences* (1939) under the title "Discours de
Sète." See *Œuvres I*, Pléiade (1957), p. 1427.

287. REMARKS ABOUT MYSELF: "Propos Me Concernant,"
foreword to Berne-Joffroy, *Présence de Valéry*, in the collection "Présences," (Paris: Plon, 1944). See *Œuvres II*, Pléiade
(1960), p. 1505.

335. MY WORK AND I: "Mon Œuvre et Moi," a typescript
from the *Valeryanum*, Paris, Bibliothèque Jacques Doucet.
Published in a translation by Malcolm Cowley, *The Herald
Tribune*, New York, April 8, 1928. Unpublished in French.

343. THE AVENUES OF THE MIND: "Les Avenues de l'Esprit,"
an interview by S. Bach, *La Petite Gironde*, April 3, 1927.
344. *Tristan, votre cœur...*:

> Tristan, yours is a heart of bronze.
> I reckon more days than goods I've won
> Since the day when I was born
> Thirtieth October, seventy and one.

See *Collected Works*, Vol. 1, pp. 372–373.

349. REPLY: "Réponse," Paris, *Commerce*, No. 29, Winter 1932. See *Œuvres II*, Pléiade (1960), p. 1601.

354. MEMORIES OF PAUL VALÉRY: "Souvenirs sur Paul Valéry," by Pierre Féline, Paris, *Mercure de France*, July 1954. An expansion of Féline's article, "Rue Urbain-V en 1890," published in *Paul Valéry Vivant* (Marseilles: Cahiers du Sud, 1946).

356. *Only the passers-by...*: see the *Collected Works*, Vol. 6, p. 16. Féline misquotes "Les passants semblaient en liberté."

357. *Que fait Sennachérib...*:

> What is Sennacherib doing, a King greater than fate?
> King Sennacherib is doing this—he is dead.

358. *La nature, Madame...*:

> Nature, Madam, is quite beautiful today.

379. *...no longer intoxicates me*: In the letter quoted, Valéry says, "il ne me drogue plus." Here, Féline substitutes "griser."

380. *Centre de ressort...*:

> Center of resilience, of scorn, and of purity
> I sacrifice myself inwardly to what I would be.

INDEX

INDEX

Academy, French, 11, 266, 267, 269–70, 276
Adam, Mme Juliette, 8
L'Adolescent confidentiel (Michel Féline), 356*n*
Africa, colonies, 282
Agatha (La Sainte du Sommeil, Valéry), 103*n*, 194*n*, 196, 221–24, 229, 245
Agence Havas, 9–10, 102 & *n*, 220*n*, 225, 243, 246, 373
Album de vers anciens (Valéry), 114*n*
algebra, 359, 360
Algiers, 258
"L'Âme et la danse" (Valéry), 348, 367, 387, 388
America, 281; American drinks, 144; American pens, 243
Ampère, André Marie, 162, 280
Amphion (Valéry), 380, 388
Analects (Valéry), 393
analysis, 312
Annecy, 147
L'Antique (Gide), 129
anti-Semitism, 192
Antwerp, 218
Aphrodite (Louÿs), 40
application of forces, 306–08
"L'Après-midi d'un faune" (Mallarmé), 357, 381

Archimedes, 279
architecture, 4, 6
A Rebours (Huysmans), 5, 37, 75*n*, 89*n*
"Arion" (Valéry), 133 & *n*
Aristotle, 336
Arles-sur-Tech, 251
art, 133, 159; classical, 235; realism in, 256
Astarté (Louÿs), 134*n*
Aude, 250
"L'Aurore" (Valéry), 11, 258*n*, 345
Auvergne, 376
Auzillion, Charles, 60, 90, 94, 96, 98, 101, 104
Aventures du roi Pausole, Les (Louÿs), 229*n*
Aveyron, 204
Azemmour, 243

Bach, Johann Sebastian, 358
Bach, S., 343–48, 406
Bachelard, Gaston, 361
Bailly, 265
Balzac, Honoré de, 47, 125, 129, 131, 162, 335
Banville, Théodore de, 130, 202, 249
Barnes, 56
Barrès, Maurice, 114, 119

411

Barthou, Jean Louis, 269, 270
Batavia, 147, 155
"Bateau ivre, Le" (Rimbaud), 242
Baudelaire, Charles, 13, 80, 82, 257, 325
Bauër, Henry, 187
Bayard, Chevalier, 12, 76n
Bayreuth, 121, 134, 137
Beardsley, Aubrey, 43
Beethoven, Ludwig van, 7
Belgians, 133
Belgium, 218, 219n
Belle Jenny (Gautier), 69
Bérenger, Victor Henry, 89
Berger-Levrault, 366
Bergson, Henri, 345, 346
Berlin, Congress (1881), 282
Bernanos, Georges, 347
Bernard, Professor, 69n, 71–72
Beyer, Adolphe Van, 239n
Béziers, 90n
Bilitis, see Chansons de Bilitis
Biskra, 145, 148, 163n
Bismarck, Otto von, 282–83
Blanche, Jacques-Emile, 225
"Blasphèmes" (Mallarmé), 249
Blavet, Alcide, 77n, 85n, 86
Bloy, Léon, 223
Boccaccio, Giovanni, 70
Bonnel, 66
Bonnières, Robert de, 144
Bonniot, Edmond, 226n, 249
Bonniot-Mallarmé, Mme Geneviève, 9, 226n
Bordeaux, 182
Boulanger, Gen. Georges, 64
Bourget, Paul, 248, 270, 273
Bourgogne, Sergeant, memoirs, 215n
Bouvard, 176
Boxhill, 44–45

Boylesve, René, 269
Bréal, Michel, 189n
Bremond, Henri, 269, 270, 343
Brieux, Eugène, 269
Bruges, 218
Brulard, Henri, 219
Bug-Jargal (Hugo), 12
Burne-Jones, Sir Edward, 159
Byron, George Gordon, Lord, 47

Cabella, Gaeta, 61n
Cabella, Gaetano, 61n, 62n, 138
Cabella, Vittoria (Grassi), 61n, 62n
Cahiers (Valéry), 103n, 348, 393, 402
Cairo, 161
calculus, 360, 361, 365
Cambridge, 157
Candide (Voltaire), 180
Cantor, Georg, 381, 382n
Casablanca, 365
Caserne des Minimes, 37
Cassandra, 155
Castiglione (place), 176
Cathédrale, La (Huysmans), 191
Catholicism, 13, 61; literature and, 347
Caves du Vatican, Les (Gide), 248 & n
Centaure, Le, 102n, 180–81, 183, 185, 224
Centaure group, 220n
Cette, see Sète
Cévennes, 75
Chansons de Bilitis, Les (Louÿs), 40, 164n, 190
Chantavoine, Henri, 6
Chanvin, Charles, 197
Chaouïa, 366
Charles V, Emperor, 61

Charmes (Valéry), 11, 65*n*, 367, 371, 373, 377, 378–79
Chartered Company, 9, 51–52
"Chercheuses des poux" (Rimbaud), 109
Chimère, La, 114*n*
Chopin, Frédéric François, 168
Christianity, 13, 119
Church, the, 122, 229
"Cimitière marin, Le" (Valéry), 4, 346, 369
Clairville, 175*n*
Claudel, Paul, 142, 270
Clay, theory of consciousness, 70
Clignancourt, 142
Cocteau, Jean, 347
Coles (Meredith's servant), 45–46
Collège de France, 381
"Communiants, Les" (Rimbaud), 131
Congo, 282
Connaissance, La, 343
Conque, La, 6, 112, 114*n*, 131, 356
"Conquête allemande, La" (Une Victoire méthodique," Valéry), 243
"Conquête méthodique, Une" (Valéry), 59, 367
Conrad, Joseph, 53
Constantine (Algeria), 145
Constantinople, 161, 177, 367
"Conte vraisemblable, Le" ("La Folle Journée," "A Likely Story," Valéry), 83 & *n*; text, 398–402
Contes drôlatiques (Balzac), 65
Cook, James, voyages, 215*n*
Corneille, Pierre, 21
Coste, Albert, 140, 159, 404

Cousine Bette (Balzac), 224
Cowley, Malcolm, 406
Criquetot-l'Esneval, 219
Critique of Pure Reason (Kant), 103
Cuverville, 198, 219, 221, 243, 255*n*
"Cygne, Le" (Mallarmé), 357
"Cygnes, Les" (Vielé-Griffin), 128

Daillan, 71, 82
Darwin, Charles, 148, 149
Daudet, Alphonse, 273
Daudet, Léon, 8
Daumas, General, 149
Davray, Henry D., 203
death, 133, 166
Debussy, Claude, 358
Dècle, Lionel, 8
Degas, Edgar, 100, 146*n*, 187, 196, 242; and dedication of *Monsieur Teste,* 185; letter to Valéry, 241; photographs by, 195, 241
Deheil, 347
Delille, Jacques, 81
Démon de Midi, Le (Bourget), 248
Derème, Tristan, 344
Descartes, René, 227, 279, 344, 347, 397
Deschanel, Paul, 266
Dickens, Charles, 42
Dierx, Léon, 89
Dinner in London (*Supper in Singapore,* Valéry, never written), 196
Discourse on Method (Descartes), 161, 344
Divagations (Mallarmé), 219*n*
Djérid desert, 145

Doria, Andrea, 61
Dragomirof, General, 187
Draguignan, 105, 106
Dreyfus affair, 9, 100n, 195–96, 217, 268
Drouin, 131, 172, 183, 237, 247
Drouin, Mme, 188, 237, 247
Dubus, 89
Du Fondement de l'Induction (Lachelier), 184 & n
Dujardin, Édouard, 202
Durand-Ruel gallery, 195
Dürer, Albrecht, 89
"Durtal" (Valéry), 190, 194, 197
dynamo, 279–80

L'Eclair de Montpellier, 355
education, 158, 278–79, 283–85
"L'Église" (Valéry), 76 & n
Einstein, Albert, 371, 372
Elpénor (Giraudoux), 346
Emaux et Camées (Gautier), 81
England, 41–58, 73, 76–77; see also London
English literature, 42, 158
Ennery, 175n
En route (Huysmans), 170
Entretiens (Valéry), 128, 131
L'Ermitage, 114, 224
Euclid, 99, 236, 383
Eupalinos (Valéry), 365 & n, 367, 377, 379
Eureka (Poe), 132, 226, 375, 377
Euripides, 271
Europe: Bismarck's idea of, 282–83; youth and the State, 284
events, dislike of, 290–91, 314–15, 328

Fabre, Lucien, 346–47

Faraday, Michael, 162, 280
Fashoda, 9
Fatinitza (Suppé), 41
Faust (Goethe), 81
Féline, Michel, 356n
Féline, Pierre, 90 & n, 243, 244, 403; letters from Valéry, 366, 368–76, 384–89; memories of Valéry, 354–89, 407
Fénéon, Félix, 172n, 192
Feuilles d'automne (Hugo), 12
"Feuillets" (Gide), 405
Fez, 386
"Fileuse, La" (Valéry), 133 & n
Fille Élisa, La (Goncourt), 69
fishing, 23–24
Flahault, Professor, 77 & n
Flaubert, Gustave, 167
Flers, Marquis de, 269
Florence, 154
Foch, Gen. Ferdinand, 332
"Folle Journée," see "Conte vraisemblable"
Fontainas, André, 203
Fontaine, Arthur, 231
Fontainebleau, 147
Fourment, Gustave, 60, 393, 403; Valéry's correspondence with, 60–107, 396
"Fragments du Narcisse" (Valéry), 65n
France, Anatole, 269, 270
France: African colonies, 282; government of, 9, 179, 192–93, 243, 385; Nietzsche's idea of female genius, 203–04; translations of foreign books in, 203
friendship, 8, 11, 36, 75, 94–95, 101, 104–05, 122, 133, 181–82, 260, 263, 300

Gabès, 145
Galileo Galilei, 279
Gallimard, Gaston, 10, 243, 247, 253n
Gascony, 376
Gautier, Théophile, 4, 67, 69, 80
Gavarni (Sulpice Guillaume Chevalier), 69
Genoa, 20, 26, 61, 62n, 63, 90n, 138, 154, 176, 178, 204, 241
geometry, 99, 143, 221, 360–61
Georgics (Virgil), 26
German language, 147, 148
Germans, 204
Germany, 57, 281; colonies, 282; Williams's articles on, 53, 57–58
Ghéon, Henri (pseud. Henri Vanglon), 246
Gide, André, 6, 10, 270, 347, 350, 364, 402–403; analysis of Valéry's character, 205–09; *La Jeune Parque* dedicated to, 253n; *Journal*, 260, 332; marriage, 176, 177; in North Africa, 145, 148, 163n; Valéry summarizes his relationship with, 165–67, 209–13; Valéry's correspondence with, 108–264, 403
Gide, Charles, uncle of André, 404
Gide, Mme, mother of André, 143, 148, 404
Gide, Mme (Madeleine Rondeaux: Émmanuèle), wife of André, 120n, 176, 177, 180, 188, 221, 238, 245, 246, 247, 255n, 258, 405
Gillet, Father, 347
Giraudoux, Jean, 346

Gladiator (unfinished book, Valéry), 325
Gobillard, Jeannie, *see* Valéry, Mme (Jeannie Gobillard)
Gobillard, Mlles, 9
Gobillard, Paule, 250, 253
God, 13, 119, 124, 127
Goethe, Johann Wolfgang von, 47, 81, 162, 166
Goldberg, 194
Goncourt brothers, 69, 139
Gosse, Sir Edmund, 43, 394–395
Gotterdämmerung (Wagner), 132
Gourmont, Rémy de, 158, 191
Grassi, Cardinal de, 12
Grassi, Charles-Joseph de, 76n
Grassi, Giulio de, 62n, 68n, 74n, 76n
Grassi, Mme de (Jeanne Lugnani), 74n
Greek language, 128
Grève des Forgerons, La (Banville), 130
Guerne, M. de, 89
Guignon, Le (Mallarmé), 249
Guilbert, Yvette, 130

Hades, 279, 288
Hamlet (Shakespeare), 119
Han d'Islande (Hugo), 12
Hanotaux, Gabriel, 11, 269
Hardouin, Jean, 333
d'Haussonville, Comte, 269, 270
"Hélène" (Valéry), 114 & n
Helmholtz, Hermann von, 38–39
Henley, William Ernest, 52–53, 56–58
Henri-Robert, 270
Henry, Mme Hubert, 100
Heredia, José María de, 8, 15, 93, 154, 216, 217, 357, 359n;

monument, 247; salons, 265–66

Hermès, 191

Hérodiade (Mallarmé), 85, 115, 201–02, 250 & *n*, 357, 381

Herodotus, 286

Hérold, André, 128, 130, 191

Hérold family, 162

Hervieu, Paul, 266, 267

Histoire de la Révolution Française (Michelet), 242

history, 291, 294, 316–17

Hugo, George, 49, 396

Hugo, Victor, 4, 47, 48, 67*n*, 162, 163, 215, 328, 335, 357–58, 405

Huysmans, Joris-Karl, 5, 8, 75*n*, 76*n*, 89, 99, 121, 170, 344; letter from Valéry, 402; Valéry's article on, 190*n*, 191–92

L'Idee fixe (Valéry), 384*n*

idols, 294–95

Illuminations, Les (Rimbaud), 129, 132, 162, 242

India, 143

Indies, 77

Indo-China, 368

Ingres, Dominique, 255–56

Introduction to the Method of Leonardo da Vinci (Valéry), 8, 49, 171, 172, 243, 344, 346, 367, 396; *Note and Digression*, 344, 367

Irmion, Abbé, 77*n*

Italia (battleship), 61–62

Italy, 7, 59, 62, 75–76, 137, 143, 150, 154, 157, 178, 281

Jaloux, Edmond, 255

Jameson Raid, 52

Japan, 59, 367

Jean-Aubry, G., 53

Jeanbrau, Dr., 250, 251

Jeune Parque, La (Valéry), 10, 11, 253*n*, 345, 367, 381

"Jeune Prêtre, Le" (Valéry), 363*n*

Jews, 192, 204

Joan of Arc, 47

Journal des Débats, 6

Journal des Savants, 70

Kant, Immanuel, 70, 103, 125

Katanga, 282

Keyserling, Count Hermann, 332

King Lear (Shakespeare), 132

Kipling, Rudyard, 203

Kitchener, Horatio Herbert, Lord, 49

Kolbassine, Eugène, 100 & *n*, 142, 147, 155, 173, 178, 181, 217

Lachelier, J., 184*n*

Ladysmith, 48

Laforgue, Jules, 162

"Lagunes" (Gide), 134*n*

Lamalou, 221, 223

Lamartine, Alphonse de, 12, 47, 57, 325

Lamoureux concerts, 8

language, 293, 306–07, 324; *see also* words

Laplace, Pierre Simon de, 143, 162

Lapras, 162

La Preste, 250, 251, 252

Larbaud, Valery, 254

La Rochefoucauld (place), 106

La Spezia, 61, 63

Laurens, Paul-Albert, 163*n*, 190

law studies, 4, 6, 7, 36, 37, 74n, 77n, 90n, 114n, 134, 136, 354
Lazare, Bernard, 130, 138, 158
Léautaud, Paul, 239
Lebanon, 369
Lebey, André, 9, 102n, 220n
Lebey, Édouard, 9–10, 102n, 220n, 228–29, 230, 234 & n, 373, 377
Leclerc, Charles-Alfred, 247n
Lefèvre, Frédéric, 348
Legion of Honor, 376n
Lemerre, Alphonse, 265
Leonardo da Vinci, 89, 139, 170, 176; see also Introduction to the Method of Leonardo da Vinci
Leopold II, 282
literature, 158, 214–15, 227–28, 257–58, 296, 301, 311, 329, 341, 351, 382; see also poetry; writing
Lobengula, 51
Lohengrin (Wagner), 7, 114, 115, 359 & n
Lombardo-Venetia, 177
Lonato, 176
London, 8, 41–44, 49, 50, 52, 53, 55, 74n, 87, 120, 156, 157, 159, 161, 164
Lorrain, Claude, 20
Louis XV, 37
Louis Lambert (Balzac), 125, 161
Louÿs, Pierre (Pierre Louis), 7, 11, 83 & n, 84, 85, 87, 89, 111, 120–21, 125, 126, 128, 130–34, 137, 140, 142, 144, 150, 159–60, 169, 173, 178, 181, 184, 186, 187, 190, 196, 222, 224, 229n, 237, 247, 254, 344, 350, 364, 393; letter from Valéry, 84; letter to Valéry, 403–404;

and Meryem, 163, 163–64n; Valéry meets, 6, 39–40, 108n
love, 94–95, 116–17, 118, 124; Valéry's love affairs, 169, 356, 357n, 402–403, 404
Loyola, St. Ignatius of, 159

"Made in Germany" (Williams), 53, 57–58
Maeterlinck, Maurice, 132
Mallarmé, Geneviève, see Bonniot-Mallarmé
Mallarmé, Mme (Marie Gerhard), 9, 226
Mallarmé, Stéphane, 89, 93, 122, 145n, 190, 214, 219n, 223, 227, 228, 242, 244, 298, 344, 361–64; death, 105, 201; funeral, 201, 405; and Gide, 130; and Henley, 56, 58; letter from Valéry, 404; letter to Valéry, 404; Louÿs sends Valéry's poem to, 403–404; Rimbaud compared with, 249; and Valéry's marriage, 99; Valéry's plans for family after his death, 202–03; Valéry's relationship with, 7, 8, 97, 120, 147, 156, 173; writings, 5, 6, 13, 15, 41, 123n, 325–26, 357
Mallet, Robert, 108n, 406
Malta, 172
Malthus, Thomas R., 316
Manet, Édouard, 99 & n, 146n
Manet, Eugène, 99n
Manton, M. and Mme, 93n, 100n
Margherita, Queen of Italy, 62
Mardrus, 203
Marseille, 20, 140
Masques et visages (Gavarni), 69
Masson, 87

mathematics, 8, 90*n*, 359–63, 365, 381, 384, 385
Mathilde, Princess, 163
Mauclair, Camille, 89, 155
Maupassant, Guy de, 273
Mauriac, François, 347
Maurras, Charles, 347
Maxwell, James Clerk, 162
Mazel, Henri, 87, 158
medicine/doctors, 231–32
Mediterranean sea, 19, 32–35
Mélanges (Valéry), 247
memory, 288–90, 323–24
Mendès, Catulle, 187
Mendiant, Le (Mallarmé), 249
Mercier, Louis, 100
Mercure de France, 184, 189*n*, 190*n*, 191, 194, 197, 223, 228, 244, 386*n*
Meredith, George, 8, 42, 50; letters to Valéry, 44, 49, 395–96; Valéry visits, 44–48
Merrill, Stuart, 89
Meryem (Arab girl), 163, 163–64*n*
Mesnil, Dr., 245
Mesnil, 236, 238, 246, 252
Mettman family, 225
Meunier, 89
Meynial, Professor, 77 & *n*
Michelet, Jules, 242
Milan, 176
Milhaud, Gaston, 359*n*
military service, 5, 15–16, 37–38 74*n*, 106, 108*n*
Minkowski, Hermann, 372
Mme Vénus, 69
Mockel, Albert, 131
Molière, Jean Baptiste Poquelin, 335
Mondor, Henri, 404
Monet, Claude, 146

"Mon Faust" (Valéry), 374*n*, 389
Monod, Julien P., 393
Monsieur Teste (Valéry), 7, 100*n*, 183, 184, 198, 200, 204*n*, 219, 243, 245, 295, 306, 308, 344, 367; dedication offered to Degas, 185; Gide's criticism of, 186–87
Montesquieu, Charles de Secondat, Baron, 346
Montesquiou-Fezensac, Robert, Comte de, 89–90
Montpellier, 3–5, 37, 60*n*, 67*n*, 73, 131, 145, 146, 149, 151, 159, 191, 204, 225, 250, 251, 252, 283, 354, 355, 389, 404; University, 6, 38–39, 74*n*, 100*n*, 108*n*, 251
Morand, Paul, 346
Moreno, Marguerite, 191
Morice, Charles, 89
Morisot, Berthe, 9, 99*n*, 100*n*, 219*n*
Morocco, 244, 365, 386
Mounier, Albert, 175*n*
Muhlfeld, Mme Lucien, 254*n*, 268, 269
Munich, 131
music, 7, 168, 178, 207, 239, 312, 387; conversation as, 223; literature compared with, 329, 345; Valéry's admiration of Wagner, 358–59
Musset, Alfred de, 12, 325, 328
Mylius, Mr., 138–39

Nadal, Octave, 61*n*, 396, 398, 402
Naples, 20, 154
Napoleon, I 47–48, 61

"Narcisse parle" (Valéry), 6, 111–12, 115, 356, 367
Narcissus (Gide), see Traité de Narcissus
Natanson, Mme Thadée, 226
Natanson family, 203 & n
Naval Esthetics (Valéry), 128, 132
Nerval, Gérard de, 245
New Review, The, 52–53, 57
Newton, Isaac, 279
Nietzsche, Friedrich Wilhelm, 47, 203–04
Nîmes, 108, 147
Nordmann, 371
Notre-Dame de Paris (Hugo), 12
Nouvel esprit scientifique, Le (Bachelard), 361
Nouvelle Revue française, La, 171, 187, 247, 259, 260, 405
novels, 302, 307, 328, 346

"Octobre" (Gide), 134n
Oersted, Hans Christian, 280
Oran, Parc d'Artillerie, 366n
Orange Republic, 52
Orient, 161
Orsay, 245
Oxford, 157

Painlevé, Paul, 268, 373
Palavas, 90n, 108n, 251
Pall Mall Gazette, 48
"Palme" (Valéry), 11, 345
Paludes (Gide), 168, 170, 172, 226
Paris, 7, 86–87, 93n, 97, 110, 120, 124, 125, 131, 137, 139, 140, 142–43, 145, 148, 150, 151, 152, 157, 164, 182, 184, 225, 230, 252, 365, 370, 373, 380, 387, 388; Exposition of 1900,

154; Mallarmé's house, Valéry's residences, 93n, 100n; in World War II, 389
Parnassians, 362
Parsifal (Wagner), 121, 358, 363n
Pascal, Blaise, 328, 360, 375, 377
Pastoral Symphony (Beethoven), 7
Péladan, Joseph, 130
Pennell, Mrs. Joseph (Elizabeth Robins), 43, 44
Péra, 162
Persius, 159
Peschiera, 176
Pétain, Marshal Henri Philippe, 380n
Petrarch, 70
Peyrou, 75, 140, 171
Phalanges, 244
philosophy, 7, 29, 79, 220, 306–14, 320–22, 339, 345
Pindar, 117
Plaisance, 225
Plume, La, 356n
Poe, Edgar Allan, 6, 110, 119, 122, 124, 125, 162, 226–27, 249, 257, 326, 357, 362, 363; Love Letters, 143
Poésies d'André Walter, Les (Gide), 109, 111, 112, 113, 135n
Poètes d'aujourdhui, Les (Van Beyer and Léautaud), 239n
poetry, 79, 85–86, 126, 297–98, 324, 329, 349–53, 357–58; Prévost's taste in, 270–72; speech in, 331–32; writing, 10–11, 36–37, 167, 337, 338, 345–46, 349–53
Poictevin, Francis, 145 & n
Poincaré, Henri, 360

Poisson, Siméon Denis, 162
Pollock, Sir Frederick, 47, 48, 49, 395
Pollock, Lady, 47, 48, 49, 395
Polyptique d'Irmion, La, 77*n*
"Pour la nuit" (Valéry), 403
"Pour votre Hêtre 'Suprême'" (Valéry), 255*n*
Pranzini, 64
Prats-de-Mollo, 251
Prétextes (Gide), 237
Prévost, Marcel, 265–73, 406
Princesse Maleine (Maeterlinck), 112
Protagoras, 28
Proust, Marcel, 290
Psalms, 63, 65*n*
Pugno, Raoul, 239, 240
"Purs drames" (Valéry), 128*n*, 129
Pyrénées-Orientales, 250

Quillard, Pierre, 161, 162, 191

R——, Mme de, 402–403, 404
Rabeval (Fabre), 347
Racine, Jean Baptiste, 358
Ravachol, 355
Redon, Odilon, 231
Regards sur le monde actuel (Valéry), 204*n*
Régnier, Henri de, 120, 128, 130, 131, 134, 142, 144, 164, 225, 255, 269
religion, 13
Renan, Ernest, 92
Renouvier, Charles Bernard, 70
revolutionaries, 191, 192
Revue, La, see *Nouvelle Revue française, La*
Revue Blanche, La, 192, 199, 226*n*

Revue de Paris, 164, 168
Revue Hebdomadaire, 375
Rhodes, Cecil, 51
Rhodesia, 51, 52
"Rhumbs" (Valéry), 348
Richepin, Jean, 249
Rimbaud, Arthur, 6, 56, 109*n*, 122, 129, 131, 141, 143, 242, 249; compared with scientists, 162, 326
Rin, Angelo de, 74*n*
Rin, Mme de (Pauline de Grassi), 74*n*
Rin, Pinetta de, 74*n*
Ring of the Nibelungs (Wagner), 345
Rivière, Jacques, 249
Rogery, Professor, 62, 63*n*
Rolla (de Musset), 13
Romances sans paroles, Les (Verlaine), 129
Romans, ancient, 204
Romanticism, 357
Rome, 154, 384
Rossetti, Dante Gabriel, 159
Rothomago, 175 & *n*
Rouart, Eugène, 146 & *n*, 148, 161, 163, 164, 167, 174, 178–79, 183, 184, 187; letter from Valéry, 185
Rouart, Henri, 146*n*
Rouart-Valéry, Agathe, 250, 253
Rouen, 114
Roustan, 283
Royan, 231
Russia, 59, 281; National Assembly, 239

Sade, Marquis de, 70
St. Aulaire, M. de, 53
Saint-Denis, 142

Saint John (Leonardo da Vinci), 139
Sand, George, 124
Sanguines (Louÿs), 237
Santa Margherita, 240
Sappho, 137
Sardinia, 62n, 68n
Sardinoux, 88, 101
Satan, 13
Saül (Gide), 198–99, 200
Schopenhauer, Arthur, 125
Schumann, Robert, 168, 358
Schwob, Marcel, 8, 42, 44, 53, 175, 394–395
science, supreme law of, 362 & n
sea, 25–31, 179
self, 29, 138, 259–60, 291–92, 297, 303–05, 320, 333, 335
Sémantique, La, science des significations (Bréal), 189n
"Sémiramis" ("Air de Sémiramis," Valéry), 380, 387, 388
sentiment, 13, 328
Sète (Cette), 3, 4, 19–22, 62n, 67n, 68n, 140, 251, 253, 285–86, 389; Collège de, Valéry's address at, 274–86, 406
Shakespeare, William, 335
ships, 22, 25
Siberia, 367
Siegfried (Wagner), 132
Signoret, Emmanuel, 190, 191, 195
Si le grain ne meurt (Gide), 163n, 256n, 403
Sisyphus, 288
sky, 28, 31, 32
snails, 186
Soirée avec Monsieur Teste, see *Monsieur Teste*
"Solitude" (Valéry), 75n
Soriano, Marc, 397

Souday, Paul, 347, 405
Souf desert, 145
"Souvenirs de la classe de Philosophe" (Valéry), 397–398
Spain, 140, 250, 252
speech, rapidity of, 331–32
spiders, 232
Spinoza, Benedict, 347
State, the, 284
Steevens, George Warrington, 48–49
Stendhal (Marie Henri Beyle), 47, 162, 228
Stevenson, Robert Louis, 42
Suarès, André, 255
sun, 28, 31–32
Suppé, Franz von, 41, 394
swimming, 26–27
Switzerland, 372
Symbolism, 357, 362
Syria, 369
"Syrinx, La" (Valéry), 133n, 139

Taine, Hippolyte Adolphe, 47
Tannhäuser (Wagner), 358
Tantalus, 288
Tel Quel (Valéry), 382n
Tennyson, Alfred, Lord, 92, 93
Tentative amoureuse, La (Gide), 148n
Teste in China (Valéry, unfinished), 204n
Théorie des ensembles (Cantor), 381, 382n
Thibaudet, Albert, 345
Thompson, Benjamin, Count Rumford, 162
Thousand and One Nights, 203n, 237
Tinan, Jean de, 200
Tintoretto, 176, 178

"Toast funèbre" (Mallarmé), 123n
Tolstoi, Count Leo, 47
tortoises as ornaments, 195
Toulouse-Lautrec, Henri de, 43
Traité du Narcisse (Gide), 125, 126n, 133, 135n
Transvaal, 48, 51
Trappists, 170
trees, 179–80, 255, 256
Trente-six mille Nuits, Les, see *Thousand and One Nights*
Trieste, 74n, 176
Tristan, 159
Tristan and Isolde (Wagner), 345, 359
Tunis, 154, 387, 388
Tunisia, 282
Turner, Joseph Mallord William, 42, 44
Tussaud, Mme, Museum, 41

Ubu, 181, 217
Ubu, 191
Umberto I, King of Italy, 62
United States, *see* America

Valéry, Barthélémy, father of Paul, 3–4, 12, 60n, 68n
Valéry, Claude, son of Paul, 107, 239, 253, 258, 259
Valéry, Mme (Fanny de Grassi), mother of Paul, 12, 60n, 68n, 137, 143, 151, 176, 187, 189, 225; Gide's condolences on her death, 261, 264
Valéry, Jean, son of Jules, 203n
Valéry, Mme (Jeannie Gobillard), wife of Paul, 9, 10, 99, 103, 220, 225, 228, 230–31, 233, 236, 239, 246, 250–52,
258, 259, 261, 358; marriage, 99n, 101, 219n
Valéry, Jules, brother of Paul, 60n, 68n, 77n, 86n, 100n, 203n, 250
Valvins, 201, 202
Van Dyck, Anthony, 139
Vanier, Leon, 356n
Venice, 176, 178
Verlaine, Paul, 5, 37, 53, 55, 56, 96, 129, 145n, 357
Vernet, Joseph, 20
Verona, 176
"Victoire méthodique, Une" ("La Conquête allemande," Valéry), 243
"Vieilles Ruelles, Les" (Valéry), 75–76n
Vielé-Griffin, Francis, 128, 180, 203
Ville, La (Claudel), 142
Ville sans maîtres, La (Rouart), 146n
Villiers de l'Isle-Adam, Auguste, 5, 145n, 162, 173, 238
Villon, François, 42, 394
Viollet-le-Duc, Eugène Emmanuel, 4
Virgil, 67, 70, 174, 271
Visconti, Federico, Cardinal, 76n
Visconti, Galeazzo, Duke of Milan, 12, 76 & n
Vogue, 131
Voix intérieures (Hugo), 12
Volta, Alessandro, 280
Voltaire François (Marie Arouet), 346
Voyage d'Urien, Le (Gide), 171

Wagner, Richard, 7, 87, 122, 212, 345, 358–59, 362

Walcknaër, 131, 163
Walkyrie (Wagner), 359
Wallonie, La, 133 & *n,* 134*n*
Walter, André, see *Poésies d'André Walter*
war, 385; visions of, 170
War Ministry, 9, 98*n,* 102*n,* 103, 172, 176, 225, 268
Wells, H. G., 203
Whibley, Charles, 48
Whistler, James Abbott McNeill, 44, 93
Williams, Ernest E. G., articles on Germany, 53, 57–58
With Kitchener to Omdurman (Steevens), 49
women, 14, 119, 123, 299
words, 299, 300, 301, 303, 304, 321; abstractions, 318; study of, 220–21
World War I, 10–11, 252

World War II, 388–89
writing, 229–30, 296, 298, 301–02, 307–08, 324–25, 329–30, 335–42; of *Agathe,* 193–94, 222, 223; aims of, 214; author as person, 336; for *Le Centaure,* 180–81, 183; haste in, 194; of *Leonardo da Vinci,* 171; of *Monsieur Teste,* 186–87, 198; publication of works, 244–47; see also poetry, writing
Wronski, Jozef Maria (Hoëné Wronski), 162, 355, 362*n*

"Yalou, Le" (Valéry), 204*n*
Yellow Book, The, 43

Zola, Émile, 223, 273
Zurich, University, 373

LIBRARY OF CONGRESS CATALOGING IN PUBLICATION
DATA

Valéry, Paul, 1871–1945.
    The collected works of Paul Valéry.

    (Bollingen series, 45)
    CONTENTS: v. 1, Poems, translated by D. Paul. On poets
and poetry, selected and translated from the Notebooks, by J. R.
Lawler. [etc.]
    I. Title. II. Series.
PQ2643.A26A23   848'.9'1209   56–9337
ISBN 0-691-09859-X (v. 1)

This colophon was chosen from a number of drawings by Paul Valéry of his favorite device.